ON MUSIC AND MUSICIANS

Robert Schumann

ON MUSIC

and

MUSICIANS

UNIVERSITY OF CALIFORNIA PRESS

Berkeley and Los Angeles

University of California Press
Berkeley and Los Angeles, California

© 1946 by Pantheon Books, Inc., New York

EDITED BY KONRAD WOLFF

TRANSLATED BY PAUL ROSENFELD

First California paperback edition published 1983

ISBN 0-520-04685-4
Library of Congress Catalog Card Number 82-70650

Printed in the United States of America
1 2 3 4 5 6 7 8 9

CONTENTS

ON MUSIC

ON MUSICIANS

CONTENTS

CONTENTS

Introduction

IT IS *certainly no exaggeration to call Robert Schumann one of the great writers on music and one of the great writers, generally, of his time. Imagination and expression, the two elements required for any manifestation of art, were his in writing as well as in composing, and his literary gifts were so spontaneous that what he wrote can be enjoyed and understood quite independently of his music. As Robert H. Schauffler* (FLORESTAN, *p. 274) put it: "If he had never written a note of music, Schumann's aphorisms, letters, and essays alone would constitute a priceless legacy to mankind."*

As a writer Schumann was a disciple of the German Romantic School, and in particular of Jean Paul and E. T. A. Hoffmann. He once said that he had learned more counterpoint from Jean Paul than from his music teacher. As an adolescent, he broke off a romantic attachment to a young girl because she had spoken slightingly of this writer. The novels of Jean Paul—who was ten years older than Schumann's father and died when Robert Schumann was fifteen—are today nearly forgotten, even in his native Germany, because of their peculiar, involved style, but nobody has ever denied him his magic of imagination, the poetry of his style, and his purity of sentiment. Schumann's inner life was more attuned to Jean Paul than to Hoffmann or the other romantic writers. Hoffmann was an intellectual. Gifted, like Schumann, for both literature and music— indeed, even for painting—he confined his artistic activity to his spare time. By profession he was a councillor of the Court of Appeal (the famous KAMMERGERICHT *in Berlin). The discipline, occasionally even the dryness of the legal mind, are at times perceptible in his novels and sketches. The well-constructed plots, macabre and full of tension, have kept his works alive to this day, and many of them have inspired later generations of writers. In Hoffmann, Schumann found the model for his particular type of music criticism, for Hoffmann was the first critic who spoke of music as a writer as well as*

15

a musician. Thus he succeeded in conveying the meaning of certain works of the one art in terms of the other. His analysis of Mozart's DON GIOVANNI, *for instance, is written in the form of a short story. Hoffmann relates the tragic death of the primadonna, which follows her performance of "Donna Anna" and is caused by her unrequited love for the baritone who sang the title rôle; and in the telling of this story he expresses his conception of Mozart's opera. Many of Hoffmann's descriptions of Mozart's and Beethoven's works, while precise and analytical in content, were, in form, narrative prose. Schumann adopted the same method.*

The dialogue form employed in so many of Schumann's writings, where he speaks with the voices of the different "Davidites" (DAVIDS-BÜNDLER), *may equally be considered Hoffmannesque. The revival of Greek philosophy in Germany in the first decades of the 19th century took a new impetus from the translation of Plato's work by the great Protestant philosopher Schleiermacher. The basic method of the dialogues—the acquirement and communication of philosophical knowledge through discussion—was subsequently used as an art form by many romantic writers. Hoffmann wrote a series of short novels under the collective title* DIE SERAPIONSBRÜDER. *The book—which contains some of his best-known tales—is written in the form of a record of club meetings uniting some young writers and their friends. Each reads to the others his newest stories and essays, and between readings the stories as well as general topics are discussed. The dialogue form is applied to the criticism of art and literature, and much valuable material for aesthetic appreciation is presented with charm and wit.*

Here Schumann found the prototype of a literary form allowing him to express his opinions on music and musicians clearly and attractively. Remarks in his letters (carefully collected by Gustav Jansen, DIE DAVIDSBÜNDLER, *1883) make it abundantly clear that he adopted the form of dialogues between club members in his journal* (NEUE ZEITSCHRIFT FÜR MUSIK) *as a deliberate device for making his criticism more lively reading, and for added suspense and mystification. For nobody could know whether the members of the Club of Davidites, listed on the title page as contributors, were real or fictitious characters. In reality they were both: on the one hand, Schumann signed his own articles, not only with his three pen names Florestan, Eusebius, and Master Raro, but also occasionally with the*

16

pen names of his friends (Jeanquirit: St. Heller; Julius: Julius Knorr, etc.). On the other hand, these friends themselves contributed articles and reviews to the journal under their Davidite names. To enhance the spirit of mystification Schumann at one time inserted the following notice in the journal: "Various rumors are circulating concerning the undersigned club. As unfortunately we are forced, for the time being, to withhold our reasons for secrecy, we ask Herr Schumann (in case such a person is known to the honorable board of editors) to be kind enough to represent us, whenever necessary, with his name. DIE DAVIDSBÜNDLER."

However, Florestan, Eusebius, and Raro had existed prior to the foundation of the NEUE ZEITSCHRIFT (1833). In Schumann's diary of 1831 we find the following entries: "June 8th [his birthday]. From today on I want to give to my friends better, more beautiful names. Therefore I will call you as follows: Wieck becomes Master Raro and Clara becomes Cilia [Caecilia]." "July 1st. Entirely new personages will be featured in this diary from now on—two of my best friends, whom, however, I have never set eyes on—Florestan and Eusebius."

As is well known, Schumann gradually identified himself to such an extent with the personalities of Florestan and Eusebius, whose characters he describes in the introduction to the complete edition of his writings (1853; see p. 25) that he even came to write two of his greatest piano works, the DAVIDSBÜNDLERTÄNZE and, partly, the CARNAVAL, in form of a discussion between the stormy Florestan and the lyrical Eusebius. The two personalities clearly show the influence of Jean Paul who, in two of his novels (FLEGELJAHRE and SIEBENKÄS) had introduced two similarly contrasting pairs. The third prominent member of the club, Master Raro, who endeavors to give a finished, poised solution to the arguments of the other two, is to this day an unsolved mystery. In view of the feud that gradually developed between Schumann and his future father-in-law, Friedrich Wieck, it seems probable that Schumann soon ceased to identify Raro with his first prototype. Hugo Riemann, great German musicologist, has advanced the theory that the name of Raro actually was taken from the combination ClaRA-RObert, and was intended to symbolize the complete and integrated personality which Schumann hoped to become after his desired union with Clara Wieck. The substance of this theory, if not the etymological explanation, *is certainly correct, and is further supported by the fact that all the later epigrams and aphorisms signed by Schumann himself—in particular the* HOUSE-RULES FOR YOUNG MUSICIANS—*are similar in style and spirit to the utterances of Raro in the early Davidite dialogues.*

That Schumann depended so largely on the romantic literature of the preceding generation makes him by no means an imitator in a derogatory sense. It is an often observed phenomenon that what has been a general literary movement in one generation becomes, in the following, an instrument of expression for the reflections in some of the more specialized fields of writing. Many of the greatest writers among philosophers and historians were born some thirty or fifty years later than the great poets or novelists whose style they adopted. In nineteenth century Germany Ranke thus became the Goethe of history, Nietzsche the Heine of philosophy. Of Schumann, however, it can be said that, as a writer, he is more alive to posterity than his revered model, Jean Paul.

It is not the purpose of an editorial introduction either to anticipate the contents of the book, saying systematically and indirectly what the author has said spontaneously in the natural order of a creative mind, or critically to appraise the value of the conclusions and formulations reached in the ensuing pages. It may, however, attempt to describe the character of the book by defining its principal aims.

In this instance, they were clearly formulated by Schumann himself in his introduction (p. 25) and elsewhere (p. 224), and even in the very name of the DAVIDSBÜNDLER *which refers to the slaying of the Philistines by David. The Philistines, in the current use of the German language, are employed as a symbol of everything stuffy, narrow, prejudiced, reactionary. It was not only (not even principally) as a composer that Schumann suffered from the prevalence of Philistinism in music: his whole nature as an artist revolted against this attitude wherever he encountered it. In his furiously ironical description of the reactions of "connoisseurs" to Beethoven's Ninth Symphony (p. 100) we find a characteristic example of the things that Schumann went out to combat.*

It was in order to embark on this fight that Schumann decided to become a professional writer. Writing was in his blood, for his gifted father, August Schumann, one of the leading publishers of the time, had also written several successful novels. (One of them, with the Jean-Paulish title JUNKER KURT VON KRÖTENSTEIN'S VERLIEBTE HELDENFAHRT, *was published under the humorous pen name of Legaillard.) At the age of sixteen Schumann, as we know from his diary, seriously contemplated becoming a poet: "What I really am I myself do not know clearly. I am certain of having some imagination, and nobody has denied me this. I am not a profound thinker: I can never logically proceed along a line of thought which I may have started well. Whether I am a poet—one has to be a poet, never can one become one—posterity will have to judge." At that time, Robert Schumann frequently helped his father write articles for encyclopedias, do research work, correct proofs, etc., and thus thoroughly learned the publisher's trade before he left Zwickau at the age of eighteen, after his graduation from school, in order to study law, first in Leipzig, then in Heidelberg. Two years later he returned to Leipzig in order to devote himself entirely to music and after only one year of study started his fight against Philistinism with a fanfare: his famous article on Chopin's Variations, opus 2 (p. 126). The many difficulties that confronted him when he tried to have this article published in Breitkopf & Härtel's* ALLGEMEINE MUSIKALISCHE ZEITUNG *was one of the main factors which prompted him, two years later, to found a musical journal of his own. For the* ALLGEMEINE MUSIKALISCHE ZEITUNG, *the leading musical journal of the time, founded by the great Rochlitz (whom Schumann sincerely admired, see p. 199) became, under the direction of G. W. Finck, increasingly narrow and reactionary. It refused to discuss Schubert's instrumental works as well as all non-German compositions. The same spirit pervaded the criticisms of a contemporary writer, Ludwig Rellstab, author of musical novels and the inventor of the infamous title* MOONLIGHT SONATA. *Schumann's aggressively enthusiastic article was finally printed, but with elisions.*

The foundation of the NEUE ZEITSCHRIFT FÜR MUSIK *is best described by Schumann himself, p. 25. Because Schumann's personality was infinitely stronger than that of his collaborators, the* NEUE ZEITSCHRIFT *remained his personal "organ" during the decade in which he directed it. Not only did he contribute his own articles, but he provided each issue with fitting motti and aphoristic quotations "On Music and Related Arts," taken from Goethe, Jean Paul, Novalis, and other poets and writers.*

19

Inseparably united with his fighting spirit are his educational aims. It was not enough to defeat Philistinism. The public in general and particularly the student of music had to be given a standard of true values by which to judge musical works, performances, and methods of learning. It is in this respect that Schumann is unique as a writer on music. Today we may disagree with his appreciation of certain works (such as Schubert's Impromptu in B-flat) or of certain composers (such as Haydn), but we continue to accept the standards by which he judged them and which he better than any other writer has clearly and creatively formulated. In other words: we may answer differently the questions which Schumann put to himself when reviewing a work of music, but we continue, at our best, to ask the identical questions as to the artistic value of a composition. These standards are established in a given order: workmanship, e.g., though of value, is subordinated to imagination, sincerity, and form. If we analyze, from this point of view, the more important of Schumann's reviews (e.g., those of Berlioz' SYMPHONIE FANTASTIQUE, Schubert's C major Symphony, Liszt's Etudes) we cannot but admire his intuitive gift for applying and adapting this order of values to each and every case. There can be no doubt that he was conscious of his educational mission. Not only his HOUSE-RULES AND MAXIMS FOR YOUNG MUSICIANS prove it: in the innumerable reviews which he was called upon to write about the second-rate output of the day, he frequently took time to illustrate in a general way one or the other aspect of his aesthetic system. (See OBSERVATIONS, p. 70 ff.)

To combat mediocrity and to promote true standards of art it took more than a brilliant, imaginative writer and musician: it took a man of the highest moral integrity. It was for moral reasons that Schumann decided never to judge his contemporaries and competitors as a fellow composer; never to allow his personal tastes and preferences to interfere with the objectivity of his judgment. He tried, and succeeded, to keep his mind open to anything that could indicate a progress in art, no matter how alien to his nature. To an incredible degree he makes us forget that it is Schumann, the great composer of KREISLERIANA, DICHTERLIEBE, the SPRING SYMPHONY, who is speaking with such loyal admiration of Mendelssohn's orchestral works, of Chopin's piano pieces, and of Brahms' first attempts in composition—to name only a few. What distinguishes him from all the other great composers who wrote about music—notably from Berlioz and Debussy—is precisely this self-denial in judging others. Only in perhaps two or three instances in the entire collection of Schumann's writings do we find traces of Schumann's own conception of musical creation applied to the work of fellow composers.

This renunciation of the creative musician in favor of the impartial critic is all the more striking as Schumann's critical activity coincided with a most fertile period in musical creation. From the age of twenty-four to the age of thirty-four, in the ten years in which he directed the journal, he composed the DAVIDSBÜNDLERTÄNZE, *the* CARNAVAL, *the* FANTASIESTÜCKE, *the* SYMPHONIC ETUDES, *the* KINDERSZENEN, *the* KREISLERIANA, *the* FANTASIE, *all his chamber music with the exception of the violin sonatas, his First and Fourth Symphonies, the great song cycles, etc. With the exception of the Paganini transcription, which he could discuss as the work of Paganini, none of these compositions were reviewed in his journal (see the letter p. 260), and nowhere did he allude to them even by way of comparison with the works of others. One feels that he must have successfully kept such comparisons even from his thoughts.*

*If we consider the style of Schumann's writings, however, we immediately feel that it is Robert Schumann, the composer, who speaks to us. The same fire, poetry, directness of expression, the same inventiveness we love in his compositions also animate his prose. He handles it with the sparkling touch, the ease that distinguishes his musical creations. And if Donald Tovey (*ESSAYS IN MUSICAL ANALYSIS, *vol. II, p. 47) could speak of the "antithetic sententiousness" of Schumann's compositions and call him "a master of epigram" in music, he might have said exactly the same about the aphorisms with which the present collection opens and which, among his writings, constitute the most personal expression of his true nature. Tovey's observation that Schumann's ideas "normally take the shape of gnomic sayings" is also supported by the form and spirit of most of these aphorisms, especially those written as arguments between the* DAVIDSBÜNDLER.

A word, finally, about the purpose of the present edition. More than a century has passed since Schumann wrote the bulk of his articles, reviews, and epigrams, and much of it has lost its immediate appeal to the reader because it concerns itself with music which is today forgotten. On the other hand, the chronological order of the writings, which Schumann had adopted in his complete edition of 1854 and which has been preserved in all later German editions, does not allow a comprehensive survey of the various articles written on the works of the same composer. In the only existing English edition, that of 1877–1880, the editor, Mrs. Fanny Raymond Ritter, tried to replace this order by systematically grouping the articles according to the art form discussed. This, however, was not consistently carried through, and the lack of an index to the second volume makes it almost impossible to find any specific subject. A new edition was all the more indicated as the old translation was swarming with misunderstandings and errors.

The present edition is to our knowledge the first in any language to group Schumann's articles and observations on musicians by individual composers. The edition is complete as far as Schumann's writings on the great composers is concerned. All his reviews of the works by the masters, from Beethoven to Brahms, are to be found here—some of them translated for the first time into English; so are his observations regarding the older masters from Palestrina to Mozart. Of his articles on music, those which are of present-day interest have been reprinted in the first part of this volume. Here are to be found a number of relatively unknown passages culled from reviews concerned with minor and forgotten artists. Of these reviews only quotations of general interest or indicative of Schumann's approach to the less important music of his time have been included. (See the articles on Lachner, Gade, Franz.) The important parts of Schumann's concert reviews are grouped in the chapter on Mendelssohn as a conductor (p. 218 ff.). They convey a true picture of concert life in Leipzig, at that time the most important music center in Germany.

As the picture would be incomplete without at least some of Schumann's remarks on his own works, the present edition concludes, in the form (dear to Schumann) of an epilogue, with a few excerpts of letters in which Schumann speaks of his composing. Extracts from letters have been inserted wherever they helped complete the picture conveyed by Schumann's articles (on Bach, for instance, and on Wagner).

The German text has been newly translated by the late Paul Rosenfeld. It was the last work undertaken and finished by this great lover of music and romanticism. It was his aim faithfully to render Schumann's thought, while preserving as much as possible of the romantic flavor of his style. The translation is based on the latest German edition of Schumann's complete writings, GESAMMELTE SCHRIFTEN ÜBER MUSIK UND MUSIKER, *Breitkopf & Härtel, Leipzig, 1914.*

The editor gratefully acknowledges the help and stimulation which he received from THE NEW FRIENDS OF MUSIC, *who sponsored this book.*

K. W.

To distinguish it from Schumann's own writings, the editor's text has been set in smaller type in italics, or inserted in square brackets. Footnotes by Schumann are so marked. All other footnotes are by the editor.

Foreword

Schumann wrote this foreword in 1854, shortly before his last illness broke out, for the complete edition of his collected articles originally published from 1834 to 1844 in his NEUE ZEITSCHRIFT FÜR MUSIK.

IN LEIPZIG toward the end of 1833 a few musicians, mostly young men, met as though by accident every evening. What brought them together chiefly was their pleasure in each other's company; also their desire to discuss the art which was the meat and drink of life to them, music. The musical situation in Germany at the moment was anything but inspiring. Rossini reigned in the opera-houses, and nothing was to be heard on the pianoforte save Herz and Huenten. Yet merely a few years had passed since Beethoven, C. M. von Weber, and Franz Schubert had lived among us.

It is true that Mendelssohn's star was rising and wondrous tales were told of a Pole named Chopin. But neither of these composers had as yet begun to exert his future far-reaching influence. So on a day the following idea came to these musical young hot-heads: "Let us not be mere spectators! Let us lend a hand ourselves for the glory of things! Let us bring the poetry of our art into honor once again!" Thus the first pages of a new musical journal (*Neue Zeitschrift für Musik*) saw the light.

But the joy of this close contact and union of young forces did not last long. Death removed Ludwig Schunke, one of the group's most beloved members. Others left Leipzig for a while. The journal was about to be discontinued. At this point one of the group, actually its musical visionary—who till this moment had spent his life in dreams, and rather at the pianoforte than over books—decided to assume the editorship. He directed the journal for about ten years, until 1844.

Thus there came into existence a series of articles and aphorisms: it is from these that this collection had been formed. Most of the opinions expressed in them have remained the writer's to this very day; and much of what was felt and ventured concerning manifestations of art in them, in fear and hope, since then has proved to have been true.

Here I must mention another society, a more than secret one, since it never existed anywhere save in the imagination of its founder: that of the *Davidsbündler* (The Davidites). In view of the desirability of dramatizing the different points of view from which works of art may be discussed, it seemed opportune to invent antithetic artist-characters to whom these different views might be ascribed. The most important of these characters were *Florestan* and *Eusebius:* between them as a mediator stood *Master Raro*. Like a scarlet thread this society of *Davidsbündler* ran through the entire journal, mingling "Truth" and "Poetry" in humorous fashion. The public enjoyed these likable fellows; but afterward they disappeared from the journal's pages, and since the day a Peri[1] led them away to distant climes, none of them has given sign of further literary activity.

Should these collected pages, the mirrors of an eventful epoch, draw attention to certain musical events which otherwise might be submerged in the current of the present age, the purpose of their editor will have been thoroughly achieved.

[1] One of "those beautiful spirits of the air who live on perfumes," represented by Tom Moore in *Paradise and the Peri,* the poem turned into a cantata by Schumann in 1843.

ON MUSIC

Neue
Zeitschrift für Musik.

Herausgegeben

durch einen

Verein von Künstlern und Kunstfreunden.

Siebenter Band.
(Juli bis December 1837.)

Mit Beiträgen
von

Dr. A. J. Becher, C. F. Becker, den Davidsbündlern, Heinrich Dorn, A. Gathy,
W. R. Griepenkerl, Dr. A. Kahlert, Oswald Lorenz, Joseph Mainzer, C. Montag,
W. Schüler, R. Schumann, J. v. Seyfried, J. F. C. Sobolewsky,
A. W. v. Zuccalmaglio u. A.

Leipzig,
bei Robert Friese.

Title page of the seventh volume of
Schumann's Musical Journal

Aphorisms

HOUSE-RULES AND MAXIMS FOR
YOUNG MUSICIANS

*This famous collection of didactic aphorisms was published
by Schumann in connection with his* ALBUM FÜR DIE JUGEND,
opus 68. A French edition was arranged by Liszt.

THE CULTIVATION of the ear is of the greatest importance. Endeavor, in good time, to distinguish tones and keys. The bell, the windowpane, the cuckoo—seek to discover what tones they produce.

You must practice scales and other finger exercises industriously. There are people, however, who think they may achieve great ends by doing this; up to an advanced age, for many hours daily, they practice mechanical exercises. That is as reasonable as trying to recite the alphabet faster and faster every day. Find a better use for your time.

"Dumb keyboards" have been invented; practice on them for a while in order to see that they are worthless. Dumb people cannot teach us to speak.

Play in time! The playing of some virtuosos resembles the walk of a drunken man. Do not make these your models.

Learn the fundamental laws of harmony at an early age.

Do not be afraid of the words "theory," "thorough-bass," "counterpoint," etc.; they will meet you halfway if you do the same.

Never strum! Always play energetically and never fail to finish the piece you have begun.

Dragging and hurrying are equally great faults.

Try to play easy pieces well; it is better than to play difficult ones poorly.

See to it that your instrument is always in perfect tune.

It is not enough for your fingers to know your pieces; you should be able to hum them to yourself, away from the pianoforte. Sharpen your power of imagination so that you may be able to remember correctly not only the melody of a composition, but likewise its proper harmonies.

Try to sing at sight, without the help of an instrument, even if you have but little voice; your ear will thereby gain in refinement. If you possess a sonorous voice, however, do not lose a moment's time but cultivate it immediately, and look upon it as a most precious gift bestowed by Heaven.

You must reach the point where you can hear the music from the printed page.

When you play, do not concern yourself with who may be listening.

Always play as though a master were present.

Should anyone place an unknown composition before you, asking you to play it, first read it over.

If you have finished your daily musical work and feel tired, do not force yourself to labor further. It is better to rest than to practice without joy or freshness.

When you grow older, avoid playing what is merely fashionable. Time is precious. It would require a hundred lives merely to get acquainted with all the good music that exists.

No children can be brought to healthy manhood on sweetmeats and pastry. Spiritual like bodily nourishment must be simple and solid. The masters have provided it; cleave to them.

Virtuoso tricks change with the times; only where proficiency serves higher purposes has it value.

You ought not help to spread bad compositions, but, on the contrary, help to suppress them with all your force.

Never play bad compositions and never listen to them when not absolutely obliged to do so.

Do not seek to attain mere technical proficiency—the so-called *bravura*. Try to produce with each composition the effect at which the composer aimed. No one should attempt more; anything further is mere caricature.

Look upon alterations or omissions, or the introduction of modern embellishments in the works of good composers as something detestable. They are possibly the greatest insults that can be offered art.

Question older artists concerning the choice of pieces for study; thus you will save much time.

You must gradually learn to know all the most important works of all the important masters.

Do not let yourself be led astray by the applause bestowed on great virtuosos. The applause of an artist ought to be dearer to you than that of the majority.

All which is fashionable again becomes unfashionable; and should you cultivate fashion until you become old, you will become a dandy whom no one respects.

To play overmuch in society is more injurious than advantageous. Study your audience; yet never play anything of which in your own heart you feel ashamed.

Lose no opportunity for making music in company with others, in duos, trios, etc. This will render your playing more fluent and sweeping. Accompany singers oftentimes.

If all were determined to play the first violin, we should never have complete orchestras. Therefore respect every musician in his proper field.

Love your instrument, but do not vainly consider it the highest and only one. Remember that there are other and equally fine ones. Remember also that there are singers, and that the highest expression possible in music is reached with chorus and orchestra.

As you grow older, converse more frequently with scores than with virtuosos.

Industriously practice the fugues of good masters; above all, those of J. S. Bach. Let *The Well-tempered Clavichord* be your daily meat. Then you will certainly become an able musician.

Seek out among your comrades those who know more than you do.

Rest from your musical studies by industriously reading the poets. Often take exercise out in the open.

Much is to be learned from singers male and female. But do not believe all they tell you.

Behind the mountains there also dwell people. Be modest. You have never invented or discovered anything that others have not invented or discovered before you. And even if you have, consider it as a gift from above which it is your duty to share with others.

The study of the history of music and the hearing of masterworks of different epochs will speediest of all cure you of vanity and self-adoration.

Should you pass a church while the organ is being played, go into it and listen. If you long yourself to sit on the organ-bench, try out your little fingers, and marvel at this omnipotence of music.

Lose no opportunity of practicing on the organ; there is no instrument which takes a swifter revenge on anything unclear or sloppy in composition and playing.

Regularly sing in choruses, especially the middle voices. This will make you musical.

What do we mean by being musical? You are not so when, with eyes painfully fixed on the notes, you struggle through a piece; you are not so when you stop short and find it impossible for you to proceed because someone has turned over two pages at once. But you are musical when, in playing a new piece, you almost foresee what is coming; when you play an old one by heart; in short, when you have taken music not only into your fingers, but into your heart and head.

How may one become musical in this sense? Dear child, the principal requisites, a fine ear and a swift power of comprehension, come, like all things, from above. But this foundation may and must be improved and enlarged. You cannot do this by shutting yourself up all day like a hermit, practicing mechanical exercises, but by a vital, many-sided musical activity; especially by familiarizing yourself with chorus and orchestra work.

You should early come to understand the compass of the human voice in its four principal sorts. Listen to it in the chorus; seek to discover in which intervals lies its principal strength and through which of them it best expresses softness and tenderness.

Listen attentively to all folk songs. These are mines of the most beautiful melodies and will teach you the characteristics of the different nations.

At an early age practice reading in the old clefs. Otherwise many treasures of the past will remain hidden from you.

Start early to observe the tone and character of the different instruments; try to impress the tone color peculiar to each upon your ear.

Never miss an opportunity of hearing a good opera.

Highly honor the old, but also meet the new with a warm heart. Cherish no prejudice against unknown names.

Do not judge a composition on a first hearing; that which pleases most at first is not always the best. Masters call for study. Many things will only become clear to you when you are old.

In judging compositions decide as to whether they belong in the realm of art, or merely in the domain of superficial entertainment. Stand for the first and do not let the other irritate you.

"Melody" is the amateur's war cry, and certainly music without melody is not music. Therefore you must understand what amateurs mean by this word: anything easily, rhythmically pleasing. But there are melodies of a very different type; at whatever page you open Bach, Mozart, Beethoven, etc., they will appear to you in a thousand different guises. If you study these, you will soon tire of the monotony of modern Italian opera melodies.[1]

It is very nice indeed if you can pick out little melodies on the keyboard; but if such come spontaneously to you, and not at the pianoforte, rejoice even more, for it proves that your inner sense of tone is awakening. Fingers must do what the head wills; not vice versa.

When you begin to compose, do it mentally. Do not try the piece at the instrument until it is finished. If your music comes out of your inner self, if you feel it, it will be sure to affect others similarly.

If heaven has gifted you with a lively imagination, you will often, in lonely hours, sit as though spellbound at the pianoforte, seeking to express your inner feelings in harmonies; and you may find yourself mysteriously drawn into a magic circle proportionate to the degree to which the realm of harmony is still vague to you. These are the happiest hours of youth. But beware of losing yourself too often in a talent that will lead you to waste strength and time on shadowy pictures. You will only obtain mastery of form and the power of clear construction by firm strokes of the pen. Therefore, write more often than improvise.

Acquire knowledge of conducting early; frequently observe good conductors; and nothing forbids you to conduct silently along with them. This will give you clarity.

[1] See p. 236.

Have an open eye for life as well as the other arts and sciences.

The laws of morality are also those of art.

You will steadily progress through industry and perseverance.

From a pound of iron which costs only a few pennies, thousands of watch-springs worth many times more can be made. Faithfully use the pound entrusted to you by Heaven.

Nothing worth while can be accomplished in art without enthusiasm.

Art was not created as a way to riches. Strive to become a true artist; all else will take care of itself.

Only when the form is quite clear to you will the spirit become clear to you.

Possibly genius alone entirely understands genius.

Someone has declared that a perfect musician ought to be able to picture a piece which he is hearing for the first time, even the most complicated of orchestral pieces, as though he had the score before him. This is the limit of the imaginable.

There is no end to learning.

♯

You must invent new and bold melodies.

People say, "It pleased"; or "It failed to please." As though there were nothing more important than the art of *pleasing* the public!

It is the artist's lofty mission to shed light into the very depths of the human heart.

No one is able to do more than he knows. No one knows more than he is able to do.

People who are unfamiliar with the most significant manifestations of recent literature are considered uncultivated. The same should apply to music.

Can that which has cost the artist days, weeks, months, and even years of reflection be understood in a flash by the dilettante?

FROM MASTER RARO'S, FLORESTAN'S AND EUSEBIUS' JOURNAL OF POETRY AND THOUGHT [1]

Schumann used the aphoristic form not only for the instruction of the young, but it also served him in his battle against the critics and in his fight for the appreciation of genius.—The order of the aphorisms in this as in the preceding section is the one established by Schumann. The continuous change of topic obviously corresponds to his literary intention. Only those aphorisms pertaining to specific composers (Bach, Chopin, etc.) have been transferred to the chapters dealing with these composers.—The initials F. and E. at the end of each aphorism stand for Florestan and Eusebius.

ON READING SCORES IN CONCERTS

As Eusebius observed a young student of music, diligently following a rehearsal of Beethoven's Eighth Symphony, score in hand, he remarked: "There is a good musician!"—"By no means," said Florestan. "He is a good musician who understands

[1] Most of these entries were written prior to the foundation of the *Neue Zeitschrift für Musik*, partly as early as 1833, and hitherto have not been published; they may be regarded as the beginnings of the Davidites. [Schumann]

the music without the score, and the score without the music. The ear should not need the eye, the eye should not need the (outward) ear."—"A lofty postulate," concluded Master Raro, "but how I agree with you, Florestan!"

There are untalented people who, driven to music by external circumstances, have learned a good deal. They are the artisans. *F.*

What is the use of dressing a hair-brained youth in his grandfather's furred dressing-gown, and sticking a long pipe in his mouth, to make him more steady and orderly? Leave him his flowing locks and his easy attire. *F.*

I do not love the men whose lives are not in harmony with their works. *F.*

Let the youth who composes be warned. Prematurely ripened fruit falls from the tree. The young mind must often unlearn theory before it can apply it. *Raro*

Knowledge is not enough; that which I have learned has to gain strength and certainty by its application to life. *F.*

The wealth of youth: What I know I throw away; what I have I give away! *F.*

Let every man defend his own skin. If a man is my enemy, I need not be his, but rather his Aesop who will make a fable of him, or his Juvenal who will turn him into a satire. *F.*

CRITICS

Music impels nightingales to sing, pug-dogs to yelp.

Sour grapes—bad wine.

They cut up timber, turning the lofty oak into sawdust.

Music speaks the most universal of languages, that through which the soul finds itself inspired in a free, indefinite manner, and yet feels itself at home.

THE PLASTIC ONES

In the end you will tell us that you can actually hear the grass growing in Haydn's *Creation!* F.

Like a Greek god, the artist must associate in a friendly fashion with mankind and with life; but when life dares touch him, let him also disappear and leave nothing behind him save clouds. F.

It is a characteristic of the extraordinary that it cannot be easily understood; the majority is always attuned to the superficial, i.e., to the enjoyment of virtuoso display. E.

Music resembles chess. The queen (melody) has the greatest power, but the king (harmony) decides the game. F.

The artist should preserve his equilibrium with life. Otherwise he will have a difficult stand. F.

GENIUS

We forgive the diamond its sharp edges; it is most costly to round them. F.

It is the curse of talent that, although it labors with greater steadiness and perseverance than genius, it does not reach its goal, while genius, already on the summit of the ideal, gazes laughingly about.

It is the misfortune of the imitator that he dares only appropriate the obvious in the original. As though intimidated by a natural awe, he dares not imitate the truly beautiful. E.

It is not good when human beings acquire too great a facility in any sphere. *Raro*

We are at the goal? What an error! Art shall be the great fugue in which the peoples will succeed one another while singing. *F.*

One voice that blames has the strength of ten that praise. *F.* Alas! *E.*

It is foolish to say that we cannot understand the music of Beethoven's last period. And why? Is his last music too difficult for comprehension in point of harmony? Too singular in form? Is the contrast of thoughts too bold? Something of that sort it must be—for total nonsense in music is an impossibility, and even a madman cannot suppress harmonic laws. But he can be more insipid. *F.*

The extraordinary in an artist is, to his own advantage, not always readily appreciated. *Raro*

The man who has set himself certain limits is unfortunately expected to remain within them. *E.*

Comparisons lead to results by detours; rather judge everything on its own merits and demerits. *F.*

PURITANS IN MUSIC

It would be a puny art, indeed, that merely possessed sounds and no speech nor signs to express the state of the soul. *F.*

Everything that is new has spirit in it. *E.*

THE FRIENDS OF COUNTERPOINT

Do not deny to the spirit what you permit to reason; do not torment yourselves with pitiful trifles and confusing harmonies.

41

Yet whenever anyone who is not indebted to your school dares write in another style, you vent your wrath on him. A time may come when that saying, already denounced by you as the saying of demagogues, "That which sounds well is not wrong," may be altered to "All that does not sound well *is* wrong." And then woe to your canons—and particularly to the *cancrizans*. F.

The Anti-chromatic School should remember that once upon a time the seventh startled just as much as the diminished octave now does, and that through the development of harmony, passion received finer nuances by means of which music has been placed among those high mediums of art which have language and symbols for all spiritual states. E.

Psyche in repose, her wings folded, is only half of beauty; she must soar. E.

Similar forces annul each other; dissimilar ones enhance each other. *Raro*

Piano Playing: The word "playing" is appropriate here, for the *playing* of an instrument must be an integral part of it; he who cannot play with it, cannot play it at all. E.

The triad=times. The third bridges past and future, as does the present. E.
A daring comparison! *Raro*

Men like S. (a rather dissolute artist) should be careful householders. The richer their powers may have been in comparison with those of others, the more painfully will they miss their wasted strength in old age. *Raro*

How little is given with a disinterested heart! E.

Forgive the errors of youth! There are ignes fatui which show the wanderer the right path; the very one that the ignes fatui fail to follow. F.

The youthful works of masters who have become great are looked upon with very different eyes than are the works of composers who promised as much, but failed to keep their promise. *Raro*

It is remarkable that weak points, which even as boys we noticed in others, later appear as lapses of intelligence, lack of talent etc. *Raro*

Dare talent permit itself to take the same liberties as genius? *F.*
Yes; but the former will fail where the latter triumphs. *Raro*

Mannerism is already displeasing in the original, let alone in imitators (Spohr and his pupils). *E.*

The emptiest head thinks it can hide behind a fugue; fugues are only for great masters. *Raro*

Consider how many circumstances must favorably unite before the beautiful can emerge in all its dignity and splendor. We need lofty, serious intention and great ideality; enthusiasm in presentation; virtuosity of workmanship and harmonic cooperation; inner desire and need of the giver and the receiver; momentarily favorable mood in audience and artist alike; a fortunate combination of time, place, and general conditions, as well as of the auspicious moment; direction and communication of impressions, feelings, views; a reflection of the joy of art in the eyes of others. Is not such a combination a happy throw with six dice of sixes? *E.*

A SYMPHONY BY N. (1833)

How it moves me when an artist—whose development cannot be called unsound or unnatural—receives nothing from the public for the sleepless nights he has devoted to his labor, destroying, rebuilding, despairing, here and there encouraged by a flash of genius—nothing, not even appreciation for the youthful faults from which he has escaped! How I felt for him as he stood there, intense, nervous, sad, hoping for one encouraging voice which would give him a little applause. I was indeed moved. *E.*

Talent labors, genius creates. *F.*

CRITICS AND REVIEWERS

The armed eye beholds the stars; the unarmed only sees fog shadows. *F.*

The great is admirable even in ruins. Dismember a symphony by Beethoven and one by Gyrowetz [1], and observe what remains. Works of mere talent or compilation, when destroyed, seem but card houses overturning one another; while, after the expiration of centuries, pillars and capitals of ruined temples still stand. *E.*

A drama without a living representation will always appear dead, foreign to the public, like a musical tone poem, deprived of the hand which realizes it. But when the performer comes to the help of the creator, half the battle is won. *E.*

The cultivated musician may study a Madonna by Raphael, the painter a symphony by Mozart, with equal advantage. Yet more: in sculpture the actor's art becomes fixed; the actor again transforms the sculptor's work into living forms; the painter turns a poem into a painting; the musician sets a picture to music. *E.*

The aesthetic principle is the same in every art; only the material differs. *F.*

It is difficult to believe that music, the essentially romantic art, can form a distinctly romantic school within itself. *F.*

[1] Gyrowetz, contemporary of Beethoven, was a Bohemian composer who wrote 60 symphonies, 30 operas, 40 piano sonatas, etc.

Paganini is the turning point of virtuosity. *F.*

Fingers and hands must be made easy and rapid in movement during childhood; the lighter the hand, the more perfect the performance. *E.*

What we learn in childhood is never forgotten. *F.*

THE COUNTERPOINTERS

They are not satisfied when a young student works out the old classic form as a master in his own medium; what they want is that he should work it out in theirs. *E.*

Music is the latest of the arts to have developed; her beginnings were the simple moods of joy and sorrow (major and minor). Indeed, the less cultivated man can scarcely believe that there exist more specialized emotions, whence his difficulty in understanding the more individual masters such as Beethoven and Schubert. We have learned to express the more delicate nuances of feeling by penetrating more deeply into the mysteries of harmony. *E.*

The masses want the massive. *F.*

If you wish to understand a man, ask him who are his friends; if you want to judge a public, observe what it applauds, what is its expression when listening to music. Since music—so different from painting—is the art which we enjoy most in company with others (a symphony, presented in a room with one listener, would please him but little); which is comprehended by thousands at one and the same time; an art which lifts mankind above life, as above the sea; which, instead of engulfing and destroying us, mirrors us as flying genii, until we are laid to rest in the groves of the Greek gods—so are there works, to be regarded as the highest, exerting equal power over different minds, young and old alike. I remember having been

45

present at a performance of the C minor symphony, and when the passage that leads toward the finale was played—exciting every nerve to the utmost tension—a little boy pressed closer and closer to me; when I asked him why he did so, he answered —"I am afraid!" *E.*

Great thoughts often make the round of minds in similar words and tones. *F.*

The oldest man was the youngest; the last-comer is the oldest; how is it, then, that we accept as laws the rules of past centuries? *F.*

Your declaration, Florestan, that you admire the *Pastoral* and *Heroic* Symphonies less, because Beethoven has so designated them and thus put limits to our imagination, seems to me to be founded on a just feeling. But if you should ask me why, I would scarcely know the answer. *E.*

Nothing worse can happen to a man than to be praised by a rascal. *F.*

IMPERTINENT MODESTY

The saying, "I have thrown it into the fire," is an example of shameless modesty; the world is not rendered unhappy by an unworthy work; besides, it is merely a phrase: one ought really to be ashamed. I detest people who throw their compositions into the fire! *F.*

ABOUT REVISING COMPOSITIONS

Two different readings of the same work are often equally good. *E.*

The original one is generally the better. *Raro*

There is a *School of Politeness* (by Rumohr); I wonder that nobody has ever thought of writing a "School of Polemics," which would be much richer in ideas. The arts should be cultivated only by people of talent. As talent would speak of talent, the language of good will would become a natural consequence in musical criticism. Nowadays, combat too often becomes inevitable. Musical polemics still present a wide field, because few musicians know how to write well, and few authors are practical musicians, neither party knowing how to take hold of the matter; consequently, musical controversies often end with a retreat on both sides or a general embrace. If only the right people would enter the field—those who know how to fight! *F.*

REPRESENTATION OF THE MOMENT, WHILE IT LASTS

A frenzied Roland could not write *Orlando Furioso;* a loving heart cannot discourse of love. If only Franz Liszt understood this, his compositions would be less extravagant, more coherent. The most curious secrets of creation might be investigated with this thought in mind. In order to move something, we must not stand upon it. Opposed to this is the crass materialism of medieval figures from whose mouths issue placards with explanatory speeches. *F.*

Why not forge every great Prometheus to the rock because he called down the light of heaven too soon! *F.*

It is not enough that a journal mirror the present. The critic must outstrip fleeing time, and from the future fight the present as if it already were the past. *E.*

We yet need a publication to defend the "music of the future." Only such men as the late blind cantor of the Thomas School and the deaf conductor who lies in Vienna could aptly edit it. *F.*

He who is too eager to preserve his originality is already in the course of losing it. *E.*

47

Only a small number of works of genius have become popular (Don Giovanni). *F.*

Do not forestall time; give the old masters to the young for study, but do not expect them to carry simplicity and severity to the verge of affectation. Teach them to make an intelligent use of the recently extended facilities of art. *Raro*

GOTTSCHALK WEDEL'S [1] PROPOSED GERMANIZATION OF FOREIGN MUSICAL TERMS

Our highly esteemed and witty friend Wedel must already have observed that we think this subject deserves consideration. Our periodical always germanizes as much as possible the titles of compositions; the eye will grow accustomed to the change, and people will at last wonder why *mit inniger Empfindung* is not as suitable as *con gran' espressione*—nor need it then be written on every page.

But we doubt whether such extraordinary translations as *Bardiet* [2] for "symphony" will ever be accepted, and we do not approve of them; no one can deprive us of our *Lied,* while, on the other hand, we should accept "sonata" and "rondeau" as they are; it would not be possible to give the same significance to a German translation of them as, for example, the affected *Klangstück* or *Tanzstück*.[3] Don't carry things to extremes, but throw the *composées et dédiées* overboard!

In my opinion it would be a good plan to express these musical terms by a series of symbols, which have more affinity with the notes than have the letters. How much more quickly the eye takes in the symbol ――――― than its Italian verbal equivalent *crescendo;* there is a pretty charm in the different signs, bows, lines, etc. used with musical characters, and I have oftentimes thought that the manner of illustrating a work by symbols

---

[1] "Gottschalk Wedel" was the Davidite name of Schumann's friend Zuccalmaglio.

[2] Obsolete German word meaning bard song.

[3] "Sound piece" or "dance piece."

of expression throws more light upon a composer's aesthetic culture than do the very tones. *F*.

Among the causes of the decline of music are bad opera houses and bad teachers. It is almost incredible how the latter affect whole generations either beneficially or destructively through primary and secondary education. *Raro*

Falconers tear out the feathers of their hawks lest they fly too high. *F*.

Red is the color of youth. Bulls and turkeys become enraged when they see it. *F*.

Critics and reviewers differ; the former stand closer to the artist, the latter to the artisan. *F*.

Just so that genius exists it matters little how it appears, whether in the depths, as with Bach; on the heights, as with Mozart; or simultaneously in the depths and on the heights, as with Beethoven. *F*.

Apollo is the God of both Muses and doctors. *F*.

♯

THAT WHICH RULES

Long ago I was struck by the scarcity of trills in Field's compositions—except slow ones; beats, rather. Field habitually practised the trill with great zeal in a pianoforte establishment in London. One day a robust fellow entered, and leaning over an instrument, standing played a trill with such roundness and rapidity that Field left the place, observing that if such a fellow could trill with such skill, it was not worth *his* while to learn the trick. May we' not deduce from this and other instances the deep sense of reverence with which men bow only before that which is not to be imitated mechanically? *F*.

DILETTANTISM

Beware, Eusebius, of despising the better kind of dilettantism, so inseparable from artist life. The saying, "No artist, no connoisseur," can only be regarded as a half truth; for we cannot point to any period in which art has really blossomed without this reciprocity. *Raro*

♯

Experience has proven that the composer is usually not the finest and most interesting performer of his own works, especially his most recent ones, which he has not yet mastered from an objective point of view. Other people often know how to express our meanings better than we do ourselves. *E.*

Right. And should the composer, who needs rest at the conclusion of a work, strive at once to concentrate his powers on its performance, his judgment—like overfatigued sight that tries to fix itself on one point—would become clouded, if not blind. We have seen instances when composers have wholly misinterpreted their own works by such a forced operation. *Raro*

LOOKING AT MUSIC

While playing Kalkbrenner's four-part one-handed fugue, I thought of the excellent Thibaut, author of the book, *On the Purity of Music*, who told me that once, at a concert given by Cramer in London, a polite Lady Somebody, an art amateur, actually rose, against all English convention, and stood on tiptoe to stare at the artist's hands. The ladies near her imitated her example, until finally the whole audience was standing; and the lady whispered ecstatically into Thibaut's ear: "Heavens, what trills!—what trills! and with the fourth and fifth fingers!—and with both hands at once!" The whole audience murmured in accompaniment: "Heavens! what a trill! what trills!—and with both," etc. *Raro*

This seems to me a very common characteristic of the public at concerts where the listeners like to see the virtuoso in person. *E.*

Would to heaven that a race of freaks could arise in the world of artists, with one finger too many on each hand; then the dance of virtuosity would be at an end! *F*.

PLAYING IN PUBLIC FROM MEMORY

Whether out of daring or charlatanism, it is always a proof of uncommon musical powers. Wherefore the prompter's box, wherefore fettered feet, when the head has wings? Do we not know that a chord played from notes—no matter how freely— is never half so free as one played from the imagination? We are all alike; and I, because a German and therefore wedded to tradition—I also would be astonished, had I seen the actor or dancer produce his or her written part in public in order to perform it with more assurance; and yet, I, too, am like the Philistine, who, upon seeing a virtuoso quietly continue to play after the score had fallen from the desk, cried out in hot excitement, "Look, look, that is indeed art! He knows it by heart!" *F*.

DEPENDENCY

Had Shakespeare not existed, would Mendelssohn's *Midsummer Night's Dream* have seen the light—even though Beethoven has written many a one without title? The thought might make me sad. *F*.

Yes. Else why does it happen that so many characters only display their individuality after they have looked to others for support? Like the great Shakespeare himself, who, it is well known, found much of the material of his plays in novels and works of older writers. *E*.

Eusebius speaks true. Many people act freely only when they feel themselves conditioned. *Raro*

Articles

ON CERTAIN PROBABLY CORRUPTED PASSAGES
IN THE WORKS OF BACH, MOZART,
AND BEETHOVEN

*Schumann rarely took the pen to express himself on general
subjects. The article which follows was inspired by practical considerations. In all the instances mentioned therein,
further research has proved the accuracy of Schumann's in-
tuition. It is because the method of detection proved itself
correct, rather than because of the particular instances to
which it was applied, that this essay has remained important for over a century.*

WERE we acquainted with all of these, folios might have to be
written about them; and if earthly tones penetrate beyond the
grave, I think the masters must often smile when they hear the
errors that custom, tradition, and even anxious reverence, have
permitted to continue in their works. It has long been my intention to refer to a few in some of the better-known works of the
masters mentioned above, with the request that all artists and
connoisseurs test them, whenever possible, by comparisons with
the original manuscripts. Even these themselves are sometimes
incorrect. No composer would dare swear with certainty that
any manuscript of his is entirely free from errors. It is quite
natural that among the hundred thousand skipping dots that
he writes in an incredibly short space of time, a dozen or so
should be jotted down a little too high or too low; indeed, composers oftentimes set down the maddest harmonies.

Despite all this the original manuscript remains the authority
which must be consulted first. I should be glad if all persons
who are in possession of the doubtful passages I am about to
mention, would compare the original manuscript with the

printed copies, and kindly communicate the result to me. In some cases this comparison is not even necessary, so obvious are the errors.

The greatest number of these errors will be found in the editions of Bach's works, particularly the older ones. It would be a meritorious task—though one requiring much time—for some musical connoisseur, thoroughly conversant with Bach, to undertake the correction of all hitherto incorrectly printed passages . . . A criticism on *The Well-tempered Clavichord* with an addition of the different readings (Bach himself made many alterations) would alone demand a volume by itself. I shall refer only to a few other instances.

In the grand and beautiful *Toccata with Fugue for the Organ* commencing thus,

both parts move on the keyboard, over an organ point, in strictly canonical progression. Is it possible that this has been overlooked by the proofreader? For he has allowed a number of notes to stand that are not compatible with the canon. Similar oversights occur in the course of the piece in the corresponding passages on pages 4 and 5 [of the Peters Edition]. Though these may be easily corrected, the explanation of another passage in the same piece is more difficult. My readers will no doubt remember the grandiose pedal solo; by comparing this with the parallel passage on the fourth below, they will find that a number of errors have crept in. Two measures are wholly wanting on page 4, between measures 3 and 4; these may be seen in the transposition on page 5, staff 6, in the second and third measures. The solution of this question can only be found in the original manuscript.

To tolerate such errors would be like permitting a rent to remain in a picture, a leaf to fall out of a favorite book. No one ought to consider as immaterial the possession of a piece as extraordinary as this composition in its true reading.

Another curious accident, which only Bach's manuscript can explain, is to be found in the *Art of the Fugue*. Fugue No. 14, four pages long, already appears in No. 10. How did this happen? Bach would surely not have included four pages, note for note, twice in the same work! . . . The fact that this repetition has remained so long unobserved is only to be explained by the unchanging key and theme throughout the work.

But who, when he is reveling in Bach's harmonies, can think of everything,—most of all, of errors? Thus I for years overlooked one in a Bach fugue which was very familiar to me, until a master—who certainly possesses an eagle eye [Mendelssohn]—directed my attention to it. The fugue is in E minor, on a wonderful theme.[1] . . . If we insert, between the third and fourth measures, the single note ____ it will be correct. This admits of no doubt.

Let us now mention passages, still more interesting, perhaps, to our readers, in works which they may have heard and played countless times without suspecting that anything was amiss. I must request them, however, to refer to the scores in question since the passages would occupy too much space for reproduction here and a correct judgment cannot be arrived at without the closest examination.

Our first doubtful passage will be found in Mozart's G minor Symphony, a work in which every note is golden, every movement a treasure. And yet, strange to say, four entire measures have slipped into the andante, which, according to my firm conviction, do not belong to it. From the twenty-ninth measure on (excepting the eighth-note up-beat) there occurs a period of four measures, leading from D-flat major to B-flat minor, which is repeated in the following four measures, with simplified in-

[1] Peters, vol. 2, No. 9.

strumentation; it is not possible that Mozart intended this. The wholly un-Mozartean, unmasterful linking of the thirty-second with the thirty-third measures must often have struck musicians, even when they listened superficially. The question is which of the two four-measure periods ought to be cut out, the first or the second? At a first glance it looks as if the first should be retained. The sudden entrance of the wind instruments, rising to a *forte*, is not without artistic meaning. But in the other version the progression of the parts seems to me far more natural; clearer, simpler, yet similarly not without intensification; and according to this the twenty-ninth to the thirty-second measures would be cut out so that all instruments, after a clear *crescendo*, might unite in a *forte*. The same four superfluous measures are also to be found on the repetition in the second part where the measures 48 to 51 of this part should be omitted. How these errors crept in can only be revealed, if at all, through the original, now in the possession of Councillor André. In our opinion the most probable theory is that Mozart first wrote the passage in the form which to us appears to be the correct one; that he then introduced it into the score more fully instrumentated; and that later, returning to his first idea, he forgot to strike out the earlier reading. Other musicians should express their opinion regarding this point, which is of much consequence; so that by a general agreement the andante might everywhere be played in the manner designated. And also to request publishers to leave the four extra measures, but within parentheses, in the score, with a remark explaining the reason why they do so. I have been told that when the andante is performed at the Paris *Conservatoire*, the four measures are omitted in both places. Mendelssohn has also long come out in favor of this custom.

Finally I will mention some passages in Beethoven symphonies that may be recognized almost at first sight as errors of the copyist. One of these is to be found at the close of the first movement of the B-flat major Symphony, where, of the three measures, *fortissimo* (eight measures before the end), one is evidently superfluous. The error was probably very easily committed because of the complete similarity of the notes in all the parts. Beethoven may have made it himself.

But the fact that we listen, year after year, to the following passage in the *Pastoral* Symphony—fixed, indeed, in the score—without violently protesting, can only be explained by the magic influence of Beethoven's music which moves us so deeply that, while immersed in it, we almost forget to think and hear.

In the first movement we find:

How would it be if, instead of the sudden rest in the first violins, we made *simili* signs ($\simeq$)? Would it not sound different and better? Is not this suggested by the inversion from measure 5 on where the violas play the passage first given to the first violins? *Certainly* it should be so. Either the copyist mistook the *simili* signs for rests, or some impish spirit was at work. Ries tells us how enraged Beethoven became over a passage in the *Eroica* Symphony which Ries had altered with the best intentions. If Beethoven had once really heard this passage in the *Pastoral* Symphony, I think the orchestra and the director would have excited similar emotions in him.

Enough for today; may the instances cited above seriously be taken into consideration! How can we better express our admiration and reverence for our great masters than by endeavoring to remove from their works those injuries that may have accrued to them by accident or error? It was only for this end that the above lines were written.

ON THE COMIC SPIRIT IN MUSIC

This article was inspired by Schumann's friend Keferstein who had written on the same subject in the journal CAECILIA.

HALF-EDUCATED people are generally unable to discover in music, without an accompanying text, more than the expression of grief and joy and perhaps melancholy (which lies midway between the two). They are deaf to the finer shades of passion—anger, remorse on the one hand, satisfaction, quietude, etc. on the other. On this account it is difficult for them to understand great masters like Beethoven and Schubert, who have translated almost every possible condition of life into the language of tone. I have fancied, in certain *Moments musicaux* of Schubert's, to perceive a suggestion of unpaid tailors' bills, so much do these breathe the bad moods of a *bourgeois*. Eusebius even declares that in one of his marches he sees the whole Austrian national guard pass by, preceded by the bagpipers, and carrying sausages and hams on the points of their bayonets. But this interpretation is an excessively subjective one!

Among purely comic instrumental effects I must mention the kettledrums, tuned in octaves, in the scherzo of Beethoven's D minor Symphony—the horn passage [in D]

in the A major Symphony, and generally, the repeated entries in D major in slow tempo with which he suddenly stops and thrice startles us (indeed the whole last movement of this symphony is the highest instance of humor that instrumental music has to show), and the *pizzicato* in the scherzo of the C minor Symphony, though you feel a droning behind it. The members of a well-known and experienced orchestra always begin to laugh at a passage in the last movement of the F major Symphony, because in this bass figure  they think they hear the name (Belcke) of one of its honored members.[1]

The questioning figure of the double basses in the C minor Symphony has a comic effect:

The figure in the adagio of the B-flat major Symphony

is a veritable Falstaff, in particular when occurring in the bass

[1] Christian Gottlieb Belcke was a distinguished flutist of the *Gewandhaus* Orchestra in Leipzig.

or the timpani. A comic effect is produced by this snappish figure

in the last movement of the quintet, opus 29, up to the sudden entrance of the 2-4 time measure which tries to beat down the struggling 6-8. Certainly Beethoven enters personally in the andante *scherzoso* . . . or else begins a soliloquy with the words: "Heavens! What have I done here! The bagwigs will shake their heads" (or just the reverse, rather), and so on. Comic indeed are the conclusions of the scherzo of the A major Symphony, and of the allegretto of the Eighth. We can picture the composer throwing down his pen, not good to begin with. Then, the horns at the close of the scherzo of the B flat Symphony,

which here seem to indicate an entirely fresh start! How many such examples may be found in Haydn! Fewer in the idealistic Mozart. Among the moderns one should not forget, besides Weber, Marschner whose comic talent seems by far to exceed his lyric gift. *Florestan*

CHARACTERIZATION OF THE KEYS

The following study was based on an article which Schumann had contributed to a general dictionary in 1834.

THIS HAS BEEN advocated and opposed. Reason, as usual, lies in the middle. It is as inadmissible to say that this or that feeling, in order to be correctly expressed in music, must be translated in this or that key (anger, for example, in C-sharp minor) as to agree with Zelter who declares that any feeling may be expressed in any key. The analysis of this question was already begun in the last century; the poet Schubart especially professed to have found in some keys the characteristic expression of definite feelings. Though a great deal of poetic tenderness is to be found in his characterization, though he was the first to signalize the great differences that exist between the major and the minor scales, he piles up too many adjectives, epithets, and specifications in his work. However, this would not be of great concern had they all been correctly applied. For instance, he calls E minor a girl dressed in white, with a rose-colored bow at her bosom! In G minor he finds discontent, discomfort, worried anxiety over an unsuccessful plan, ill-tempered chewing of the lips. Now compare this idea with Mozart's Symphony in G minor, full of Hellenic grace! . . . No one will deny that a composition, transposed from its original key into another, produces a different effect or that this alteration is produced by a difference in the character of the keys; only try the *Désir* Waltz [1] in A major, or the "Bridal Chorus" [2] in B major! The new key seems contradictory to the feeling; the normal state of mind in which these compositions were written has been carried into a foreign sphere. The process by means of which the composer selects this or that principal key for the expression of his feelings is as little explicable as the creative process of genius itself, which selects a certain form as the mould which most accurately embodies the thought. The composer selects the correct key with no greater reflection than does the painter in selecting his colors. It would be a good idea—had we space for it—to compare the predominant character of classic masterworks set in the same keys, to discover whether or not certain moods, in the course of time, had not conventionally referred themselves to certain keys. The difference between major and minor must be allowed beforehand. The former is the active, virile principle; the latter, the passive, the feminine. Simple feelings demand simple keys; the more complicated ones re-

[1] By Schubert, in A-flat major.
[2] From Weber's *Freischütz*, in C major.

quire those which are less frequently heard. Thus one might observe the rising and falling [of the temperature of feeling] in the interwoven succession of rising and falling fifths, and accept F-sharp—the middle point in the octave, the so-called tritonus—as the highest point, which again descends through the flat keys to the simple, unadorned C major.

Surveys

In the beginning of some of his reviews of recently published compositions, which Schumann grouped by art forms (symphonies, concertos, variations, études, etc.), he would take the opportunity of surveying the general picture of each form as it appeared to him at the time. The most important of these surveys, when taken together, amount to a clearly defined theory of the evolution of forms in general.

[SYMPHONIES]

This survey was written two years before Schumann began to compose symphonies himself.

WHEN THE GERMAN speaks of symphonies, he means Beethoven; the two names are for him one and indivisible—his joy, his pride. As Italy has its Naples, France its Revolution, England its Navy, etc., so the Germans have their Beethoven symphonies. The German forgets in his Beethoven that he has no school of painting; with Beethoven he imagines that he has reversed the fortunes of the battles that he lost to Napoleon; he even dares to place him on the same level with Shakespeare. Since the compositions of this master have become an integral part of us, since some of his symphonic works have become popular, one could suppose that they had left deep traces behind them and begotten works of the same nature during the period following that of Beethoven. But this is not so. We find imitations—and, oddly enough, principally of his earlier symphonies, as if each one needed a certain time to be understood and copied; we find many too close imitations, but very, very seldom, with few exceptions, any true maintenance or mastery of this sublime form in which, bound in a spiritual union, continually changing ideas succeed one another. The great number of recent symphonies drop into the overture style, especially in their first movements; the slow movements are there because slow movements are required; the scherzos have nothing of the scherzo about them save the name; the last movements completely forget what the former ones contained. Berlioz was announced to us as a phenomenon. Little more than nothing is known about him in Germany; what is known of him by hearsay seems to have so alarmed the Germans that a considerable time must pass before he will be accepted here. Assuredly he has not labored in vain; no phenomenon comes singly. This will be shown in the near future. Mention of Franz Schubert must not be omitted; his achievements in the symphonic field, however, still remain unpublished [1839]. The Viennese contest for a prize symphony gave us significant proof of the existing level of symphonic talent. One may say against them what one will, such contests are always useful and can never do any harm; and the laws of intellectual creativeness are little understood by those who declare that productiveness is not increased by incitation, even the most prosaic. Had one of those rare and priceless diamonds, such as are only to be found in imperial and royal treasure vaults, been offered as prize for a symphony during the lives of Haydn, Mozart, and Beethoven, I wager that the masters would have girded their loins and given their best for the occasion. But who could have served as judge? Enough of this. . . .

[PIANO CONCERTOS]

This survey was written in the beginning of 1839. In 1841, Schumann wrote the first movement of his Piano Concerto in A minor. The work was completed only in 1845.

PIANOFORTE composition holds a considerable place in the modern history of music; in it there is displayed the first dawn of a new spirit in music. The most talented composers of the present day are pianists; an observation that was also made during former epochs. Bach and Handel, Mozart and Beethoven, all grew up at the pianoforte; and, like sculptors who first model their statues in small, soft masses, they may often have sketched at this instrument what they afterwards worked out in orchestral forms of grander scope. Since their time the pianoforte has been perfected to a high degree. With the improvement of pianoforte technique and with the bolder swing and sweep which composition had won through Beethoven, the instrument has gained in range and significance; and should pedals be added to it, like the organ's (and this, I believe, will eventually be the case), new possibilities will suggest themselves to the composer. Freeing himself more and more from the support of the orchestra, he will learn how to write more richly, fully, idiomatically. We realize that this separation from the orchestra has for a long time been in process; in defiance of the symphony modern pianoforte playing can only dominate through its own resources, and this may be the reason why recent times have produced so few piano concertos and generally so few original compositions with orchestral accompaniment. Our journal, since its establishment, has reported the appearance of practically all new piano concertos; during the past six years their total number cannot have exceeded sixteen or seventeen, a very small number in comparison with the past. What was formerly considered as an enrichment of instrumental forms, as an invention of consequence, has recently been voluntarily neglected—so greatly do times change. It might certainly be considered as a loss were the piano concerto permitted to become entirely obsolete; but we could scarcely contradict piano players should they say: "We do not need the assistance of others; our instrument is the most effective when heard alone." And so we must wait patiently for the genius who may show us in a new and brilliant fashion how the orchestra ought to be combined with the piano; who may make it possible for the pianist to reveal the riches of his instrument and his art, while raising the orchestral rôle to something more than that of a bystander and permitting it artistically to suffuse the scene with manifold colors. We would gladly insist, however, that young composers should give us, as an indemnification for that serious and dignified concerto form, equally serious and dignified solo compositions; no caprices, no variations, but finely rounded characteristic allegro movements which in any case might be used for the opening of a concert. But, until then, we shall often return to those older works that open a concert in so worthy a manner and so fully test the powers of an artist; to those admirable concertos of Mozart and Beethoven, or—should a highly refined and select circle desire to gaze again on the countenance of a great man too little and too seldom honored —to one by Sebastian Bach. Or, should we wish to produce something new, to one of those later ones in which the old traditions, especially those of Beethoven, have been skilfully and felicitously extended.[1]

[PIANO SONATAS]

These lines were written shortly after Schumann, following a pause of several years, had completed his second and last piano sonata, opus 22. They may serve to explain why Schumann never wrote piano sonatas again, except for the three sonatinas, opus 118, which he composed for his three little daughters.

IT IS strange that those who write sonatas are generally unknown; and it is also strange that the older composers still liv-

[1] Schumann here is thinking of Mendelssohn and Moscheles.

ing among us, who grew up when the sonata was at its peak, and among whom only Cramer and Moscheles retain some importance, least of all cultivate this form. It is easy to guess the reason why the components of the former class—usually young artists—write sonatas: there is no better form in which they can introduce themselves to the higher class of critics and please them at the same time. Therefore most sonatas of this kind must be regarded as samples, so to speak, or as studies in form; they are seldom the result of an irresistible inward impulse. As for the older composers, there is doubtless a reason why they no longer write sonatas. We leave it to others to guess what this reason may be.

It was Hummel who bravely built along the old Mozartean lines, and whose F-sharp minor Sonata alone will outlive his name. Franz Schubert, above all, sought and found a new departure from Beethoven. Ries [1] worked too quickly. Berger [2] gave us a few excellent compositions which, however, never attained an extended circulation, and Onslow [3] shared the same fate. Weber became fierily and rapidly successful, establishing a style of his own, and many of our young writers are merely continuations of Weber. Such was the status of the sonata ten years ago, and such it remains. A few fine works in this style have since appeared and may yet be made public; but, on the whole, it looks as if this form had run its course. This is as it should be, for we cannot repeat the same forms for centuries, and ought rather to think about creating something new. So let them, if they will, write sonatas or fantasies (what's in a name?). Only do not let music be forgotten, and pray to your good genius that the rest may follow.

[1] Pupil of Beethoven.
[2] Well-known teacher.
[3] French composer.

[VARIATIONS FOR THE PIANO]

It is to be remembered that, at the time of this survey, Schumann was working on his SYMPHONIC ETUDES EN FORME DE VARIATIONS, *opus 13.*

WHOEVER invented the first variations was certainly no bad fellow (and after all, was it not Bach?). One can neither write nor listen to symphonies every day, and so imagination discovered that graceful form from which Beethoven's genius evolved such ideal works of art. But the actual period of the variation is approaching its end and making room for the capriccio. May it rest in peace! For no musical form has produced more insipid results than these—and so will it continue. One has little conception how much shameless vulgarity, how much poverty has grown to rank profusion in these depths. At least before we had good boring German themes; now we are forced to swallow hackneyed Italian ones in five or six watery decompositions. And lucky you are if you get off with so few! For you can see what happens when the Müllers, the Mayers, and whatever they are called, emerge from their provinces! Ten variations, double repetitions. If only that were all! But then comes the variation in the minor and the finale in 3/8 time—ugh! Not a word more! Into the fire with it all! We consider ourselves and our readers far too good to be burdened with such trash . . .

[PIANO STUDIES]

The music market, in Schumann's time, was swamped with collections of piano études of all kind; a great part of his reviewing activity therefore had to be devoted to this type of composition.

No PIANOFORTE MUSIC contains so much that is excellent as the study (étude). The reasons are simple: its form is one of the easiest and most attractive, and its aim is so clear and firmly fixed that it is almost impossible not to succeed in it . . . In a broad sense every piece of music is a study, and the simplest is oftentimes the most difficult. In a narrower sense we require a special purpose in the study; it must develop technique in a special phase and lead to the mastery of some particular difficulty, of technique, rhythm, expression, presentation, or what not. If the étude contains many difficulties, it enters the domain of the caprice; one would then do better to devote one's time to practicing broader, inwardly connected movements like those of the concerto, which in these days presents much matter for study and contains all sorts of difficulties. . . .

The following is part of a review of Hummel's ETUDES, *written in the form of an argument between Eusebius, Florestan, and Raro.*

THE MOST LAUDABLE Bach, who knew a million times more than we even suppose, was the first to undertake to write for students; but he did it in so gigantic a manner that only after many years did he become known to the world as the founder of a severe, thoroughly healthy school through a few men who, in the meanwhile, have been developing in their own ways.

Bach's son Emanuel inherited a fine talent. He filed, refined, added a beautiful cantilena to the then predominating harmony and figurated melody; but as a creative musician he remained very far behind his father. As Mendelssohn once said, "It was like the advent of a dwarf among the giants."

Clementi and Cramer followed. The former, on account of his contrapuntal, often cold art, could find no acceptance among young minds. Cramer was preferred on account of the transparent clearness of his étude music.

Although later on certain musicians were allowed specific merits, the general ability to train the head and hand was ascribed only to Cramer's school.

67

But now many wished to do something about feeling. They realized that all these études were unsatisfactory because of their intellectual monotony; they also discovered, thank Heaven! that it was not necessary to learn them all seriatim in order to improve.

The subtle Moscheles then contrived his interesting character-pieces, by means of which he also excited the imagination.

Then came Hummel. Eusebius, I shall speak out! His studies came a few years too late . . . Who will deny that most of these studies are put together and finished in a masterly fashion; that a certain idea is developed in each of them; that all of them were created with that masterly ease which is the result of a long, well-spent life. But that charm of the imaginative which causes youth to lose itself in the beauty of the piece and forget its difficulty while mastering it is utterly wanting.

Believe me, Eusebius—and it may be told in your own colorful language—if Theory be the faithful yet lifeless mirror that reflects truth silently, remaining dead, without an object to animate it, Imagination is the seeress with blindfolded eyes from whom nothing is withheld and whose errors often add to her charm. What do you say to this, master? *Florestan*

[STRING QUARTETS IN GERMANY]

These lines were written in 1842, the same year in which Schumann composed his three string quartets, opus 41.

THE QUARTETS of Haydn, Mozart, Beethoven! Who does not know them and who dare cast a stone at them? Though it is definite evidence of the indestructible vitality of those creations that, after the lapse of half a century, they still delight all hearts, it is not to the credit of the recent artistic generation that in so long a period of time nothing comparable has been created. Onslow's quartets alone found a response, and after him, Mendelssohn's, whose aristocratic-poetic nature was especially adapted to this musical form; moreover in Beethoven's later quartets treasures may be found unknown as yet to the world, and among which we may search for many years.

We Germans are, therefore, not poor in quartets; but very few among us have known how to augment the existing capital.
Florestan

[DANCE MUSIC]

The following survey was written by Schumann under his own name in 1835 but in a style very close to that of Eusebius. Although it precedes a review of short piano pieces, it stands by itself in the original, and is to be understood as a literary effort of particular intensity of feeling.

MUSICAL like political revolutions penetrate every sphere of life, including the smallest. In music we observe the new influence even there where art is sensuously allied with common life—in the dance. As the monarchy of counterpoint disappeared, miniature sarabands and gavottes, like hoops and patches, went out of fashion, and queues became much shorter. Then the minuets of Mozart and Haydn rustled by in their long trains, while people stood facing each other decorously and silently, bowing often, and finally taking leave of each other; a grave peruke was still to be seen here and there, but the hitherto stiffly laced figures now began to move more gracefully and elastically. Then young Beethoven broke in, breathless, hesitant and disturbed, with long, disorderly hair; neck and brow free as Hamlet's; and people were greatly astonished at the asocial fellow. But the ballroom was too close and oppressive for him, so he rushed out into the darkness, heeding no obstacles, impervious to fashion and ceremony, yet moving aside lest he should step on a flower; and those who were pleased with such a temperament called it caprice, or whatever they liked. Now a new generation has come to the fore; the children have become youths and maidens, so shy, so dreamy, that they scarcely venture to look at one another. One of them, by the name of John [Field], sits at the pianoforte on which the moonbeams shine broadly and kiss the keys; another sleeps upon stones and dreams of his re-arisen country [Chopin]; no longer are they concerned with sociability, with sympathy, for each one thinks and acts only for himself; nor are wit, irony, and egotism wanting. A clear high string still resounds in the joyous Strauss [the elder]; but the deeper ones, plucked by time, are only momentarily submerged: how will it all end, and where is it leading me?

Observations

[COMPOSERS AND COMPOSITIONS]

These observations are epigrams, aphorisms, reflections, and maxims which Schumann inserted in some of his reviews of second-class music of the time. While these reviews no longer present the same general interest today, the general observations contained therein may help to complete the picture of Schumann's musical credo.

Artists, like some mothers, frequently love those of their children best who have caused them the greatest pains.

♯

People compose for many reasons: to become immortal; because the pianoforte happens to be open; to become a millionaire; because of the praise of friends; because they have looked into a pair of beautiful eyes; or for no reason whatsoever.

♯

Nature would burst should she attempt to produce nothing save Beethovens.

*The following reflection is mainly directed against Spohr
and his school, but was applied by Schumann to others,
even to Beethoven, see below, p. 98.*

We must speak a word in favor of every one of the more
powerful, masculine expressions in music today (which so
preponderantly and in its most beloved masters tends to the
contrary); as if Beethoven had not lived a short time ago and
plainly said: "Music must strike fire from the spirit of a man; emo-
tionalism is only meant for women." Few remember what he
said; the majority aim at emotional effects. They ought to be
punished by being dressed in women's clothes.

♯

I have discovered a truth: that we often wish we might recall
a genius *à la mode,* of whose injurious and narrowing influence
we have always been convinced, merely because his own dis-
appearance leaves a vacancy which men of even lesser talents
seek to fill—and how badly! The critics only began to praise
Rossini when Bellini appeared; and he will be lauded because
Caraffa and the others cannot displace him. So with Auber,
Hérold, Halévy.

♯

It is most difficult to manage those people who succeed in
forcing polite treatment from us by means of their own politeness, who bow away our half-expressed criticism, and who
slip through our fingers when we try to get down to essentials
with them. In life, in society, and at court they find and keep
their positions, and it is impossible to exclude them from the
domain of art. Moreover, when, like Thalberg, they belong to
the aristocracy by birth, when, like Döhler, they possess dip-
lomatic connections, they are certain to succeed and speedily obtain a reputation, and there is no end to the praise that is
lavished on them. At times, especially in later years, when incense no longer intoxicates, when even the body begins to lose

its flexibility, these favored ones may occasionally breathe a sigh of longing for better things; of regret for the lost opportunities of their youth. A loftier desire, then, stirs its wings, a new courage arises; they try to recover what they have missed and to make up for what they have lost. Sometimes they succeed, but oftentimes the effort comes too late.

♯

A flower may be painted merely in blue and green, a waltz may be built on tonic and dominant, but when painting a landscape one must know how to use colors freely. Let the musician courageously strike the keys. A passing false tone will quickly be covered up by a powerful idea . . . For aught I care the fifths may ascend or descend chromatically, the melody may be doubled in every interval in octaves. Yes, lately I heard (in a dream) an angelic music filled with heavenly fifths, and this happened, so the angels assured me, because they had never found it necessary to study thorough-bass. Those for whom my words are intended will understand my dream.

The relation of the following lines to Schumann's own compositions is obvious; the same subject is discussed regarding the titles to Beethoven's PASTORALE *(p. 96) and Berlioz'* SYMPHONIE FANTASTIQUE *(pp. 180-81).*

Titles for pieces of music, since they again have come into favor in our day, have been censured here and there, and it has been said that "good music needs no sign-post." Certainly not, but neither does a title rob it of its value; and the composer in adding one at least prevents a complete misunderstanding of the character of his music. If the poet is licensed to explain the whole meaning of his poem by its title, why may not the composer do likewise? What is important is that such a verbal heading should be significant and apt. It may be considered the test of the general level of the composer's education.

♯

Scorn not the short piece. A certain broad basis, a leisurely development and conclusion may be the ornament of many a work. But there are tone-poets who know how to express in minutes what for others requires hours. The interpretation and reception of such concentrated compositions, however, are exacting matters for the performer and for the listener, and they call for a special effort and for a favorable hour and time. Beautiful, broad form may be enjoyed at all times, but profundity of meaning is not communicable at every moment.

In his Fantasy for Violin and Orchestra, opus 92 and opus 134, Schumann, at the end of his life, attempted to compose in a form approaching that outlined below. It is strange that Schumann does not mention Weber's CONZERTSTÜCK *in this connection.*

There is a lack of smaller pieces in concerto form in which the virtuoso can give us all in one his performance of an allegro, adagio, and rondo. It would be well to think out a new genre consisting of one longer movement in a moderate tempo, in which the preparatory passage might take the place of the first allegro, the *cantabile* that of the adagio, and a brilliant close might replace the rondo. This idea is full of suggestions which we ourselves would gladly realize in a composition out of the common order. One could even write the piece as a pianoforte solo.

♯

There exist men of undoubted talent who, subject neither to the power of the great contemporary geniuses nor to fashion, live and create according to their own laws. They have in common with men of genius what is common to all powerful, noble natures; but they despise fashion; and the independence and obstinacy with which they reject everything that looks like courting popular favor may be the cause which prevents their names from reaching the public, to the possible detriment of both parties, though it is of course the public which is the greater loser.

\#

I must express a thought which I mention unwillingly, and so introduce it with Goethe's words: *"Wer sich der Einsamkeit ergibt,—ach! der ist bald allein."* Too long an absence from the world in the end harms the artist; he accustoms himself to certain forms and mannerisms until he becomes an eccentric, a dreamer. So far all may still go well with him. But should a voice from the public cry to him, "Beware, my friend!" he begins to brood, to doubt himself: thus pedantry is followed by discouragement and by hypochondria, this most deadly enemy of creativity.

\#

Young artists, always striving for something new and, if possible, eccentric, esteem too lightly the easily conceived and perfected works of finished masters, and they are greatly mistaken in supposing that they can do likewise. There is always a difference between master and disciple. The quickly tossed-off pianoforte sonatas of Beethoven, and still more those of Mozart, in their heavenly grace exhibit the same degree of mastery that do their deeper revelations. The perfected talent of the master shows itself in that it loosely plays round the outlines which it has projected from the beginning of the work, while younger, less cultivated talent, whenever it leaves the foothold of custom, strains ever tighter at the ropes, and so often comes to grief.

*Here Schumann formulates the principle of his own use of
the piano in songs and song cycles.*

Paralleling the development of poetry, the Franz Schubert
epoch has already been followed by a new one which has
utilized the improvements of the simultaneously developed
instrument of accompaniment, the piano . . . The voice alone
cannot reproduce everything or produce every effect; together
with the expression of the whole the finer details of the poem
should also be emphasized; and all is well so long as the vocal
line is not sacrificed.

♯

Good singers of *Lieder* are almost rarer than good composers
of them.

[ADVICE TO COMPOSERS]

HE WHO constantly confines himself to the same forms and relations finally becomes a mannerist or a Philistine; nothing is
more injurious to an artist than stagnation within a convenient
form; in later years the power of creation tends to decline in
any case, and it is too late to make a formal change—many a
good talent only then discovers that it has but half accomplished its task. Another way of progressing and of enriching
oneself for new creations is the study of other great individuali-
ties. Mozart is often cited as a contradiction of this statement,
and we are told that neither this study nor, indeed, any other
is necessary to genius. But who can say what further masterworks Mozart would have written, had he, for example, known
Sebastian Bach in his entire greatness? [1] If Haydn spurred him
on, how much more would Bach have done so! We cannot
originate everything from within ourselves. What a length of
time it took to evolve the fugue! Must the artist experience

---

[1] Since Schumann wrote these lines it has been established that Bach's music
did influence Mozart in his later years; see A. Einstein, *Mozart*, p. 149.

and examine everything himself, and will he not reach his goal more quickly by studying and imitating the best works attainable, until he has completely conquered their form and spirit? But he must also know all his contemporaries, from the first to the last; that includes, for instance, Strauss [1] who is, in his way, most representative of his time. He who omits to do this, must continually remain in uncertainty with regard to his own relation to the present and with regard to the compass of his own powers, and will in the end have nothing better to offer the world than what is already antiquated and obsolete.

♯

In order to understand thoroughly a composition we must first strip it of its elaborations. Then only can we judge whether it is beautifully formed, how much nature has bestowed, and how much art has added. And if we can still find a pure melody, borne by sound and noble harmony, the composer has passed the test and we will pay him our tribute. This test appears to be such a simple one, and yet, how few pass it.

♯

Display of "learning" betrays a first attempt, and honest beginners generally give us too much of a good thing. Then, as if the whole of counterpoint had to be eliminated from their systems from the start, they threaten us with the opening of fugues (principally rattled off by the double basses); we are given three, four, and more themes, superposed one upon the other; and ultimately we cannot help remarking how happy the composer must be to have managed a return to the principal key. The writer of these lines understands this all too well; he knows it from his own experience . . . and what effect is produced in the end? To be sure, Mozart and Beethoven worked out their themes; but with what material, for what reasons, in what places! Everything is achieved easily, as if in

[1] Johann Strauss, Sr., composer of the *Radetzky* March, was as popular at the time as his son was to be thirty years later.

jest and play. They, too, had to learn by experience; but they never wrote merely for the eye and paper. How I wish that some young composer would sometime give us a gay, light symphony, in a major key, without trombones and double horns! Of course, that is even more difficult; only he who knows how to control the orchestral masses can also dispose of them at his will. But let no one, because of what we have said above, declare in the future that we are not looking for endeavor; we want the profoundest; we merely do not want profundity for its own sake; we do not wish to see the seams. Gluck's observation "that nothing ought to be written *that is not effective*" is, taken in its right sense, one of the most golden of rules, the true secret of the master.

The idea that young composers should write four-part chorals and other choral music seems to have been an obsession with Schumann: see the various fragments from letters reprinted below.

[*Reviewing a Pianoforte Capriccio Entitled* "Adieux à la Patrie"]
MUCH AS WE love the characteristic, we would prefer a young composer to bring us four-part chorals for criticism rather than tone-pictures whose descriptivity lies exclusively in their titles. . . . If only we could have our Federal Parliament order . . . that no publisher print the work of young composers before they have delivered a volume of decent four-part chorals! In that case we should have far better capriccios.

[*Letter to T. G. Herzog, August 4, 1842*]
"You SEEM to be particularly at home with the organ. This is a great advantage, and the greatest composer in the world has written most of his most glorious compositions for this instrument. But, on the other hand, the organ rather tempts one to a certain comfortable way of composing because almost anything sounds well on it. At all events, don't write too many

small things and try your hand at something bigger, such as a fugue, a toccata, etc., of which Bach has left us the loftiest examples.

But, if you don't want to become exclusively a composer of organ music, try a piano sonata or a string quartet and, above all, write for the *voice*. That will further you more than anything and bring the musical being to fruition.

Read a good deal of music: it sharpens your ear. Never play a piece until your *mind* has first grasped the sound. For this purpose I would particularly recommend Bach's three hundred and twenty *Chorals* and *The Well-tempered Clavichord*.

However, do not do too much at once; always bring all your compositions to a conclusion, especially those on a larger scale, even when you are not quite satisfied with them . . ."

[*Letter to Carl Reinecke, January 22, 1846*]
"I HAVE read your compositions with great interest and have found a good deal in them that pleased me very much . . . Don't be put out by the fact that as yet you cannot produce work *entirely your own* and that recollections of earlier models are often to be found there. At such an early age as yours creation is always more or less reproduction. The ore has to go through a great many washings before it becomes sterling metal.

To develop your individual sense of melody it is always best to write a great deal for the voice and unaccompanied chorus; in fact, to *invent* and develop as much as possible *mentally* . . ."

[*Letter to L. Meinardus, September 16, 1848*]
"ABOVE ALL things, persevere in composing mentally, not with the help of the instrument, and keep on twisting and turning the principal melodies about in your head until you can say to yourself: 'Now they will do.' To hit upon the right thing all in a moment, as it were, does not happen every day, and the sketchbooks of great composers, especially of Beethoven, prove how long and how laboriously they often worked over a simple melody and kept on improving upon it.

I see from your letter that you yourself feel the defects of the sonata. However, my advice to you is to correct nothing and rather to begin something new. Write especially for chorus . . ."

[*Letter to the same, December 28, 1853*]

"I WISH you composed in the same style as you write your letters—so easily, thoughtfully, and full of natural humor . . . Above all, you must strive to write new and beautiful melodies. The combinations ought to be merely accidental . . . Then cut yourself loose from the 'subjective' piano. Chorus and orchestra take us out of ourselves . . . So write for orchestra, and especially for chorus . . ."

♯

Every artist's life has its vacation period when all he asks is to feather his oars; but the voice which rouses him to new effort will not fail. The German has great examples of lofty manliness before him; to these let the disciple sometimes look up; to Bach, for instance, who declared that all his works written before his thirtieth year were non-existent; to Beethoven who, even in his last years, could not bear his own *Christ on the Mount of Olives*. Do you not tremble, young artists, when you reflect what your opinion regarding your own compositions may be fifty years from now? What kings throw away, however, is still good enough for tradesmen to pick up. To be sure, you refuse to burn any of your immortal works. So rejoice in your short lives, but do not blame the future if it forgets.

♯

The endeavor to interest as a harmonist, even in small details, may become very dangerous, particularly to an operatic composer. Such rapid, artistically interwoven, often enharmonic changes of chord may be used in complicated ensemble scenes. But in the choruses many sharps and flats are undesirable, and the singers are sure to undertake them unwillingly and intone

79

them erratically; nor are such numerous modulations necessary in a simple song . . . How effective is a simple triad when freely and naturally sung by the human voice! All the enharmonic art of Spohr is nothing beside Handel's freely flowing triads. Therefore a composer must, above all things, guard himself against an overemphasis on harmony; such an overladen chromatic maze in the middle voices can be dangerous even to the instrumental parts; to say nothing of the passages where the voices should predominate and *sing*.

♯

Simplicity alone does not make a work of art; indeed, it may be as blameworthy as its opposite—complexity. The sound tonemaster, however, employs all means deliberately at the right moment.

♯

The fate of a concert piece depends on half minutes; one too many, and somebody begins to cough—and gone is all enthusiasm. Better too little.

♯

An occasional reminiscence is preferable to a desperate independence.

♯

Let us be certain that were a genius like Mozart to be born today, he would write concertos in the manner of Chopin rather than in the manner of Mozart.

♯

Toward the close of a composition, when the primary ideas should, as it were, reçede, the composer ought to avoid overloading the hearer's attention with new feelings or impressions. Such pointed endings are sometimes called original, but nothing is easier than to write an original close (or, for that matter, any close at all), even if one does not carry it to such lengths as Chopin, who lately closed on a chord of the sixth and fourth.

♯

German composers usually fail because they are too anxious to please the public. Let only one of them give us something personal, simple, and deeply felt, and he will see for himself that he can accomplish more in this way. The public is apt to turn a cold shoulder on the man who always approaches it with outstretched arms. Beethoven went about with bowed head and folded arms; the crowd respectfully made way for him and gradually became familiar with, and fond of his extraordinary speech.

[MUSIC AND TECHNIQUE]

The public has lately begun to weary of virtuosos, and, as we have frequently remarked, we have too. The virtuosos themselves seem to feel this, if we may judge from a recently awakened fancy among them for emigrating to America; and many of their enemies secretly hope they will remain over there; for, taken all in all, modern virtuosity has benefited art very little.

♯

Young composers can never learn too soon that music does not exist for the fingers but the reverse, and that no one dare be a bad musician in order to become a good virtuoso.

♯

[Analyzing Hiller's Pianoforte Studies]
As a pedagogue, I must search for three objects—root, flower, and fruit; or for the poetical, the harmonic-melodic, and the technical content; or for the gain offered to heart, ear, and hand.

81

Many works are wholly above discussion; for instance, Mozart's C major (*Jupiter*) Symphony with Fugue, many works by Shakespeare, some of Beethoven's. Those, however, which are principally intellectual, individually characteristic, or stamped with mannerism give us cause to ponder.

♯

In proportion as pieces for four hands disappear from the pianoforte literature of the day, pieces for one hand, characteristically enough, begin to appear. Our opinion regarding this manner of composition may be presumed.[1] If works written with this aim are not of the very best, . . . it is not worth while to publish them. It is of a tragic-comic, almost unnatural effect to see one hand working away, when the introduction of the other would instantly facilitate matters, as is shown in the following example: [2]

Place a clever child near the pianoforte while this is being played, and he will certainly cry out, "Why don't you play it with both hands?" Why uselessly disable oneself?

♯

The older I grow, the more convinced I am that the piano expresses itself mainly in the following three styles: (1) richness

---

[1] On a former occasion Schumann had written: "It is not quite as bad as if someone wanted to study dancing with one foot, but it always remains funny and somewhat foolish when the right hand remains idle and appears to say: 'If I only were willing to work a little, you would not have to struggle so hard.'"

[2] From Eduard Marxsen, *Impromptus for the Left Hand Alone*.

of sound and varied harmony progressions (made use of by Beethoven and Franz Schubert); (2) pedal effect (as with Field); (3) volubility (Czerny, Herz, and others). In the first category we find the expansive players; in the second, the fanciful ones; and, in the third, those distinguished by their pearly technique. Many-sided, cultured composer-performers like Hummel, Moscheles, and, finally, Chopin, combine all three, and are consequently the most beloved by players; those writers and performers who neglect to study any of these fall into the background.

♯

The most difficult things written by one perfectly versed in the difficulties of the keyboard are far easier to play than the easiest things conceived by an amateur.

♯

[*Reviewing the Concert given by a Child Prodigy*]
WE LOVE child prodigies. Whoever accomplishes extraordinary things in youth will, if he continues to learn, bring about in his age things even more extraordinary. Also certain technical abilities should be developed to the point of virtuosity as early as possible. But that to which our young artist especially owes his reputation we oppose as thoroughly false—we mean public improvisations during childhood and youth. We do not address ourselves to him, whose uncommon talent we recognize, but to his mentor, his teacher, or whoever he may be.

Who would seek gain to close the bud that has once unfolded? It would be useless. It would be unnatural to repress a powerful, early-matured inclination. It is common enough to see some particular sense sooner developed in one person than in another. But the rare flowers of January should be patiently fostered and cherished in still seclusion before they are exhibited to the gaze of the cold world.

Our delightful young artist, if thoughtful and thoroughly musical, must feel that much is still lacking; even the correct

83

use of his instrument; besides, the technical repose which betrays a perfected schooling; certain execution which is only attained by continuous study; and above all things a healthy tone, which no one can acquire instinctively. If we are not mistaken, a few years hence he will thank us for placing firmly before him the future, which is not to be jested with. But even if mistaken, we would be forced to say that in him a talent had been lost deserving of a better fate.

In any case, I would like to remind him of a significant old legend. Apollo once bestowed his friendship on a beautiful mortal who grew more and more god-like, more and more akin, in form and spirit, to his divine protector. But he betrayed his secret to men prematurely. The enraged god appeared to him no longer, and the youth, overwhelmed by grief, looked unceasingly into the eyes of the sun, his beloved friend, until he died. Betray not thy divine gifts to men until commanded by the Muse who bestowed them upon thee and of whom thou hast become worthy. For the artist, the beautiful mortal, the god transforms himself into imagination. *Eusebius*

ON MUSICIANS

Old Music

[*Letter to F. Brendel, July 3, 1848*]
"AT TIMES it really sounds like the music of the spheres, and then, what art! I verily believe he is the greatest musical genius ever produced by Italy."

DOMENICO SCARLATTI

THE PIANO WORKS of Domenico Scarlatti, fingered by Carl Czerny, are nicely presented in single issues. The first four contain thirty-three pieces, most of them allegro movements, which present an accurate picture of his style. Scarlatti possesses many excellent qualities which distinguish him from his contemporaries. The order of the ideas—armored, as it were—such as we find in Bach, is missing; he is much less substantial, more ephemeral, rhapsodic. One has difficulty in always following his music, because he quickly knots and then unties again the musical threads. Compared to that of his contemporaries, his style is brief, pleasing, and piquant. His works certainly take an important place in piano literature—by continuing much that was new at the time; by the many sided use they made of the instrument; and in particular by a more independent use of the left hand—but we confess that much in this music no longer pleases us nor ought to please us.

How can any of these compositions be compared with those by our better composers! How clumsy is the form, how rudimentary the melody, how limited the modulation! Especially

87

in comparison with Bach! As one spirited composer [Mendelssohn] once said about Ph. Em. and J. Seb. Bach—their relation equals that of a dwarf and a giant. However, the true pianist, if he wants to be an artist, should become acquainted with the leaders of all different schools, and particularly with Scarlatti, who obviously raised the art of piano playing to a higher level. Yet one should not play too many of these pieces in succession, because they are very similar in movement and character. If presented in one measure and due time, they will continue to sound fresh and new to the listener . . . Mr. Czerny's addition consists of a new fingering. Little do we know to what purpose a fingering for these works—as well as for Bach's piano compositions—may possibly serve.

SELECTED PIANO PIECES BY FAMOUS MASTERS OF THE 17TH AND 18TH CENTURIES

AT A TIME when all eyes are fixed more than ever upon J. S. Bach as one of the greatest creators of all times, it is well to call attention also to his contemporaries. Although nobody in his century can be compared to him in regard to composition for piano and organ—indeed everything else assumes dwarfish proportions when measured with the giant figures he produced —there are some few isolated voices of his time which we should not entirely disregard; they have a quality of inwardness which is still of interest to us. The new heralds of old music mostly make the mistake of singling out those pieces in which our ancestors frequently were clever at the expense of music: I mean the different types of fugue and canon; they harm their own interests and defeat the good cause of old music when they pass over the more spiritual, imaginative, and musical products of the time as less important. The present collection avoids this mistake, containing a series of independent, genuine compositions which in their naïve and unadorned style appeal to more than the mere intellect. The most important of these pieces, in our opinion, are those by Couperin (who died in 1733), Kuhnau (who died in 1722), and G. Böhm (about 1680). The one by Couperin even has a touch of *Provençal* folklore and a delicate melody, while the stiff adagio by Kuhnau almost makes your flesh creep; G. Böhm, finally, provides a climax with his ghost-like capriccio.

Bach

[*Czerny's Edition of* The Well-tempered Clavichord]
CZERNY'S SHARE in this consists of a preface, fingering, metronome markings, and intimations regarding character and performance. The preface is rather brief and written too hastily: it would be possible to connect all kinds of rich thoughts with this work of works. As to the fingering, this is Czerny's business, and he understands it well; of course we have not tried out all of his fingerings. We approve, for the most part, of his tempo indications and also of his introductory remarks on the performance of the whole, as well as of his indications for shading of each piece; the latter instructions we consider especially desirable, for nothing can be more tiresome or contrary to the meaning of Bach than to drone out his fugues or to restrict one's representation of his creations to a mere emphasis on the successive entries of the principal theme. Such rules are suited to students. But most of Bach's fugues are character pieces of the highest type; some of them truly poetic creations, each of which demands its individual expression, its individual lights and shades. A Philistine accentuation of the entries of the fugue subject is far from sufficient. A pleasing portrait of Bach adorns the title page; he looks like a schoolmaster with a world at his command.

[*Various Piano Compositions*]

WE ARE GREETED by several new things by Sebastian Bach. The wish recently expressed in this paper that a complete edition of his works might be published seems to have borne fruit at least in so far as his piano compositions are concerned. The first two volumes containing *The Well-tempered Clavichord* have been followed by two more volumes. One of these contains the well-known *Art of the Fugue*—complete except for two fugues for two pianos—and, at the end, two fugues from the *Musical Offering*. As to the *Art of the Fugue,* it is known that the work consists of a series of fugues as well as a few canons on one theme. This theme does not warrant such multiple use and particularly does not seem to contain in itself the possibility of overlapping imitations. Bach therefore used it differently in inversions, simultaneous augmentations and diminutions, etc. Frequently his endeavors become almost artificial; thus, for instance, there are two fugues which in all four parts are inverted—a most difficult task which makes one's eyes smart. He has constructed marvels with the theme, and possibly all this may have been only the beginning of a giant structure since the divine master, as everyone knows, died while working at it. The last unfinished fugue which suddenly breaks off has always moved me deeply. It is as if he, the ever-creating giant, had died while writing these pages.

The fourth volume of the new edition contains a collection of important single pieces . . . Piece No. 10, *On the Departure of My Beloved Brother,* is of particular interest, and evidence of the master's heart. It has divers subtitles, such as "Farewell to the friends because it has to be . . ." The publication of Bach's piano concertos also has begun, and the first volume presents the very famous one in D minor; this is the piece which Mendelssohn played a few years ago in Leipzig in public, to the delight of certain individuals, but in which the public did not appear to participate. The concerto belongs to the greatest masterpieces, particularly the close of the first movement has

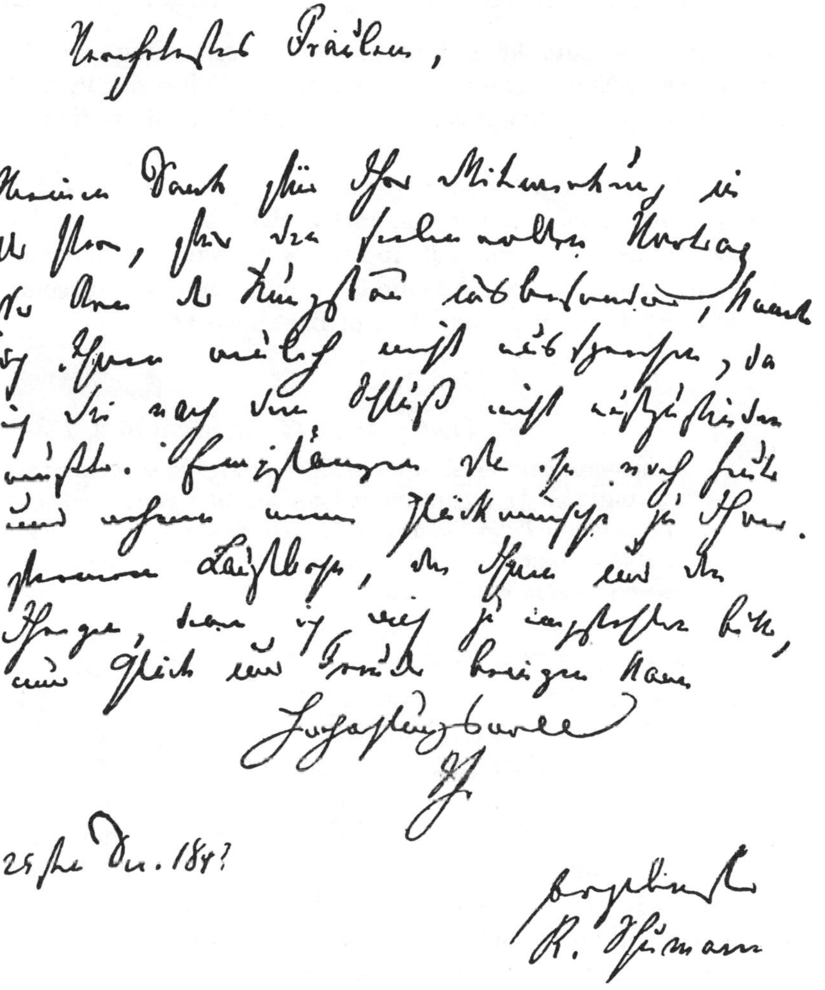

Schumann's Autograph

a vitality comparable to that of the corresponding part in Beethoven's Ninth. Thus it remains true, as Zelter put it, that "this cantor of Leipzig is an incomprehensible manifestation of divinity."

However it is only at his organ that he appears to be at his most sublime, most audacious, in his own element. Here he knows neither limits nor goal, and works for centuries to come.

Apart from Germany, England is the only country that seems to have furthered the circulation of Bach's works.

[Letter to D. G. Otten, April 2, 1849]

Schumann became so fond of Bach's PASSION ACCORDING TO ST. JOHN *that he organized and conducted a performance of the work on Palm Sunday, 1851. His supposition, however, that the* PASSION ACCORDING TO ST. MATTHEW *was the earlier work is undoubtedly wrong.*

"DO YOU KNOW Bach's *Passion According to St. John,* the so-called little one? I am sure you do! But don't you think it is much bolder, more powerful and poetical than the *Passion According to St. Matthew?* To me the latter seems to have been written some five or six years earlier. I think it contains some shallow parts and is inordinately long. But the other—how condensed, how full of genius, especially the choruses. And what consummate art! . . . But nobody writes about it . . . That's how it is and always will be. But some pieces must be left for the minority, for the few widely scattered, truly artistic minds, and they have Palestrina, Bach, Beethoven's last quartets, etc."

♯

In the course of time the distance between sources diminishes. Beethoven, for instance, did not need to study all that Mozart studied—Mozart, not all that Handel—Handel, not all that Palestrina—because these had already absorbed the knowl-

edge of their predecessors. But there is one source which inexhaustibly provides new ideas—Johann Sebastian Bach.
Florestan

[*Letter to Keferstein, January 31, 1840*]
"IF I MAY be allowed to confess it, I have often doubted whether you still take the same interest in the efforts of the younger generation of artists which I once observed in you. A remark you made lately in the Stuttgart paper rather confirmed these doubts. You said that it was only through Bach and Kuhnau that one could understand where Mozart's and Haydn's music came from; how much less, then, could one imagine whence modern composers derived theirs. At least, that was the drift of it. But I don't quite share your opinion. Mozart and Haydn only had a partial and imperfect knowledge of Bach, and we cannot know how Bach, had they known him in all his greatness, might have stimulated their creative powers. But the thoughtful combinations, the poetry and humor of modern music, originate chiefly in Bach. Mendelssohn, Bennett, Chopin, Hiller—in fact, the whole so-called Romantic School (of course I am speaking of Germans) is far nearer to Bach in its music than Mozart ever was; indeed, it has a thorough knowledge of Bach. I myself make a daily confession of my sins to that mighty one, and endeavor to purify and strengthen myself through him. And then, however honest and delightful Kuhnau may be, one can hardly place him on a level with Bach. Even if Kuhnau had written *The Well-tempered Clavichord*, he would still be but a hundredth part of him. In fact, to my mind Bach is unapproachable—he is unfathomable . . ."

Haydn and Mozart

Schumann speaks very little about Haydn and Mozart because they had become universally recognized before his time, and their music was well known by all music lovers. For the same reason Schumann, when speaking of Beethoven, mainly concentrated on his late works—which were still subject to controversy—and on those that had just been published some ten years after his death.

WE LOVE youth's struggle for progress, and Beethoven, who struggled up to his last breath, gives us a noble example of human grandeur; but in the groves of Mozart and Haydn there also stand heavily laden trees that we cannot easily overlook. If we do, we deny ourselves to our own detriment that lofty pleasure until, after having vainly hunted about the world for other things, we finally return to these men—but, alas! often too late, with a chilled heart which can no longer enjoy, with trembling hands that have lost the power to form.

The following remark belongs to the very few of Schumann's with which most musicians of our day will disagree. The new appreciation of Haydn's genius is largely due to Brahms.

Today it is impossible to learn anything new from him [Haydn]. He is like a familiar friend of the house whom all greet with pleasure and with esteem but who has ceased to arouse any particular interest . . .

♯

Serenity, repose, grace, the characteristics of the antique works of art, are also those of Mozart's school. The Greeks gave to "The Thunderer" a radiant expression, and radiantly does Mozart launch his lightnings.

A true master does not develop pupils, but new masters. With reverence I return continually to *this* master whose influence has been so all-embracing and far-reaching. Even should this lucid manner of thinking and poetizing be supplanted by a more formless and mystic one, as Time—which casts a shadow even upon Art—may ordain, may that beautiful period of art never be forgotten, that period during which Mozart reigned, and during which Beethoven shook the world to its very foundations—perhaps not without the acquiescence of his royal predecessor, Wolfgang Amadeus.

Afterwards Carl Maria von Weber and a few foreigners ascended the throne. But when these had also departed, the people were led more and more astray, and now lie in an uncomfortable classic-romantic torpor.

♯

... the Overture to the *Magic Flute*—which will live on to delight mankind in centuries to come—that frolicking heavenly child prodigy which, in spite of fog and darkness, will time and again re-emerge and radiate light and gaiety ...

Beethoven

[Fifth Symphony]

LET us be silent about this work! No matter how frequently heard, whether at home or in the concert-hall, this symphony invariably wields its power over men of every age like those great phenomena of nature that fill us with fear and admiration at all times, no matter how frequently we may experience them. This symphony, too, will be heard in future centuries, nay, as long as music and the world exist.

[Sixth Symphony]

IN COMPOSING his *Pastoral* Symphony Beethoven well understood the danger he incurred. His explanatory remark, "Rather expressive of the feeling than tone painting," contains an entire aesthetic system for composers. And it is absurd for painters to portray him sitting beside a brook, his head in his hands, listening to the bubbling water! . . .

When Beethoven conceived and carried out his idea for the *Pastoral* Symphony, it was not a single short spring day that inspired him to utter his cry of joy, but the dark commingling of lofty songs above us (as Heine, I believe, somewhere says). The manifold voices of creation stirred within him.

LETTER OF AN ENTHUSIAST TO CHIARA

[Seventh Symphony]

THIS REMINDS me of Beethoven's A major Symphony, which we heard recently; and afterwards, moderately enthusiastic, we went late in the evening to Master Raro. You know how Florestan, improvising at the pianoforte, talks as if in his sleep, smiles, weeps, arises, starts over again, and so on. Zilia [1] was in the bay window, other Davidites were grouped here and there. Many things were discussed. "I laughed," Florestan began his speech and at the same time playing the opening chords of the A major Symphony, "I laughed about a dry old registrar who discovered in this a battle of the giants with an effective annihilation of them all in the last movement, but slyly passing over the allegretto because it did not fit in with his theory; and I laughed, generally, at those who eternally preach about the innocence and absolute beauty of music as such. (To be sure, art has no business to imitate the unlucky octaves and fifths of life—it should rather conceal them; yet in some arias of Marschner's *Hans Heiling*, for example, I find beauty without truth, and in Beethoven, on rare occasions, truth without beauty.) But my finger-tips itch when I hear some people say

[1] Klara Wieck (short for Caecilia).

that Beethoven, while writing his symphonies, gave himself up to exalted sentiments—lofty thoughts of God, immortality, and the course of the stars . . . whereas genius, while pointing to the heavens with its leafy crown, spreads its roots deeply into its beloved earth. But—to return to the symphony. The following description is not mine, but taken from an old number of the musical paper, *Cecilia* . . .

". . . it is the merriest wedding; the bride, a heavenly maid with one rose, only one, in her hair. Unless I am greatly mistaken, in the introduction the guests arrive, greeting each other with servile bows; and the airy flutes remind us that in the village, gay with maypoles, gawdy with ribbons, everyone rejoices for and with the bride Rosa. And again, if I am not mistaken, her mother, pale, and with a tremulous glance, appears to ask her: 'Do you not know that we must part?' and Rosa, overcome, throws herself into her mother's arms, yet without releasing the hand of her sweetheart. And now all is very quiet in the village" (here Florestan broke into the allegretto, playing fragments of it here and there), "only a butterfly flutters by, and a cherry blossom falls. The organ begins to play; the sun stands high; in the church motes dance in the shafts of light; the bells ring out; churchgoers enter, one after the other; pews are opened and shut; some peasants study their hymnbooks; others look up to the choir; the procession approaches —first the choir boys with lighted tapers and incense burners, then friends, often turning to look at the bridal pair, accompanied by the priest; behind them the parents, the bridesmaids, and all the young village people. They range themselves in order, the priest ascends the altar, and talks, now to the bride, now to the happiest of men; he tells them of the duties and purpose of the sacred bond, he describes to them the joy that is found in love and peace—and then as he asks for the all-embracing, ever-binding 'yes,' they respond firmly, slowly—I cannot continue the picture—fancy the finale as you will!" Florestan broke off, and finished the allegretto so that it sounded as though the sexton had slammed the door, causing the whole church to reverberate.

Enough! Florestan's description has awakened something within me at this moment; the letters swim before my eyes. There is much that I still have to say to you, but the outdoors summons me. So I close, hoping in my next letter for a better beginning than this conclusion. *Eusebius*

♯

There is one irritating passage in the slow movement of the A major Symphony (there is but one A major Symphony!) where the restrained melody rises and falls slowly—notes almost in the manner of Spohr [1]—that is to say, in a manner repulsive to all who dislike softness and the effeminate. I wager Beethoven meant it ironically, which is also indicated by the aggressive bass that follows. . . . *Florestan* [2]

[Eighth Symphony]

OF ALL of Beethoven's symphonies the one in F major is less performed and listened to than any of the others. Even in Leipzig, where all of them are so much at home and almost popular, there is a prejudice against this one in spite of the fact that scarcely another Beethoven symphony equals it in point of profound humor. A prepared climax such as the one toward the close of the finale is rare even in Beethoven; and as to the allegretto in B-flat, one has no choice but to be—quiet and happy. The orchestra gave a masterly performance, and even the dangerous trio of the minuet, with its strangely consoling, sad melody for the French horn went off well. . . . December 10, 1840

AFTER LISTENING TO THE D MINOR SYMPHONY

[Ninth Symphony]

I AM THE blind man who is standing before the Strasbourg Cathedral, who hears its bells but cannot see the entrance.

[1] Schumann obviously means the measures 123-138.

[2] This aphorism was not reprinted in Schumann's own edition of his literary works.

Leave me in peace, young men; I no longer understand mankind. *Voigt* [1]

Who blames the blind man if he stands before the cathedral and has nothing to say? Let him only remove his hat reverently while the bells ring above. *Eusebius*

Yes, love him, love him well, but never forget that he reached poetic freedom only through long years of study; and reverence his never-ceasing moral force. Do not search for the abnormal in him, return to the source of his creativeness; do not illustrate his genius with the Ninth Symphony alone, no matter how great its audacity and scope, never uttered in any tongue. You can do as much with his First Symphony, or with the Greeklike, slender one in B-flat major! and do not grow arrogant over rules that you have never thoroughly worked out. Nothing is more dangerous; even a man with less talent could, after a moment's hesitation, draw the mask from your reddening face. *Florestan*

And when they had ended, the master said, in a voice full of emotion: "No more words on the subject! Let us forever love that lofty spirit who looks down with benignity on that life which gave him so little. I feel that we are now nearer to him than formerly. Young men, you have a long and difficult road before you. A wonderful glow fills the sky—whether of morning or evening, I do not know. But let your creations penetrate the darkness about us!"

MARDI GRAS SPEECH BY FLORESTAN

(After a performance of Beethoven's Ninth Symphony)

FLORESTAN climbed on the piano and said: Davidites! That is, youths and men who shall slay the Philistines, the musical and the others. . . .

[1] Karl Voigt, who was the husband of Schumann's close friend, Henriette Voigt, once declared, in an outburst of enthusiasm caused by a rehearsal of the Ninth, that he would will a part of his estate to "this divine work." Schumann found this remark so touching that, to show his gratitude as an artist, he ascribed to Voigt the opening aphorism of this series.

. . . I laughed at Eusebius. Slyly he poked fun at a fat man. This individual, during the adagio, had whispered to Eusebius: "Did not Beethoven also write a Battle Symphony, sir?"--"That is the *Pastoral* Symphony, sir," Eusebius replied indifferently. "Yes, of course," the fat man said meditatively. . . . When the first chord of the finale burst out, I said to a trembling man next to me: "What else is this chord, dear cantor, but a common chord with an anticipatory dominant-note in a somewhat complicated distribution (because one is uncertain whether to take the A of the timpani or the F of the bassoon for a bass)? See Türk, 19th section, page 7." [1]

"Well, sir, you talk very loudly and certainly are not serious." Softly, yet with a terrible voice, I whispered: "Cantor, mind the thunderstorms. The lightning does not announce its visit by a butler, at the best it sends a storm before and a thunderclap afterward. These are its ways."—"But dischords like that ought to be prepared . . ." But here the next one already burst in: "Cantor, this beautiful seventh in the trumpets will forgive you. . . ." And I looked at these Beethovians, as they stood there with their eyes popping out, and said: "That was written by our Beethoven, it is a German work—the finale contains a double fugue—he was blamed for not introducing such forms —but how he did it—yes, this is *our* Beethoven." Another chorus joined in: "The work seems to contain the different genres of poetry, the first movement being epic, the second, comedy, the third, lyric, the fourth (combining all), the dramatic." Still another bluntly began to praise the work as being gigantic, colossal, comparable to the Egyptian pyramids. And others painted word pictures: the symphony expresses the story of mankind— first the chaos—then the call of God "there shall be light"—then the sunrise over the first human being, ravished by such splendor—in one word, the whole first chapter of the Pentateuch is in this symphony.

I became angrier and quieter. And as they were busy reading

[1] Türk was a famous music teacher and writer on music of the old generation. Of course there is no such passage in Türk.

the work and finally applauded, I grasped Eusebius' arm and went down the stairs with him, surrounded by smiling faces

Below, in the dark of the street lamps, Eusebius said as if to himself: "BEETHOVEN—what a word—the deep sound of the mere syllables has the ring of eternity. As if no better symbol were possible for this name!" "Eusebius," said I very calmly, "Do you too, dare to praise Beethoven? Like a lion he would have reared himself before all of you and asked: 'Who are you that you dare be so presumptuous?' I do not mean you, Eusebius, you are a good soul, but does a great man *have* to have thousands of dwarfs in his train?" Do they believe they understand him when they smile and applaud him who fought so hard in innumerable battles? Not able to account for the simplest rules of music, how dare they judge a master in his totality? . . .

#

Finally, the Ninth. At last one begins to realize that here a great man has created his greatest work. I do not recall that ever before has it been received so enthusiastically. Saying this we do not mean to praise the work—which is beyond praise—but the audience. . . . [February 11, 1841]

[*THE OVERTURES TO LEONORA*]

Schumann's four attempts to describe the LEONORA *Overtures almost parallel Beethoven's composition of them.*

WHEN IT WAS played for the first time in Vienna and almost wholly failed, it is said that Beethoven wept; in the same situation Rossini would have laughed. Beethoven was induced to write the new one in E major, which might have been written by some other composer.—Thou didst err; yet thy tears were noble. *Eusebius*

The first conception is always the most natural and the best. The understanding may err, but never the feeling. *Raro*

101

Ye peddlers in art, do ye not sink into the earth when ye are reminded of the words uttered by Beethoven on his deathbed: "I believe I am as yet but at the beginning"; or Jean Paul: "It seems to me that I have written nothing as yet"? *Florestan*

THE FOUR OVERTURES TO FIDELIO

IT SHOULD be written in golden letters that last Thursday the Leipzig Orchestra performed—*the four overtures to "Fidelio," one after another*. Thanks to you, Viennese of 1805, that the first did not please you and that Beethoven in divine rage therefore poured forth the three others. If he ever appeared powerful to me, he did so on that evening, when, better than ever, we were able to listen to him, forming, rejecting, altering in his own workshop, and glowing with inspiration. He was most gigantic in his second start. The first overture was not effective; stop! thought he, the second shall rob you of all thought—and so he set himself to work anew and allowed the thrilling drama to pass before him, again singing the joys and sorrows of his heroine. This second overture is demonic in its boldness—even bolder, in certain details, than the third, the well-known great one in C major. But it did not satisfy him; he laid this one aside also, merely retaining certain passages from which, already more certain and conscious, he formed the third. Afterwards there followed the lighter and more popular one in E major, which is generally heard in the theater as the prelude.

Such is the great four-overture work. Formed after the manner of Nature, we first find in it the roots from which, in the second, the giant trunk arises, stretching its arms right and left, and finally completed by its leafy crown. *Florestan*

OUR READERS have already been informed that we heard all the overtures which Beethoven wrote to *Fidelio*, performed in an evening concert of the *Gewandhaus*. Gladly then we acknowledged this great undertaking on the part of our orchestra. For the further information of our readers respecting these overtures and what concerns them we may observe that the one performed on the evening in question as No. 1 has already appeared in score, with this note on the title page: "From the posthumous works." It is in C major, is the first Beethoven wrote to this opera, and pleased but little on its first performance. No. 2, still in manuscript and in the possession of Messrs. Breitkopf & Härtel, is also in C, and plainly the original from which Beethoven afterwards worked out his great Overture No. 3; the fourth is the light one in F major, usually heard in opera houses. If only the different editors could agree to publish the four overtures in one volume; for masters and scholars such a work would be a memorable example, on the one hand, of industry and conscientiousness, and, on the other, of the almost playful creative and inventive power of this Beethoven in whom Nature simultaneously combined the gifts for which she usually requires a thousand vessels. To the multitude it is, of course, a matter of indifference whether Beethoven wrote four overtures to a single opera or whether Rossini equipped four operas with a single overture. But the artist should endeavor to follow every trace that leads him to the more secret workshop of a master; and that this may be facilitated (since it is not possible to find an orchestra able and willing to play all four overtures for him), I trust the idea of a collective edition of them may be taken into consideration, and that I shall not have expressed this wish in vain.[1]

THE LEONORA OVERTURES

MANY PEOPLE will recall with pleasure the evening on which the Leipzig Orchestra, under the direction of Mendelssohn, performed all four *Leonora* Overtures one after the other . . . We again speak of this on the occasion of the publication of the parts (the score will follow soon) of the second *Leonora* Overture. There can hardly be a doubt as to the order in which Beethoven composed these overtures. One might perhaps believe

[1] This wish has since been fulfilled. [Schumann]

that the one now published was the first to be written, since the work has the character of a first daring attempt, written in the liveliest joy over the completion of the opera, whose main features it mirrors on a smaller scale. But Schindler's book (p. 58) completely dispels this doubt. According to Schindler's definite assertions, these were the circumstances: Beethoven first wrote the overture later published by T. Haslinger as opus 138 [the first *Leonora*]. Played in Vienna for a small audience of connoisseurs, this overture was generally judged as being "too light." Beethoven, irritated, then wrote the one now published by Breitkopf & Härtel and again revised it; the result of this revision was the well-known No. 3 in C major. The fourth overture finally, in E major, was written only in 1815 when *Fidelio* was again taken up into the Vienna repertory.

Nearly all musicians agree that the third overture is the most effective and perfect of the four. But one ought not to underestimate the first; except for one weak passage (p. 18 of the score) it is a lively, fresh piece of music and entirely worthy of the author. Introduction, transition to allegro, first subject recalling the "Florestan Aria," and final crescendo—everything reflects Beethoven's rich feeling. The relations between the second and third overtures, however, are more interesting. Here you very distinctly get a glimpse into the master's workshop. How he changed the music; how he rejected parts of the orchestration and of his ideas; how in none of these overtures he managed to get away from the "Florestan Aria"; how the first three measures of each overture continue throughout the piece; how he cannot give up the trumpet call behind the scene but introduces it much more beautifully into the third overture than into the second; how he does not stop before in the third overture he brings the work to that perfection which we admire so greatly—all this is among the most interesting and instructive studies that any musical adept can pursue. Gladly would we compare both works step by step. But that is much more enjoyable when done with the score in hand than by written words, when we just briefly touch the essential differences . . .

"RAGE OVER THE LOST PENNY," RONDO [OPUS 129]

IT WOULD be difficult to find anything merrier than this whim; I laughed heartily about it the other day when I played it over. But how amused was I when, playing it through for the second time, I read the following remark on its contents: "This capriccio, found among Beethoven's posthumous works, is entitled in the manuscript, 'Rage over the Lost Penny, Released in a Capriccio'." [1] It is the most amiable, harmless anger, similar to that felt when one cannot pull a shoe from off the foot and perspires and stamps while the shoe very phlegmatically looks up at its owner. Now I have you, Beethovians! I could be angry with you in quite another way when you gush with enthusiasm and cast your eyes to heaven and rave about Beethoven's freedom from earthliness, his transcendental flight from star to star. "Today I feel altogether unbuttoned," was his favorite expression when he was inwardly merry. And then he laughed like a lion and beat about him, for he was always untamable! "But with this capriccio I'll get you!" You will think it common, unworthy of a Beethoven, like the melody to *Freude, schöner Götterfunken* in the D minor Symphony; you will hide it far, far beneath the *Eroica!* And should we have a new renaissance of art—the genius of truth holding the balance with this comic capriccio on one side and ten of the newest pathetic overtures on the other—the overtures would rise as high as heaven. Young and old composers, there is one thing you may learn from it of which, above all things, it is necessary to remind you—Nature, Nature, Nature!

[1] The authenticity of the title is doubtful; cf. *Musical Quarterly* 1946, p. 182.

Weber

OBERON, MARCH 18TH, 1848

TOO LYRICAL a subject. The music, too, is inferior to that of Weber's other operas in point of freshness. A slovenly performance.

EURYANTHE, SEPTEMBER 23RD, 1847

WE RAVED over this as we had not done about anything for a long time. This music is too little known and appreciated. It is heart's blood, the noblest that he had; and this opera certainly cost him a part of his life—but he is also immortal because of it. It is a chain of sparkling jewels from beginning to end—all brilliant and flawless. How splendid the characterization of certain figures, such as Eglantine and Euryanthe—and how the instruments sound! They speak to us from the innermost depths. We were full of it—talked long of it. I think the most inspired number of the opera is the duet between Lysiart and Eglantine in the second act. The march in the third act is also admirable. However, the crown must be awarded to the entire work and not to separate passages.

Schubert

SYMPHONY IN C MAJOR

The famous article in which Schumann describes his discovery of one of the great masterpieces of Schubert is as remarkable for its story as for its analysis of the music. Schumann was the first writer who recognized clearly the glory of Schubert's instrumental music, at that time generally unknown and not at all appreciated in its true greatness.

THE MUSICIAN who visits Vienna for the first time delights awhile in the festive life of the streets, and often stands admiringly before the door of St. Stephen's Cathedral; but he soon remembers how near to the city lies a cemetery containing something worthier of regard to his mind than all the city boasts—the spot where two of the glorious heroes of his art rest, only a few steps apart. No doubt, then, many a young musician, after the first few days of excitement in Vienna, has like me wandered to the Währing Cemetery to place flowers on those graves, were it but a wild rosebush, such as I found planted on Beethoven's. Franz Schubert's resting place was unadorned. One fervent desire of my life was fulfilled; I gazed long on those two sacred graves, almost envying the person buried between them—a certain Count O'Donnell, if I am not mistaken. To look into the eyes of a great man for the first time, to grasp his hand, is something everyone desires. It had never been possible for me to meet either of the two whom I venerate most highly among all modern artists; but after this visit to their graves I wished I could have had beside me a man who had been close to them—if possible, a brother of either. On my way home I remembered that Schubert's brother Ferdinand, to whom he had been much attached, was still living. I looked

him up and found that he resembled Franz, to judge from the
bust that stands beside Schubert's grave; he was shorter than
Franz, but strongly built, with as much honesty as music expressed in his face. He knew of me because of that veneration
for his brother which I have so often publicly expressed; told
me and showed me many things . . . Finally, he allowed me to
see those treasured compositions of Schubert's which he still
possesses. The sight of this hoard of riches thrilled me with joy;
where to begin, where to end! Among other things, he drew
my attention to the scores of several symphonies, many of
which have never as yet been heard, but were shelved as too
heavy and turgid. One must understand Vienna, its peculiar
attitude toward concerts and the difficulties involved in col-
lecting the necessary material for great performances in order
to forgive the city where Schubert lived and toiled that only
his songs are to be heard, today, while his great instrumental
works are seldom or never performed. Who knows how long
the symphony of which we are speaking might have lain buried
in dust and darkness, had I not at once arranged with Ferdinand Schubert to send it to the directorate of the *Gewandhaus*
Concerts in Leipzig, or rather, to the conducting artist himself,
whose discerning glance never overlooks the most modest
beauty, nor the outstanding and dominant one. My hopes were
fulfilled. The symphony went to Leipzig, was heard, understood, heard again, and joyously admired by almost everyone.

I must say at once that he who is not yet acquainted with
this symphony knows very little about Schubert; and when we
consider all that he has given to art, this praise may appear to
many exaggerated. Partly, no doubt, because composers have
so often been advised, to their chagrin, that it is better for them
—after Beethoven—"to abstain from the symphonic form." It is
true that of late we have had but few orchestral works of consequence; and those few have interested us rather as illustra-
tions of their composers' progress, than for their art or as creations of decided influence on the general public. Most of the
others have merely been pale reflections of Beethoven; not to

forget those tiresome manufacturers of symphonies who recall the powder and perukes of Mozart and Haydn, but not the heads that wore them. Berlioz belongs to France and is only occasionally mentioned as an interesting foreigner and a hothead. The hope I had always entertained—and many, no doubt, with me—that Schubert, who had shown himself in his older compositions firm in form, rich in imagination and versatile, would also turn to the symphony and find a mode of treatment certain to impress the public, is here realized in the most glorious manner. Assuredly he never proposed to continue Beethoven's Ninth Symphony, but, an indefatigable artist, he continually drew from his own creative resources symphony after symphony. The only thing that seems to us objectionable in the publication of this Seventh Symphony, or that may lead even to a misunderstanding of the work, is the fact that the world now receives it without first having followed its creator's development of this form in its forerunners. Perhaps, however, these may now be made accessible; the least among them must possess Schubert characteristics; Viennese symphony writers did not have to go so very far in search of the laurel they are so much in need of, for in a suburb of Vienna, in Ferdinand Schubert's study, they might have found sevenfold richer laurels. And here, for once a wreath was to be found! But so is it often! Should the conversation turn to—[Mendelssohn], the Viennese never cease to praise their own Franz Schubert; but when they are among themselves, they do not seem to think much of either. But enough of this! Let us refresh ourselves with the wealth of ideas which flow from this precious work! Vienna, with its Cathedral of St. Stephen, its lovely women, its public pageantry, its Danube that decks it with countless silvery ribbons; this Vienna, spreading over the verdant plain and reaching towards the lofty mountains; Vienna, with its reminiscences of the great German masters, must be a fertile terrain for a musician's imagination. Often when gazing on the city from the heights above I have thought how frequently Beethoven's eyes may have glanced restlessly toward the distant silhouette of the Alps; how Mozart may have dreamily followed the course of the Danube as it disappears into thickets and woods; and how Haydn may have looked up to the spire, shaking his head at its dizzy height. If we put together the cathedral spire, the Danube, and the distant Alps, casting over the whole a soft haze of Catholic incense, we shall have a fair picture of Vienna; and when before us lives this charming landscape, chords will vibrate that never yet have sounded within us. On hearing Schubert's symphony and its bright, flowery, romantic life, the city crystallizes before me, and I realize why such works could be born in these very surroundings. I shall not attempt to give the symphony its proper foil; different ages select different sources for their texts and pictures: whereas the youth of eighteen hears a world event in a musical work, the adult only perceives a national event; the musician himself, however, probably never thought of either, but simply gave the best music that he happened to feel within him at that moment. But everyone must acknowledge that the outer world, sparkling today, gloomy tomorrow, often deeply stirs the feeling of the poet or the musician; and all must recognize, while listening to this symphony, that it reveals to us something more than mere beautiful song, mere joy and sorrow, such as music has ever expressed in a hundred ways, leading us into regions which, to our best recollection, we had never before explored. To understand this, one has but to hear this symphony. Here we find, besides the most masterly technicalities of musical composition, life in every vein; coloring down to the finest gradation; meaning everywhere; sharp expression in detail; and in the whole a suffusing romanticism such as other works by Franz Schubert have made known to us.

And then the heavenly length of the symphony, like that of a thick novel in four volumes, perhaps by Jean Paul who also was never able to reach a conclusion, and for the best reason—to permit the reader to think it out for himself. How this refreshes, this feeling of abundance, so contrary to one's experience with others when one always dreads to be disillusioned at the end and is often saddened through disappointment. It would be incomprehensible whence Schubert had all at once acquired this sparkling, easy mastery in the handling of the orchestra, did we not know that this symphony had been preceded by six others, and that it was written in the stage of virile power (on the score is the date, "March, 1828"; Schubert died in the following November). We must grant that he possessed an extraordinary talent in attaining to such idiomatic treatment of the single instruments as well as of the orchestral masses— they often seem to converse like human voices and choruses— although he scarcely heard any of his own instrumental works performed during his lifetime. Save in a few of Beethoven's works I have nowhere in the treatment of instruments observed so striking and deceptive a resemblance to the voice; it is the exact reverse of the treatment of the human voice by Meyerbeer. Another proof of the genuine, mature inspiration of this symphony is its complete independence of the Beethoven symphonies. Here you can see how correct, how prudent in judgment Schubert's genius reveals itself! As if conscious of his own more modest powers, he avoids imitating the grotesque forms, the bold proportions which we find in Beethoven's later works; he gives us a creation of the most graceful form possible, yet full of novel intricacies; he never strays far from the central point and always returns to it. Those who closely study this symphony must receive the same impression. At first, we feel a little embarrassed by the brilliancy and novelty of the instrumentation, the length and breadth of form, the charming variety of vital feeling, the entirely new world that opens before us—just as the first glimpse of anything to which we are unaccustomed confuses us; but a delightful feeling remains, as though we had been listening to a fleeting tale of fairies and enchantment. We feel that the composer has mastered his tale, and that, in time, its connections will all become clear. This assurance is immediately produced by the elaborate romantic introduction, although here everything still appears veiled in secrecy. The passage from this into the allegro is wholly new;

the tempo does not seem to change, yet we reach port, we know not how. It would not give us or others any pleasure to analyze the separate movements; for to give an idea of the fictional character that pervades the whole symphony, the entire work should be copied. Yet I cannot without a few words take leave of the second movement, which speaks to us in such touching tones. There is in it a passage where a horn, as though calling from afar, seems to come from another world. The instruments stop to listen, a heavenly spirit is passing through the orchestra.

The symphony produced such an effect among us as none has done since Beethoven's days. Artists and connoisseurs unite in its praise, and the master who had studied it with the utmost care for its perfect success [Mendelssohn] said a few words which I should have been only too happy (had it been possible) to report to Schubert as the gladdest of glad tidings. It may take several years before the work will be thoroughly at home in Germany; but there is no danger that it will ever be overlooked or forgotten; it bears within it the seeds of everlasting youth.

And thus my visit to those hallowed graves, reminding me of a relative of one of the great departed, offered me a second reward. The first one I received on the day itself; for I found, on Beethoven's grave, a steel pen, which ever since I have reverently preserved. I never use it save on festal occasions like this one; may inspiration have flowed from it!

FIRST GRAND SONATA IN A MINOR, OPUS 42. SECOND GRAND SONATA IN D MAJOR, OPUS 53. FANTASIA OR SONATA IN G MAJOR, OPUS 78. FIRST GRAND SONATA FOR FOUR HANDS, IN B-FLAT MAJOR, OPUS 30

WE NOW COME to our favorites, the sonatas of Franz Schubert, whom many know only as a composer of *Lieder*, while the majority scarcely knows his name. We can only give hints here, for volumes would be needed to justify in full our opinion of them as works of eminent character; for these, perhaps, I may find time later.

Though, without many words, we may describe all three

sonatas as "glorious," the "Fantasia or Sonata" seems to us the most perfect of his sonatas in form and spirit. Here everything is organic, breathing the selfsame life. He who has not sufficient imagination to solve the riddle of the last movement, had better eschew it.

The one in A minor most resembles it; the first part is so still, so dreamy; it could move one to tears; yet so simply, so easily is it built of two ideas, that one must admire the wizard who so singularly well knew how to combine and contrast them.

What a different kind of life wells up from the energetic D major Sonata, seizing us and sweeping us away, stroke upon stroke! Then the adagio, wholly Schubertian, impulsive, extravagant, scarcely can he find an ending. The last movement is difficult to fit into the whole and is rather droll. To consider it from a serious viewpoint would be utterly ridiculous. Florestan calls it a satire on the Pleyel-Vanhall [1] nightcap style; Eusebius discovered in the strongly contrasting passages ugly faces like those one makes to frighten children. In fine, both take it from the humorous side.

We consider the four-hand sonata one of the least original compositions of Schubert; indeed, only occasional flashes reveal his genius. Yet how many other composers would have been crowned with laurel for this work alone, whereas in Schubert's wreath it is only a modest twig; so accustomed are we to judge men and artists in accordance with the best they have done.

Though Schubert is perhaps more original in his *Lieder* than in his instrumental works, we nonetheless highly value the latter as being purely musical and complete in themselves. As a pianoforte composer he excels others, even Beethoven, in one peculiarity (astonishingly fine though the ear of the latter was when in his deafness he listened only in his imagination): his instrumentation is more in conformity with the piano; it is *sonorous* and seems to come from the depths of the pianoforte, while in Beethoven we only receive the tone color by borrowing from the horn, the oboe, etc.

[1] Two old-fashioned pianist-composers of the time.

As for the general inward meaning of these creations, Schubert has tones for the most delicate feelings, thoughts, even events and states of life. As thousandfold as are the dreams and passions of man, as multiple is Schubert's music. That which his eye sees, his hand touches, is wrought into music; from the stones which he throws about him there sprang, as from Deukalion and Pyrrha, living human forms. He is the most eminent composer since Beethoven. The deadly enemy of all Philistinism, he practiced music in the highest sense of the word.

LAST COMPOSITIONS [1]

IF FERTILITY be a distinctive mark of genius, then Franz Schubert is a genius of the highest order. Not much over thirty when he died, he wrote in such abundance that but half of his compositions have as yet been published; another part will soon follow, while a still greater part will never, or not for a long time be given to the public. Among his first-mentioned works his songs obtained the quickest and widest popularity; gradually he would have set all German literature to music; he would have been the man for Telemann, who claimed that "a good composer should be able to set public notices to music." Whatever he felt, he poured forth in music; Aeschylus, Klopstock, so difficult to set to music, yielded to his hand, while he drew the most profound meaning from the lighter verses of Müller and others. And what a multitude of instrumental works of every form and kind!—Trios, quartets, sonatas, rondos, dances, variations, for two and four hands, large and small, full of the strangest things, and of the rarest beauties, which our journal has elsewhere characterized. Among the works that await publication, masses, quartets, a great number of songs, etc., have been mentioned to us. The last section comprises his larger compositions, several operas, sacred music, several symphonies and overtures, etc., now in the possession of his heirs.

[1] Schumann made a mistake here: the *Lieder* of the *Schwanengesang* and the String Quintet in C major, opus 163—both of which he apparently did not know—were written after the compositions reviewed in this article.

The last of Schubert's compositions which have appeared are entitled "Grand Duo for Pianoforte for Four Hands," opus 140, and "F. Schubert's Last Composition, Three Grand Sonatas for Pianoforte." [C minor, A major, B-flat major, opus posth.]

There was a time when I was loath to mention Schubert, and would only at night speak of him to the trees and stars. Who of us does not rave at some time? Enraptured with this new mind, whose wealth seemed to me boundless and incommensurable, deaf to everything that could bear witness against him, I thought of nothing but of him. With increasing years, with increasing demands, the circle of our favorites grows smaller and smaller. The cause of this is in ourselves as well as in them. Who is the master of whom one holds the same opinion all one's life? Experiences which youth has not yet achieved are necessary to the evaluation of Bach; it even underestimates Mozart's greatness. Mere musical studies are not enough to enable us to understand Beethoven, just as in certain years he inspires us with one work rather than with another. It is certain that equal ages exert a reciprocal attraction upon each other, that youthful enthusiasm is best understood by youth, and the power of the mature master by the full-grown man. So Schubert will always remain the favorite of youth. He gives what youth desires—an overflowing heart, daring thoughts, and swift deeds; he tells them what they most love, romantic stories of knights, maidens, and adventures; he intermingles a little wit and humor, but not so much that the basic softness of the mood is thereby troubled. Moreover he gives wings to the performer's own imagination like no other composer save Beethoven. His easily followed peculiarities tempt one to imitate them; we would like to carry out a thousand ideas suggested by him. Thus is it that he has a great future.

Ten years ago I should have declared, without more ado, that these lately published works were the finest in the world, —and, compared with the productions of today, they still so appear to me. But as compositions by Schubert I do not place them in the class in which I place his Quartet in D minor, his

Trio in E-flat major,[1] and many of his shorter songs and pianoforte pieces. The duo, especially (which I regarded as a symphony arranged for the pianoforte until the original manuscript,
which, by his own hand, is entitled "Sonata for Four Hands,"
taught me otherwise), still seems to me under Beethoven's
influence. And in spite of Schubert's manuscript I still hold to
my own opinion respecting the duo. One who wrote as much as
Schubert does not trouble too much about titles, and thus he
probably hastily entitled his work "sonata," while "symphony"
was what he had in mind. Then, to give a more everyday reason for my opinion, it is probable that at a time when his name
was only beginning to be known he was more likely to find
publishers for a sonata than for a symphony. And in comparing
this work with his other sonatas, in which the purest pianoforte
character is expressed, I can only, familiar as I am with his
style and his manner of treating the pianoforte, consider it an
orchestral work. We hear string and wind instruments, *tuttis,*
a few solos, the mutter of drums; and my view is also supported
by the broad symphonic form, even by its reminiscences of
Beethoven's symphonies, such as, in the second movement,
that of the andante of Beethoven's Second, and, in the last, that
of the finale of Beethoven's A major Symphony as well as several paler passages, which may have lost force in transcription.
In this way, too, I would like to save the duo from the reproach
of being imperfectly suited to the pianoforte, that something
has been attempted with the instrument of which it is inca-
pable; while, as a transcribed symphony, it must be looked at
in a different light. If we so accept it, we shall be the richer for
a symphony. I have mentioned the reminiscences of Beethoven;
but do we not all nourish ourselves from his treasures? Yet even
without this lofty predecessor, he would have still remained
Schubert; his originality might merely have shown itself at a
later time. To one who has some degree of education and feeling Beethoven and Schubert may be recognized and distin-

[1] The Symphony in C was not known at the time this article was written.
[Schumann]

guished, from the very first. Schubert is a more feminine character compared to the other; far more loquacious, softer, broader; compared to Beethoven he is a child, sporting happily among the giants. Such is the relation these symphonic movements bear to those of Beethoven, and, in their inwardness, they could not have been conceived by any other than Schubert. To be sure, he brings in his powerful passages, and works in masses; and still he is more feminine than masculine, for he pleads and persuades where the man commands. But all this merely in comparison with Beethoven; compared to others, he is masculine; indeed, the boldest and most freethinking among the newer musicians. With this conviction we should take up the duo. It is not necessary to seek for its beauties; they win us the oftener we hear them; one cannot help loving this loving poet. And though the adagio strongly reminds me of Beethoven, I know scarcely anything in which Schubert is more himself; he stands bodily before us—with the first measures his name passes our lips . . . And we will agree that from beginning to end the work sustains itself on the same level—something we should always demand of a work, though today it is achieved so rarely. No musician should remain unacquainted with such a work, and if so many among them fail to understand some creations of today, and some of the future, it is their own fault; their insight is blind to transitions. The new (so-called) Romantic School is not wrought from thin air; everything has its own good reason.

The sonatas are designated as the last work by Franz Schubert, and as such seem rather peculiar. Probably those to whom the year of their creation was unknown would judge them differently—as did I, placing them in an earlier period of the composer's career, while I always considered the Trio in E-flat major as Schubert's last as well as his most individual work. It would be something more than human in a man who wrote as much and as continuously as Schubert, were he to improve and surpass himself with every succeeding effort; thus these sonatas may indeed be the last work of his hand. I have not been able to learn whether he wrote these sonatas on his sick-bed or not; from the music I rather surmise that he did; and yet it may be that my opinion and fancy are influenced from the first by the sad ideas awakened by the word "last" on the title page. Be that as it may, these sonatas seem to me to differ from his others in their greater simplicity of invention, their voluntary resignation of novel brilliancy (just where he formerly made such great demands on his powers), and through a spinning-out of general musical ideas where he formerly joined period to period with new threads. The flow continues from page to page, ever more musical and melodious, as if it could never come to an end or lose its continuity; broken, here and there, by a somewhat livelier emotion, which, however, soon calms down again. More objective judges must decide whether or not my opinion has been influenced here by the thought of his illness; but the work affects me as I describe it. Then it closes so easily, gaily, pleasantly, as though set to begin a new day. It was otherwise ordained. He could face his last moment with serenity. And of the words written on his tomb-stone [1]—"a rich possession, but still fairer hope," we will thankfully remember only the first. It is useless to ponder what he might still have achieved. He accomplished enough; and let those men be praised who strove and accomplished as did he.

FOUR IMPROMPTUS FOR THE PIANOFORTE, OPUS 142

Schumann's supposition, outlined below, that the Impromptus, opus 142, were originally written, at least in part, as the movements of a piano sonata, is most probably true. His lack of understanding for the famous third impromptu may have been caused by his general skepticism in regard to the traditional variation form (above p. 66).

HE OUGHT to have lived to see how celebrated he is today; it would have inspired him to his best. Now that he is long since at rest, let us carefully collect and catalogue what he left be-

[1] By Grillparzer.

118

hind; and there is nothing among his works that does not testify to his creative mind. Few authors have left the stamp of their personality so clearly on their work as he. Every page in the two first of the above *impromptus* breathes "Franz Schubert." We find him here as we know him in his inexhaustible moods; as he charms, misleads, and again fetters us. And yet I can scarcely believe that Schubert really entitled these movements *Impromptus*. The first is evidently the first movement of a sonata, so perfectly carried out and concluded that no doubt is possible. I consider the second impromptu to be the second movement of the same sonata; in key and character it precisely fits it. Schubert's friends must know what has become of the conclusion of the sonata, or whether he ever concluded it at all. Perhaps the fourth impromptu may be regarded as the finale, but even if the tonality confirms one in this supposition, the casualness of the plan of the whole almost denies it. These are therefore mere conjectures, which only acquaintance with the original manuscript could determine. Yet I do not consider them of little consequence. We cannot be guided by titles and superscriptions; on the other hand, a fine sonata is so great an ornament in the wreath of a composer's works that I would gladly add yet another one to the list of Schubert's many: twenty, indeed. I should have scarcely attributed the third impromptu to Schubert, unless, indeed, as a work of his boyhood; it is a set of indifferent variations on an insignificant theme. They are wholly devoid of invention or fancy—qualities which Schubert has displayed to so high a degree in other sets of variations. But if the two first impromptus are played in succession and rounded with the fourth to make a lively close, we shall possess, if not a complete sonata, one more beautiful memory of Schubert. To those familiar with his style, it is not necessary to play it more than once in order to understand it. The light, intricate embroidery between the quiet melodic passages in the first movement might lull us to slumber; the whole seems to have been written during an hour of suffering as though in meditation on the past. The second movement has

119

a more contemplative character as have many of Schubert's pieces; the third (the fourth impromptu) is quite different; it pouts; quietly, however, and good-naturedly. A misinterpretation is impossible; it has often reminded me of Beethoven's comic, little-known piece, *Rage over the Lost Penny*.

[CHOPIN, MENDELSSOHN, SCHUBERT]

In the review of piano works which follows here Schumann combines works by the three greatest composers of his time. The order is significant: Schumann always postponed to the end the discussion of those works which he considered most important; and in this instance the closing sentence has more weight than all that precedes it.

THE DAVIDITES have for some time promised us further communications regarding Chopin, Schubert, and Mendelssohn; and repeatedly questioned about them, they have answered that they have always been particularly conscientious concerning those matters which they best understand, and are therefore slow to come to a conclusion. But as they still give us hope, I shall merely observe that Chopin seems at last to have arrived at the point which Schubert had reached long before him,— though Schubert, as composer, was not first obliged to lay aside his virtuosity, while, on the other hand, Chopin's virtuosity now serves him. I shall add that Florestan, somewhat paradoxically, declared that in "Beethoven's *Leonora* Overture there was more future than in his symphonies"; this remark may be more correctly applied to Chopin's most recent Nocturne in G minor [opus 15] in which I detect the most terrific declaration of war to the entire past; furthermore, one begins to ask oneself how gravity must be clothed if jest goes about wrapped in dark veils; while I regard Mendelssohn's Capriccio in F-sharp minor [opus 5] as a masterwork, his *Character-pieces* [opus 7] seem to me but interesting notes to the development of this youthful master, who while yet a child played in the chains of Gluck and Bach; in the latter piece I see a forecast of the *Midsummer Night's Dream;* I shall end by saying that Schubert [*Moments Musicaux,* opus 94] will remain our adoration—now and evermore.

PIANO TRIO IN B-FLAT MAJOR, OPUS 99
PIANO TRIO IN E-FLAT MAJOR, OPUS 100

A GLANCE at Schubert's trio [in B-flat], and all miserable human commotion vanishes, and the world shines in new splendor. About ten years ago a Schubert trio [in E-flat] went across the ordinary musical life of the day like an angry thunderstorm. It was his hundredth opus. Shortly after, in November 1828, he died. This recently published trio seems to be an older work. To be sure, its style does not refer to any early period, and it may well have been written a short time before the famous one in E-flat major. Intrinsically, however, they bear little resemblance to each other. The first movement, which in the other is inspired by deep indignation as well as boundless longing, is graceful and virginal in the one before us. The adagio, there a sigh tending to swell to anxiety, is here a happy dream, a rising and falling of genuine feeling. The scherzos somewhat resemble each other, but I give preference to that in the earlier (second) trio. I cannot decide as to the last movements. In a word, the Trio in E-flat major is more active, masculine, and dramatic; this one is more passive, lyric, and feminine. Let the work, which he bequeathed to us, be a cherished inheritance. Time, though producing much that is beautiful, will not soon produce another Schubert!

DIVERTISSEMENT À LA HONCROISE, FOR PIANO, 4 HANDS, OPUS 54

[*Letter to Henriette Voigt, July 3, 1834*]

". . . FRANZ SCHUBERT is the beautiful, pale youth around whose lips there always is a sign of approaching death. Indeed! In the *Divertissement* there is an entire funeral procession—perhaps

for a French marshal killed in battle—with its tall, veiled men,
its catafalque and obsequies . . ."

MESSRS. DIABELLI and Company have published some of the
more important compositions from Schubert's estate, to which
we want to draw the attention mainly of choral societies, etc.
These are:

> Opus 134: *Nachthelle* . . . for tenor solo and four-part male choir with
> piano
> Opus 135: *Ständchen* . . . for alto solo and four-part female choir with
> piano
> Opus 136: *Mirjams Siegesgesang* . . . for soprano solo and choir with
> pianoforte
> Opus 139: *Gebet* . . . for soprano, alto, tenor and bass with piano

The first two of these should make a charming effect; they are
extremely delicate and characteristic. In order to augment the
dull colors frequently encountered in four-part male choirs
Schubert here adds a solo part as well as a piano accompaniment. The idea is a happy one although it makes a performance
for any male choir not provided with a piano impossible, for
the piano is essential and cannot be left out. But when every
requirement is met, the enjoyment will be double. The *Ständ-
chen* (Serenade) has the same form as *Nachthelle* except that
it is written for female voices; when sung by fine voices well
rehearsed, it has a most beautiful effect—in spite of the fact that
a serenade sung by women is a rare occurrence in real life.
In this work, too, the piano is important and provides the
harmonies. In both compositions one again meets with Schubert's mannerism of keeping the same rhythm in the accompaniment from beginning to end. It is to be assumed that they
are well written for the voice; there are also no passages which
are particularly difficult to sing. *Mirjams Siegesgesang* is a

[1] This article was not contained in Schumann's own edition of his literary
works; the reason of his rejection is not known.

more elaborate composition, a kind of cantata, probably originally written with orchestral accompaniment; if this is the case
(as we are almost convinced it is), we regret that it was given
us only in a transcription. But even in this form the work is
effective; its keynote is strangely ancient, religious, almost
biblical. From other compositions by Schubert one may see
how successfully he mastered the most foreign topics through
his imagination. Any composer might learn the mode of writing in the old style; but it needs a poet to evoke the *spirit* of
ancient times so firmly and clearly. The work even contains a
fugue of great skill. The whole work concludes in the same way
it begins, that is, gaily and brilliantly. The *Gebet* (Prayer), on
the other hand, voices the soul of a present-day devout Christian with great inwardness and force; there are our Palestrina
songs: thus modern art expresses man in prayer, patient and
trusting, but at the same time active and ready to fight. One
will listen to this song with great inner sympathy.

Thus the laurels around Schubert's brow live forever. Who
would have thought this composer of *Lieder* had within him
such great wealth? We hope that friendly hands may cooperate
in a publication of his remaining vocal works: the masses and
operas. Vienna hides no greater musical treasures than these.

THE LITERATURE OF DANCING: FIRST WALTZES, OPUS 9, BOOK 1,
GERMAN DANCES, OPUS 33

*The choreographic sketch for the German Dances at the
end of this article clearly shows that there was in Schumann's mind a connection between Schubert's dances and
his own* PAPILLONS.

"AND NOW, play, Zilia! I want to submerge myself entirely in
the tones and only lift up my head from time to time, lest you
should think I have drowned myself in a fit of melancholy;
for dance music makes one sad and languid while church
music, on the other hand, makes one gay and active—at least

myself," said Florestan, while Zilia was already carried away
by the first of Kessler's polonaises. "It would be truly charming," he continued, half speaking, half listening, "if a dozen of
lady Davidites would make this evening unforgettable by dancing together arm in arm in a festival of the Graces. Jean Paul
has already said that girls should only dance with girls (which
might, perhaps, decrease the number of weddings) while men,
I added, should never dance at all. . . ."

Zilia held four soft moonlight chords. Everyone listened attentively. A rose lay on the grand piano, (Florestan always
keeps vases with flowers there instead of candles), which due
to the vibration fell on the keyboard. As Zilia reached towards
a bass key, she pricked herself on the thorns and had to stop
because of her bleeding finger. Florestan asked what was the
matter. "Nothing," said Zilia. "Like these waltzes it has nothing
to do with pain, but only with drops of blood, drawn forth by
roses." May she who said this never know any other! . . .

The Davidites waxed warm and in their excitement (musical
excitement is insatiable) cried out for more until Serpentin [1]
proposed a choice between Schubert's waltzes and Chopin's
bolero. Florestan went into a corner remote from the piano,
saying, "Now if running toward the keyboard I manage to hit
correctly the first chord of the last movement of the D minor
Symphony [Beethoven's Ninth],[2] it shall be Schubert." Of
course he succeeded. Zilia played the waltzes by heart.

First waltzes by Franz Schubert! lovely little genii, floating
above the earth at about the height of a flower—though I do not
much like Le Désir, in which hundreds of girls have drowned
their sentiment, nor the last three aesthetic errors which on the
whole I cannot forgive their creator. There is much beauty
in the way in which the rest circle round the Désir, entangling
it more or less in their delicate threads, also in the dreamy
thoughtlessness which pervades them all, so that we, too, when
playing the last, believe that we are still in the first.

[1] K. Banck (whom Schumann disliked intensely).
[2] See p. 100.

On the other hand, an entire carnival dances through his *German Dances.* "How admirable it would be," cried Florestan in the ear of Fritz Friedrich [1] (the deaf painter), "if you could bring your magic lantern and project this masked ball onto the wall!" He hurried away delightedly, and soon returned.

The following scene was one of the loveliest. The room, dimly lighted; Zilia, sitting at the piano, the wounding rose in her hair; Eusebius, in his black velvet coat, bending over the back of his chair; Florestan dressed similarly, standing at the table interpreting; Serpentin rested with his feet on Walt's [2] neck, sometimes riding about on his back; the bovine-eyed painter, à la Hamlet, working away at his shadow figures, of which a few spider-legged ones were already running up the wall to the ceiling.—Zilia began to play, and Florestan began to speak thus, although rather more elaborately.

"No. 1 in A major. A crowd of masks, drums, trumpets, an extinguisher, a man in a peruke: "Everything seems to work out perfectly." No. 2. A comic figure, scratching its ear, and whispering "Pst! pst!" Disappears. No. 3. Harlequin with his hand on his hips; exit with a somersault. No. 4. Two stiff, polite masks, dancing and conversing little with each other. No. 5. A slender cavalier following a mask. "Have I caught you at last, lovely zither player!"—"Let me go!" She escapes. No. 6. A stiff hussar with sabretache and plume. No. 7. Two reapers waltzing together in a happy trance. He says softly, "Are you she?" They recognize each other. No. 8. A farmer from the country, awkwardly preparing for the dance. No. 9. The doors open wide. Brilliant procession of knights and their ladies. No. 10. A Spaniard, to an Ursuline, "Speak, at least, since you may not love." She: "Better that I do not speak, in order to be understood! . . ."

But in the middle of the waltz Florestan sprang from the table and out the door. They were used to his ways. Zilia also soon ceased playing, and the others dispersed.

[1] J. P. Lyser, musician and painter.
[2] Louis Rakemann, pianist.

Florestan, as I may explain, is in the habit of breaking off at the moment of highest enjoyment, perhaps to preserve its entire freshness and fulness in his memory. This time he succeeded, for when my friends talk of their happiest evenings, they never fail to recall the 28th of December 18[35].

AN OPUS 2[1]

This was the first essay in Schumann's own chronological edition of his literary works. Schumann always remained a great admirer of Chopin's genius, but it is significant that in the final edition of his literary works Schumann here and there slightly modified some of the more emphatic epithets of praise.

EUSEBIUS came in quietly the other day. You know the ironic smile on his pale face with which he seeks to create suspense. I was sitting at the piano with Florestan. Florestan is, as you know, one of those rare musical minds which anticipate, as it were, that which is new and extraordinary. Today, however, he was surprised. With the words, "Hats off, gentlemen—a genius!" Eusebius laid a piece of music on the piano rack. We were not allowed to see the title page. Vacantly I turned over its leaves; the secret enjoyment of music which one does not hear has something magic in it. And besides this, it seems to me that every composer presents a different character of note forms to the eye; Beethoven looks very different from Mozart on paper; just as Jean Paul's prose is different from that of Goethe. But here it

[1] Although this Essay appeared in the *Allgemeine Musikalische Zeitung* in the year 1831, may it be permitted to stand here as the first one in which the Davidites made their appearance. [Schumann]

seemed as though nothing but strange eyes were looking up at me—the eyes of flowers, basilisk eyes, peacock's eyes, maiden's eyes; some passages seemed less strange.—I thought I saw Mozart's *La ci darem la mano* wind through a hundred chords, Leporelló definitely seemed to wink at me, and Don Juan flew by in his white mantle. "Now play it," said Florestan. Eusebius consented; and in the recess of a window we listened. Eusebius played as though inspired and evoked innumerable figures of actual life; the inspiration of the moment seemed to have increased the usual facility of his fingers. Florestan's whole applause, aside from a joyous smile, consisted of nothing but the remark that the variations might have been written by Beethoven or Franz Schubert, had either of these been a pianoforte virtuoso. Turning to the title page, he read the following: "*La ci darem la mano, varié pour le pianoforte par Frédéric Chopin, Oeuvre 2.*" In amazement both of us called out, "Opus 2," our faces glowing with unusual surprise. Except for several exclamations, however, nothing was to be heard save, "Here is something real again—Chopin—I have never heard the name—who can he be?—in any case a genius—is not that Zerlina's laughter?—Or is it Leporello's etc., etc." It would not be possible to describe the scene. Excited by wine, Chopin, and our discussion, we went to Master Raro who, slightly amused and displaying but little curiosity for Opus 2, said, "I know you and your new-fangled enthusiasm! But bring the Chopin piece to me, if you wish." We promised for the next day. Eusebius soon bade us good-night; I remained a short time with Master Raro; Florestan, who for some time has been without a home, hurried through the moonlit streets to my house. At midnight I found him lying on my sofa with his eyes closed. "Chopin's variations," he began as if in a dream, "are running through my head; the whole is dramatic and Chopinesque; the introduction, so self-sufficient—do you remember Leporello's leaps in thirds? —seems to me least fitted to the whole; but the theme—why did he write it in B-flat?—the variations, the finale, the adagio, these are indeed unusual; every measure betrays his genius! Naturally, dear Julius,[1] Don Juan, Zerlina, Leporello, and Masetto are the *dramatis personae;* Zerlina's answer in the theme has a sufficiently amorous character; the first variation might be called distinguished and coquettish—the Spanish grandee flirting amiably with the peasant girl. The flirtation develops in the most natural way in the second, which is much more intimate, comic, and quarrelsome, as though two lovers were laughingly chasing each other. How all this is changed in the third which again is filled with moonlight and enchantment. Masetto hovers in the distance and curses somewhat audibly, not, however, disturbing Don Juan. And now the fourth, what do you think of that? Eusebius played it very purely. Does it not leap impishly and impudently toward its goal though the adagio (it seems quite natural to me that Chopin repeats the first part) is in B-flat minor, as it should be, for it is almost a moral warning to Don Juan against his plan. It is both mischievous and suitable that Leporello should listen behind the hedge, chuckling and jesting; that oboes and clarinets should enchantingly lure and bubble; and that the B-flat major, in all its fullness, should accurately designate the first kiss of love. But all this is nothing compared to the last—have you any more wine, Julius?—that is the whole of Mozart's finale: popping champagne corks, ringing glasses! Leporello's voice between the grasping, snatching spirits; the fleeing Don Juan—and then the end, so beautifully soothing, provides a satisfying conclusion." Florestan concluded by saying that he had never experienced feelings similar to those awakened by this finale, except in Switzerland. "When the evening sunlight of a beautiful day," so he explained, "gradually creeps up towards the highest peaks, and when the last beam vanishes, there comes a moment when we think we see the white Alpine giants close their eyes. It is like a vision of heaven. And now you too awaken to new dreams, Julius, and sleep!" "Florestan dear to my heart," answered I, "these private feelings are perhaps praiseworthy although somewhat subjective; but no matter how little Chopin

[1] See note at the end of this article.

needs to be reminded of his genius, I nevertheless bow my head before such genius, such endeavor, such mastery!" Thereupon we fell asleep. *Julius* [1]

RONDO À LA MAZURKA, OPUS 5

THE RONDO by Chopin was probably written in his eighteenth year, though it has but recently appeared. The extreme youth of the composer is felt only in certain involved passages from which he has found it difficult to extricate himself (as at the end of p. 6); but the rondo is, notwithstanding, thoroughly Chopinesque, i.e., lovely, romantic, full of grace. He who does not yet know Chopin had best make his acquaintance with this composition.

FIRST CONCERTO FOR PIANOFORTE, IN E MINOR, OPUS 11;
SECOND CONCERTO FOR PIANO AND ORCHESTRA
IN F MINOR, OPUS 21

YOUNG ARTISTS, when meeting with your antagonists, rejoice in this indication of your talent, and estimate your power proportionate to the attack. It is remarkable, however, that in those arid years before 1830, when one thanked heaven for every blade of grass, the critics (but they are always behind the times, unless creative themselves), were still shrugging their shoulders at the recognition of Chopin, and one even dared say that Chopin's compositions were good only to be discarded. Enough! The Duke of Modena has not yet recognized Louis Philippe; but although the power of the barricades does not rest upon a base of gold, it continues without the help of the Duke. I may mention here in passing that a famous dyed-in-the-wool newspaper, so I hear (I say *hear*, because I do not read it, and flatter myself that in this respect I bear some resemblance to Beethoven), shoots daggerlike glances at me

---

[1] Julius Knorr, piano teacher. Schumann gives him credit here for having drawn his attention to these variations.

through its smiling mask, because I once said in jest of one of its journalists (who had written something about Chopin's *Don Juan* variations) that he, the journalist, had a couple of feet too many, like a bad verse, and that it would be a kindness to chop them off for him. But why recall these things today, just after having heard Chopin's F minor Concerto? Heaven forbid. Milk versus poison, cool blue milk! What is a musical paper compared to a Chopin concerto? What is a schoolmaster's madness compared to poetic frenzy? What are ten editorial crowns compared to an adagio in the second concerto? And believe me, Davidites, I should not think you worthy of address, did I not think you capable of composing such works as those of which you write, except a few, like this second concerto, which even with united effort we cannot hope to attain, but only to kiss the hem of its garment. Away with your musical journals! It would be the victory, the triumph of a good paper, could it so advance matters (and many are working toward this aim), that criticism would no longer be read; that the world, through sheer productivity, would not attend to what was written about it. It should be the highest endeavor of an honest critic to render himself entirely superfluous (as many try to become); the best discourse on music is silence. These are amusing thoughts of a journalist, none of whom should flatter himself that he is the Lord God of the artists since without these artists he would starve. Away with newspapers! No matter how high the quality of criticism, it primarily remains but a tolerable fertilizer of future works; but even so, God's sun would create in abundance. Once more, why write about Chopin? Why weary one's readers? Why not draw water with your own hand —play, write, and compose yourselves? For the last time, away with all musical journals, one and all! *Florestan*

If the madcap Florestan had his way, he would be capable of calling the above a review, indeed, of closing the journal with it. But he should remember that we have a duty towards Chopin, in whose behalf we have not yet written in our issues;

and the world will in the end attribute our silence—prompted by reverence—to other motives. If we have not yet in words glorified the composer who already reigns in a thousand hearts, it has been for several reasons—timidity in treating of a subject that is very close to us; fear lest we may not speak in proper terms of it, lest we may not have sufficient insight to reach its heights and depths; then there is also our relationship as artists with this artist; and, finally, we have delayed until now because Chopin in his last compositions seems to have struck a higher, if not different level, the direction and end of which we hoped to understand more clearly before giving a trustworthy account of it to our friends.

Genius creates kingdoms, the smaller states of which are again subdivided by a higher hand among talents, that these may organize details which the former, in their thousandfold activities, would be unable to perfect. As Hummel, for instance, followed the call of Mozart, vesting the thoughts of that master in a flowing, sparkling robe, so Chopin followed Beethoven. Or, to speak more simply, as Hummel imitated the style of Mozart in detail, arranging it for the virtuoso's particular instrument, so Chopin led the spirit of Beethoven into the concert hall.

Chopin did not make his appearance accompanied by an orchestral army, as is the custom of a great genius; he only possesses a small cohort, but every one in it is his to the last hero.

He is the pupil of the first masters—Beethoven, Schubert, Field. We assume that the first molded his mind in boldness, the second his heart in tenderness, the third his hand in flexibility.

Thus he was equipped with science of his art, fully armed with courage, and conscious of his power when in the year 1830 the great voice of the people arose in the West. Hundreds of youths had waited for the moment; but Chopin was the first on the ramparts behind which slumbered a cowardly Restoration, a dwarfish Philistinism. Blows were dealt right and left, and the Philistines awoke angrily, crying out, "Look at the impudent fellows!" while others, behind the besiegers, cried, "What glorious courage!"

Combined with all this and the favorable influence of the moment, Fate also distinguished Chopin among all others by endowing him with an original and pronounced nationalism—that of Poland. And because this nationalism is in deep mourning, it attracts us all the more firmly to this thoughtful artist. It was well for him that neutral Germany did not at first receive him too warmly and that his genius led him straight to one of the great capitals of the world, where he could freely poetize and nourish his wrath. If the mighty autocrat of the North [1] knew what a dangerous enemy threatened him in Chopin's works, in the simple melodies of his mazurkas, he would forbid this music. Chopin's works are guns buried in flowers.

In his origin, in the fate of his country, we find the explanation of his great qualities and of his defects. When speaking of grace, enthusiasm, presence of mind, nobility, and warmth of feeling, who does not say Chopin? But also, when it is a question of oddity, morbid eccentricity, even wildness and hate.

All of Chopin's earlier creations bear this impress of intense nationalism.

But Art requires more. The minor interests of the soil on which he was born had to sacrifice themselves to the universal ones. Chopin's later works begin to lose something of their all too Sarmatian physiognomy, and their expression tends little by little to approach the general ideal first created by the divine Greeks; so that by a different road we finally rejoin Mozart.

I say "little by little"; for he never can, nor should he completely disown his origin. But the further he departs from it, the greater will his significance in the world of art become.

If we should attempt to explain the importance which he has already partly gained, we would have to state that he has

---

[1] Schumann refers to the Czar of Russia, Nicholas I, who had crushed the Polish Revolution of 1830.

contributed to the realization of a concept the establishment of which appears ever more urgent: that progress in art will come hand in hand with the progress of the artists toward a spiritual aristocracy. This would not merely demand but presuppose a complete knowledge of technicalities; nor would anybody be admitted to its ranks who did not himself possess the qualities that he demanded of others, i.e., imagination, feeling, spirit— all these in the intention to speed the advent of higher musical culture in which the genuine would be as little mistaken as the manifold forms in which it might appear. By "musical" culture we mean that faculty of inner vital accompaniment, that creative sympathy, that faculty of quick reception and re-creation, whence comes that marriage of productivity and reproductivity to the end of artisthood; through which we shall ever more closely approach the goals of art. *Eusebius*

VARIATIONS FOR PIANO, ON A THEME FROM LUDOVIC
BY HEROLD AND HALÉVY, OPUS 12

EVEN in this genre Chopin carries off the prize. Like that great actor who, though he merely crossed the stage shouldering laths, was applauded by the audience with delight, he cannot disguise his lofty mind in any circumstance; what surrounds him derives color from him and adapts itself, be it ever so rigid, to his master hand. Still, I must confess that these variations should not be compared to his original works.

REPORT TO JEANQUIRIT IN AUGSBURG
ON THE EDITOR'S LAST ART HISTORIANS' BALL

BOLERO, OPUS 19; TWO POLONAISES, OPUS 22

READ AND MARVEL, my dearest friend! The editor of the most modern *Musical Times* is accustomed to give, at least once a year, a sort of art historians' ball; the guests believe it to be given in their honor; the rogue laughs quietly to himself, however, for this is the only way he can escape the tiresome reviewing of dance music, and, at the same time, perhaps, assure himself of the effect of this music on the public. Here, in a word, criticism of the liveliest kind is expressed.

More than ever I wished you could have attended this ball. Composers promenaded up and down, pretty mothers of young lady-amateur players, the —— ambassador with his sister, music publishers in business suits, a couple of rich Jewesses, Davidites leaning against pillars,—in short, it was difficult for me to conduct the lady co-editor (the giantess is called Ambrosia [1]) through the crowd for the first polonaise. . . . We conversed a great deal; for instance, of the peculiar nature of the polonaises, and how we show ourselves to be German since, even in dancing, we tread the measures of all kinds of peoples, and how Strauss has been our real savior in this respect (and perhaps only in this, interposed Ambrosia). . . .

. . . With all the amiability and cunning I could call up, I endeavored to draw her out favorably for my own sake and for the sake of my future works; but the oftener she turned her amorous eyes upon me, the more annoying it became. At last, thank Heaven, the dance was ended. On leaving me, she whispered, "To be led through Chopin's last polonaise by so artistic a hand would"—"Would make me very happy," I concluded, bowing. A battle had been won, but the romance was only beginning. My next thought was to secure Beda,[2] the younger sister, for the waltz by Chopin. I was enchanted by her angelic face, which I saw for the first time that evening, and was happily surprised when she agreed to dance the waltz with me, especially since Eusebius, angrily enough, had just told me that she, blushing, had refused to dance it with him. With me she did dance. If ever I floated ineffably on air, it was in these moments. To be sure, I was only able to coax a "yes" from her now and then, but it was always pronounced so soulfully, so finely shaded according to its various meanings, that I ever more loudly sang like a nightingale. Beda, thought I, would rather be silent than pronounce a contradictory no; so, dear

[1] It is not known whether Schumann had any particular person in mind.
[2] Klara Wieck.

Jeanquirit, I could scarcely understand her refusal of Eusebius. And now, while Chopin's body-and-soul-inspiring waltz
wrapped us in its dark waves, while Beda gazed in ever increasing melancholy towards the assembly, I gently led the conversation to Chopin himself. Scarcely had she heard his name
pronounced, when for the first time she looked towards me
with kind, wide-open eyes. "You know him?"—I admitted that.
—"And you have heard him?" Her whole frame seemed to grow
even lovelier. "And have heard him speak?" And then I told
her that I should never forget how I had seen him sitting at the
pianoforte like a dreaming seer, and how one seemed to become the dream created by him while he played, and how it
was his terrible habit, at the close of every piece, to travel over
the whistling keyboard with one finger as if to tear himself
forcibly from his dream, and how careful he had to be of his
delicate health. And as I held her trembling in fearful ecstasy,
she clung to me and pleaded to know more about him. Chopin,
gallant robber of hearts, never previously had I envied you, but
in this moment I did so intensely . . .

While I was attentively watching, someone came behind me
and put his hands over my eyes. I was almost rude when I
recognized in the jester a Flemish bassoon-player, a certain
Monsieur De Knapp [1]—the face of a scandalmonger if ever
there was one, not to mention his baldness, and the immoral
cast of his nose; a poor faker, who hates me because I once
gave him to understand in Brussels that "a bassoon-player who
cannot also play the violin like Paganini has no cause to exert
himself in my presence"; in short, whenever I think of him, I
discover a whole Shakespearean dictionary of abuse within me.
"Excuse the joke," said he (he is an intimate friend in the
editorial mansion and Ambrosia's acknowledged megaphone),
"but Fräulein Beda is now beginning the bolero." Reason
enough for me to turn my back on him. You know this tender
composition, this intoxicating picture of Southern warmth and
shyness, of reserve and abandonment; Beda in all her loveliness

[1] K. Banck: see p. 124, note.

and maidenly enthusiasm at the pianoforte, the picture of her beloved in, or perhaps at her heart, to show it to me . . . to me! *Florestan*

TWELVE ÉTUDES FOR PIANOFORTE, BOOK 2, OPUS 25

How COULD the name to which we have so often pointed, as to a rare star in the late hours of the night, be wanting in our Museum? [1] Who can tell whither its course may lead, how long may last its sparkling light? But no matter how often it showed itself, there was always the same core of light, the same deep dark glow, the same sharpness of contour—not to be mistaken even by a child. In these études, I have the additional advantage of having heard Chopin himself play nearly all of them, "and very much *à la* Chopin he plays them," whispered Florestan in my ear. Imagine an aeolian harp possessing all the scales, and an artist's hand combining these with all kinds of fantastic embellishments, but always with an audible deep ground bass, and in the treble, a softly flowing cantilena—and you will have some idea of his playing. No wonder, then, that we were most of all charmed with those pieces which we had heard played by himself, and particularly with the first, in A-flat major, rather a poem than an étude. But it would be a mistake to suppose that he allowed us to hear every one of its small notes.[2] It was rather an undulation of the A-flat major chord, brought out more loudly here and there with the pedal. But, exquisitely entangled in the harmony, there ensued a wondrous melody in the big notes.[3] It was only in the middle section that a tenor voice once broke clearly from the chords and joined the principal melody. And when the étude was ended, we felt as though we had seen a lovely picture in a dream, and, half awake, we strove to seize it again; but such things cannot be described, nor can they be fitly praised. Then he played the

[1] Museum (i.e., of the Davidites) is the title of the article of which this review is a part.

[2] Schumann refers to the notes in small print in this étude.

[3] See the preceding annotation.

second in the book, in F minor, again one in which his individuality displays itself in a manner never to be forgotten; as charming, dreamy, and soft as the song of a sleeping child. That in F major followed; fine again, but novel less in its character than in its figuration; here the master shows his admirable powers of the most amiable *bravura*—but what use are words? The pieces are all models of bold inherent creative force, truly poetic creations, though not without small blemishes in detail, but on the whole striking and powerful. Yet, if I give my complete opinion, I must confess that his earlier large collection seems more valuable to me. Not that I mean to imply any diminution in Chopin's artistic power or any retrogression, for these recently published studies were nearly all written at the same time as the earlier ones, and only a few were composed a little while ago, such as the first in A-flat and the last magnificent one in C minor, both of which display an increase of mastery. It is unfortunately true, however, that our friend writes little at present, and no works in large forms. No doubt the distracting Paris is partly to blame for this. Let us assume that after so many inner storms the artist must rest; later, perhaps, to hurry with new vigor toward those more distant suns which genius ever freshly unveils to us. *Eusebius*

TWO NOCTURNES, OPUS 27

AND NOW, as nocturnes are our subject, I will not deny that all the while I have been writing, I have been continually thinking of two new ones by Chopin in C-sharp minor and D-flat major. For, along with Field's, I consider these, with many of his earlier ones, especially those in F major and G minor, ideal; indeed, as the most heartfelt and transfigured creations evolved in music.

TWENTY-FOUR PRELUDES, OPUS 28

I MUST MENTION the preludes as most singular. I will confess that I expected something quite different: compositions carried out in the grand style, like his études. We have almost the contrary here; these are sketches, the beginnings of studies, or, if you will, ruins; eagles' pinions, wild and motley pell-mell. But in every piece we find, in his own pearly handwriting, "This is by Frédéric Chopin"; even in his pauses we recognize him by his agitated breathing. He is the boldest, the proudest poet of these times. To be sure, the book also contains much that is sick, feverish, repellent; but let everyone seek for what becomes him. Only let the Philistine keep away!

IMPROMPTU IN A-FLAT, OPUS 29; FOUR MAZURKAS, OPUS 30; SCHERZO IN B-FLAT MINOR, OPUS 31

CHOPIN will soon be unable to write anything without people crying out at the seventh or eighth bar, "That is indeed by him!" Many have called this mannerism, declaring that he is making no progress. They should be more grateful. Is not this the same original force that dazzled you so surprisingly in his first works, that in the first moment perplexed and then enraptured you? And now that he has given you a succession of rare creations and that you understand him more easily, must you ask something different from him? That would be like cutting down a tree because every year it produces the same kind of fruit. But his productions are not all alike; the trunk is indeed the same; its fruits, however, the most diverse in savor and form. The above impromptu so little resembles anything in the whole gamut of his works that it can scarcely be compared with any other Chopin composition; it is so refined in form; its cantilena is from beginning to end enclosed in such charming figuration; it is so unique an impromptu that it cannot be placed beside any other of his compositions. The impassioned character of the scherzo reminds us more of its predecessors; it is a highly attractive piece, so overflowing with tenderness, boldness, love, and contempt, that it may be compared, not inappropriately, to a poem by Byron. Such a thing is not fitted for all, to be sure. Chopin has elevated the mazurka to a small art form; he has written many of them, yet few resemble each other. Almost every one of them contains some poetic traits, something new in form and expression. Such, in the above mazurka, I consider that yearning of the key of B minor towards F-sharp minor, which concludes (though we scarcely observe it) in F-sharp; in the second, that indecision of the keys between major and minor, until the major third conquers; in the third, which, notwithstanding, contains a somewhat weak strophe (see page 13), that sudden close in parallel fifths, which will cause German cantors to wring their hands. By the way, different epochs have different ears. In the best church compositions of the old Italians we find progressions of fifths, which therefore could not have sounded ill to them. Even in Bach and Handel we occasionally find a few, though in arpeggios; but the great art of interweaving parts avoids the parallel progression. In Mozart's period they entirely disappear. Then the great theorists came to the attack, forbidding them under penalty of death, until Beethoven again introduced the loveliest fifths, especially in chromatic sequence. Of course such a chromatic sequence of fifths, especially when it stretches through twenty measures, is not to be considered as something excellent, but rather as something extremely bad; at the same time it would be foolish to isolate progressions of this sort from the whole; they should be heard in relation to what precedes them.

MAZURKAS, OPUS 33; THREE WALTZES, OPUS 34

OF NEW compositions by Chopin, we must mention . . . a volume of mazurkas and three waltzes. His forms seem to grow even brighter and lighter—or are we becoming accustomed to his style? These mazurkas will instantly charm everyone and seem to us more popular in character than his earlier ones. But his three waltzes will delight above all—so different in type are they from the ordinary ones, and of a kind as could occur only to Chopin—perhaps he was inspired to new creations while he gazed, great artist that he is, among the dancers whom he has just roused by playing. So throbbing a life flows in them that they seem to have been actually improvised in the ballroom.

SONATA IN B-FLAT MINOR, OPUS 35

ANYONE glancing at the first bars of this sonata and uncertain of its author would not prove himself a good connoisseur. Only Chopin begins and ends in this way: with dissonances through dissonances into dissonances. But how many beauties, too, does this piece contain! The idea of calling it a sonata is a caprice, if not a jest, for he has simply bound together four of his most reckless children; thus under his name smuggling them into a place into which they could not else have penetrated . . . Let us imagine some good country cantor visiting a musical city for the purpose of making artistic purchases. All the newest compositions are laid before him, but he does not care anything about them; finally, some sly fellow hands him a sonata: "Ah, yes, that is something for me, a composition of the good old times," says he delighted, and buys it at once. At home he takes up the piece, and I am much mistaken if he does not vow, by every musical divinity, that this is no sonata style but rank blasphemy, even before he has painfully deciphered the first page. But Chopin has achieved his end; he has penetrated into the cantor's residence; and who knows whether, in years to come, in the same dwelling there may not be born some romantic grandson who some day will dust off the sonata, play it, and think to himself, "This man was no fool!"

What I have just said is tantamount to half a valuation. Chopin no longer writes anything that we could also find in others; he is true to himself, and with good reason.

It is a great pity that most piano players, even cultivated ones, are generally unable to judge or to see beyond the limits of their own dexterity. Instead of first reading over such a difficult piece as this, they dig and hack away at it, bar by bar; and then, before they have acquired even a rough idea of its formal connections, they lay it aside and pronounce it bizarre, involved, etc. Chopin (something like Jean Paul) has his involved sentences and parentheses over which it is not well to linger on a first reading lest one lose the thread. We find such

passages on almost every page of this sonata, and Chopin's
often wild and arbitrary spelling of his chords render the disen-
tanglement of such passages even more difficult. For he is not
fond of enharmonizing, if I may so express it, and so we often
find keys and measures sharpened ten times and more, such
as none of us love save in extreme cases. He is often right, but
is often entangled without any reason, and thus keeps at a distance a considerable part of the public; for people do not care
to be continually mocked (as they fancy) and driven into a
corner. This sonata, for instance, has five flats for signature and
is in B-flat minor, a key that certainly cannot boast of special
popularity. It begins thus:

This thoroughly Chopinesque beginning is followed by one
of those stormy, passionate movements with which Chopin already has acquainted us. This must be heard often and well
performed. But even the first part of the work brings us a
beautiful cantilena; indeed, it seems as if the national Polish
flavor, which clung to most of Chopin's earlier melodies, were
dwindling, and that he now sometimes leans toward Italy via
Germany. It is known that Chopin and Bellini were friends,
that they often showed their compositions to one another, and
must necessarily have exercised an artistic influence on each
other. But as we have said, we find only a gentle inclination
toward southern melody here; when the song is over, the Sarmatian flashes from the tones in his defiant originality. One
interweaving of chords, at least, which we find after the close
of the first section in the second part, neither would nor could

have been attempted by Bellini. The whole movement ends in a manner by no means Italian; and this reminds me of a remark once made by Liszt: "Rossini and Co. always close with 'I remain your very humble servant.'" But it is otherwise with Chopin whose endings express just the reverse. The second movement is merely the continuation of this mood; it is bold, spirited, fantastic; the trio tender, dreamy, entirely in Chopin's manner; like many of Beethoven's, it is a scherzo only in name. There follows a still more gloomy *Marcia funebre* which is repellent; in its place an adagio, perhaps in D-flat, would certainly have been more effective. That which in the last movement is given to us under the name "finale" resembles mockery more than any kind of music. Yet we must confess that even from this joyless, unmelodious movement an original and terrifying spirit breathes on us which holds down with mailed fist everything that seeks to resist, so that we listen fascinated and uncomplaining to the end—though not to praise; for this is not music. Thus the sonata closes as it began, emphatically, like a Sphinx with an ironic smile.

TWO NOCTURNES, OPUS 37; BALLADE IN F MAJOR, OPUS 38;
WALTZ FOR PIANOFORTE, OPUS 42

CHOPIN might now publish anything without his name; one would nevertheless immediately recognize him. This remark includes praise and blame; praise for his gifts; blame for his endeavor. He possesses such remarkable original power that, whenever it displays itself, it is impossible for a moment to be uncertain as to its source; and he adds to this an abundance of novel forms that compel our admiration for both their tenderness and boldness. But, though ever new and inventive in the outward forms of his compositions, he remains in special instrumental effects intrinsically the same; and we almost fear that he will not rise any higher than he has already risen. And although this is high enough to render his name immortal in the history of modern art, he limits himself to the narrow sphere of piano music, whereas with his powers he might climb to far greater heights, whence to exercise an immense influence on the general development of our art. Let us, however, be content. He has already created so much that is beautiful; continues to give us so much that we ought to be satisfied; for we should certainly congratulate any artist who has accomplished merely half as much as he. To deserve the name of poet it is not necessary to write thick volumes; one or two true poems are enough for that, and Chopin has written such. The above-named nocturnes are also poems; they distinguish themselves essentially from his earlier ones through simpler ornamentation and a more modest grace. We know how Chopin formerly comported himself, as though overstrewn with spangles, gold trinkets, and pearls. He has altered and grown older; he still loves jewelry, but of a more distinguished kind, through which the loftiness of poetry gleams all the lovelier. Indeed, one must grant him taste, and of the finest, though of a kind not meant for specialists of thorough-bass on the lookout for consecutive fifths and infuriated by every one they detect. Yet they might learn much from Chopin, above all, how to write fifths. We must direct attention to the ballade as a most remarkable work. Chopin has already written one composition of the same name [in G minor]—one of his wildest and most original compositions; the new one is different—as a work of art inferior to the first, but equally fantastic and inventive. Its impassioned episodes seem to have been inserted afterwards. I recollect very well that when Chopin played the ballade here, it ended in F major; now it closes in A minor. At that time he also mentioned that certain poems of Mickiewicz had suggested his ballade to him. On the other hand, a poet might easily be inspired to find words to his music; it stirs one profoundly. The waltz finally is, like his earlier ones, a salon piece of the noblest sort; if it were played for dancers, Florestan thinks at least half of the ladies should be young countesses. And he is right, for Chopin's waltz is thoroughly aristocratic.

TARANTELLE, OPUS 43

THIS IS in Chopin's most extravagant style; we see before us the dancer, whirling as if possessed, until our senses reel. To be sure, nobody could call this music lovely, but we willingly forgive the master his wild fantasy. For is he not once in a while permitted to display the nightside of his soul? At any rate, Chopin never writes for orthodox reviewers.

CONCERT ALLEGRO, OPUS 46; BALLADE IN A-FLAT MAJOR, OPUS 47; TWO NOCTURNES, OPUS 48; FANTASY, OPUS 49

WE AGAIN find much that is fascinating in certain new compositions by Chopin. . . . Like everything that issues from his pen, these compositions may instantly be recognized as Chopin. The Concert Allegro entirely has the form of the first movement of a concerto and probably was originally written with orchestral accompaniment. Though the piece is rich in new and brilliant passage work, it lacks a cantilena for the middle section; as it stands it rambles on restlessly. We feel the need of a succeeding slow movement, an adagio, for the entire plan implies a complete concerto in three movements. The idea of raising the pianoforte to the highest possible point of independence, and of rendering the orchestra unnecessary, is a favorite one with many young composers, and it seems to have influenced Chopin in the publication of his Allegro in its present form. But this new attempt again proves the difficulty of the task—though what we say is not meant as a warning against similar attempts.[1] We place the ballade—Chopin's third—far higher than the Allegro; it differs strikingly in form and character from his earlier ones, and must be counted among his most original creations. In it we may recognize the refined and intellectual Pole, accustomed to moving in the most distinguished circles of the French capital. We cannot further analyze its poetic atmosphere. In their melancholy character, their peaceful movement, the nocturnes rank with Chopin's earlier ones. The second especially will speak to many ears.

[1] See pp. 63-64.

In the Fantasy we recognize the audacious, impassioned tone poet whom we have met before. Although there is a touch of genius in many details, the whole refused to subordinate itself to a beautiful form. We can merely guess what images were before Chopin's eyes when he wrote it. They could not have been joyous.

PIANO TRIO IN G MINOR, OPUS 8

I PRESUME that the trio by Chopin which appeared several years ago is known to most people. Can one blame Florestan that he is somewhat vain of the fact that he was the first to introduce an unknown youth to the public? And how brilliantly has Chopin fulfilled his prophecy! How triumphantly has he emerged from the battle with ignoramuses and Philistines! How continuously does he strive toward simplicity and true art! This trio belongs to Chopin's earlier period when he still made certain concessions to the virtuoso. But who could have foreseen the development of such anomalous originality, such an energetic nature, which would prefer wearing itself out rather than permit others to dictate laws to him? Chopin has already passed through several periods of development. The most difficult things have become child's play to him so that he eschews them, and, true artist that he is, prefers the simpler things. What can I say of this trio that everyone with a feeling for Chopin has not already told himself? Is it not infinitely noble, more enthusiastic than the song of any poet, original in detail and in the whole, and is not every note filled with life and music?

♯

What he views may be of diverse nature; but his viewpoint remains always the same. *Florestan*

♯

All Polish compositions which have recently appeared have been more or less influenced by Chopin. Through him Poland has obtained a seat and vote in the great musical parliament of

145

nations. Annihilated politically, it will ever continue to flower in our art.

Liszt

TWELVE ETUDES, OPUS 1; TWELVE GRANDES ETUDES SERIES 1, 2

> *In the following discussion of Liszt's composing it must be noted that his greatest works for piano—the Concerto in A major, the* MEPHISTO WALTZ, *the Rhapsodies, etc.—were not published at the time. There is no record of Schumann's reaction to Liszt's great piano Sonata in B minor, dedicated to Schumann.*

WE ARE HAPPY to acquaint our readers with a discovery of ours concerning these études which will greatly increase their interest in them. We refer to our collection, published by Hofmeister, numbered opus 1, and titled *Travail de la Jeunesse;* and to another published by Haslinger and entitled *Grandes Etudes.* But on closer acquaintance we find the latter to be, in most of its numbers, recasts of certain youthful compositions which had been forgotten because of the obscurity of the publishing house, and which have been brought to light and newly published by the German publisher. Though we cannot term this collection . . . an original work, it will remain doubly interesting, because of the aforesaid circumstances, to any professional pianist who has the opportunity of comparing it with the old edition. On making this comparison we immediately perceive the difference between the pianist of then and now, and find how the latter has gained in richness of means, brilliancy, and fullness; while we cannot fail to observe that the original simplicity, which is natural to the first flow of youthful talent, is almost entirely suppressed in its present form. In addition, the new version provides a criterion for the artist's present more intense way of thinking and feeling; indeed, it affords us a glimpse into his secret intellectual life with the result that we often remain undecided whether not to envy the boy more than the man, who appears unable to find peace.

Opinions vary so greatly on the matter of Liszt's talent for composition that an examination of its most important elements and its manifestation at various times will not be out of place here. This is somewhat difficult, for there is much confusion in the opus numbers of Liszt's compositions, the majority not even being numbered, so that it is sometimes only possible to speculate as to the time of their appearance. There can be no doubt, however, that we have here to deal with an extraordinary, multiply moved mind as well as with a mind influencing others. His own life is to be found in his music. Taken away from his country at a tender age, thrown amidst the excitements of a great city, admired already as a child and a boy, we find him, in his earlier compositions, now full of longing, as though yearning for his German home, now frivolous, with a light touch of French. He does not seem to have enjoyed the leisure necessary to persistent studies in composition. Perhaps he never found a master equal to him; all the more did he study as a virtuoso, for lively musical natures prefer quickly eloquent tones to dull scoring on paper. And while he developed his piano playing to an extraordinary degree, the composer in him lagged behind; this always leads to a disequilibrium, the consequences of which are felt in his most recent works. Other influences stimulated the young artist in still other ways. While he endeavored to present in his music the ideas of French romantic literature among whose representatives he lived, he was stimulated by the sudden appearance of Paganini to develop even more his playing and attempt the almost impossible. Thus, in his *Apparitions*, for instance, we find him brooding over somber fantasies or indifferent to the point of boredom; in other places indulging in the most extravagant artifices of virtuosity, mocking and madly audacious. The sight of Chopin, it seems, first brought him to his senses again. Chopin always has structure; through the strange forms of his music there always runs the red thread of a melody. But it was probably too late for the extraordinary virtuoso to make up for what he had missed as a composer. Perhaps no longer satisfied with himself as an original composer, he began to turn to others in order to embellish their work with his art; to Beethoven and Franz Schubert, whose work he spiritedly transcribed for his own instrument; or, in his desire to give something of his own, endeavored to improve his earlier pieces and embed them in the pomp of his acquired virtuosity.

These remarks must be taken as an attempt to explain the unclear, often interrupted, progress of Liszt as a composer by his preponderating genius as a virtuoso. But I sincerely believe that had Liszt, with his eminently musical nature, devoted the same time to composition and to himself that he has given to his instrument and to the works of others, he would have become a very remarkable composer. What may yet be expected from him is a matter of conjecture. To win the favor of his fatherland, he would, above all things, have had to return to serenity and simplicity, which so agreeably express themselves in these older études; he would have had to initiate the reverse process with his compositions—that of simplification rather than of complication. However, we must not forget that his intention was to give études, and that the difficulties and complications he has added in this new version of them are justified by the purpose, namely, the provision of difficulties to be surmounted.

To facilitate the reader's judgment of the present études, their original form, and the manner of their elaboration, we cite the following beginnings:

No. 1. As formerly.

The same now.

No. 5. As formerly.

The same now.

No. 9. As formerly.

The resemblance and the difference are obvious. The fundamental mood on which these pieces were based has been retained at the outset of nearly all of them, though richer figures have been added, and they are more abundant in harmony, with greater emphasis on color; but in the course of the pieces so many deviations crop up in the new edition that the original is often entirely submerged. Thus the second étude, in A minor, has received a number of additions and a new ending. In the third, in F major, the early étude is more difficult of recognition; its movement has undergone a change, it has acquired another melody, while the whole piece has gained in interest (except for the more trivial middle section in A major). In the fourth, in D minor, he has also added a melody above the figuration of the first original; inserted a middle section of soothing character; and at the close provided new accompaniments to that melody. The fifth has undergone a total transformation, and so on. The following three are wholly new, and the longest studies we know, not one of them covering less than ten pages. It would be useless labor to attempt to criticize them in the ordinary manner, or to seek for, and correct consecutive fifths and false relations. Such compositions must be *heard;* they were wrung from the instrument with the hands; and hands alone can make them resound. And one ought also to see their composer play them; for just as the sight of any virtuosity elevates and strengthens, so much more does the immediate sight of the composer himself, struggling with his in-

strument, taming it, making it obey every tone! These are true
storm and terror études—études for at most ten or twelve people in the whole world. Weaker executants will only excite
laughter by attempting them. Most of all they are related to
some of Paganini's for violin, certain of which Liszt has but
recently decided to transcribe for piano. The next numbers of
the new edition again base themselves on the old one. No. 9
has received an introduction and several interesting additions
in its course. No. 10 also appears more broadly carried out, and
ten times more difficult than before. No. 11, the principal idea—

is thus transposed—

In the course of the new étude a new figuration appears
above a somewhat insipid idea, while the middle cantilena is
charming, and as a melody must be called the most fervent in
the whole collection. The new figuration then appears once
more in the fullest piano sonorities.

Finally, No. 12 is a working-out of the last étude in the
earlier work in which the melody, originally in 4-4 time, is reset
in 6-8; it presents a number of highly difficult figures in the
accompaniment; and one often does not know where to find

the fingers for them. Nos. 6, 8, and 11 of the Hofmeister Edition are omitted in the new one (three numbers inserted in their stead); perhaps Liszt will introduce them in succeeding volumes, as he apparently intends to treat the entire gamut of the keys.

As we have said, all these should be heard played by a master, and, if possible, by Liszt himself. Even then, some passages in them might offend us, where he exceeds all limits, where the effect attained does not compensate sufficiently for the sacrifice of beauty. But we eagerly look forward to the visit he has promised to pay us next winter.[1] It was precisely with these études that he made such a tremendous impression during his last sojourn in Vienna; but great effects can only be produced by great causes, and a public cannot be brought to enthusiasm for nothing. So let everyone prepare himself for this artist by previsional examination of both collections. He himself will give us the best criticism on them at the piano.

BRAVURA STUDIES, AFTER PAGANINI'S CAPRICES, ARRANGED FOR THE PIANOFORTE (IN TWO PARTS)

This review was preceded by that which Schumann wrote on his own transcription of the same pieces (below, p. 254).

THE ORIGINAL WORK is entitled *24 capricci per violino solo, composti e dedicati agli artisti, da N. Paganini, opus 1*. An arrangement of twelve of these, by Robert Schumann, had already appeared (in two volumes) in the years 1833 and 1835. An arrangement of several of them was also published in Paris, but we have forgotten the name of the arranger. The Liszt collection consists of five numbers from the capriccios; the sixth is an arrangement of the well-known "Campanella" rondo. There is of course no question here of any pedantic imitation or a bare harmonic filling-out of the original violin line; the pianoforte reaches its effects through other means than those of the violin.

[1] See below, pp. 155-163.

To produce similar effects, no matter by what means, was here the paramount task of the arranger. Everyone who has heard Liszt, however, knows that he understands all the means and effects of his instrument. It must therefore be highly interesting to find the compositions of the greatest violin virtuoso of our century in regard to bold *bravura*—Paganini—illustrated by the boldest of modern pianoforte virtuosos—Liszt. A glance into the collection, at the strange chaos of notes, is sufficient to convince the eye that there is nothing easy to be found here. It is as though Liszt had resolved to put all his experience into the work, to bequeath the secrets of his playing to posterity; nor could he better evince his admiration for the great deceased artist than by this transcription, carefully worked out into the smallest detail and most faithfully reflecting the spirit of the original. If Schumann's arrangement was intended to bring out the more poetic side of the composition, that of Liszt, without having sacrificed the former, rather aims to stress the virtuoso side. He correctly titles the pieces *Bravura* Studies, such as may be performed in public for purposes of display. To be sure, very few persons will be able to master them; perhaps only four or five in the world. But this would not justify us to ignore the matter. There is a pleasure in facing the highest pitch of virtuosity, even from a distance. If we look more closely at many pieces in the collection, we undoubtedly find that the purely musical content is often entirely disproportionate to the mechanical difficulties. But the word "study" excuses much. You should practice, no matter at what cost.

Let us say it outright: this collection is probably the most difficult thing ever written for the pianoforte, just as its original is the most difficult ever written for the violin. Paganini probably wanted to express this with his charmingly brief dedication, *agli artisti*—that is to say, "I am accessible only to artists." And so it is with Liszt's transcription; it will convince only virtuosos of the first rank. The collection can only be judged from this point of view. We must deny ourselves a comparative analysis of the original and the arrangement; it would take too much space; this is most feasible with both scores before us. But it is interesting to compare the first étude here with Schumann's arrangement of the same, a comparison Liszt has thoughtfully invited by printing Schumann's above his own, measure for measure. It is the sixth caprice in the Italian edition. The last number gives us the variations with which the original edition also closes, the same that apparently inspired H. W. Ernst [1] to his *Venetian Carnival*. We consider Liszt's transcription of these musically the most interesting number of the whole work, but even here we often find difficulties of the greatest sort within the small space of a few bars; of such a nature that even Liszt himself might have to work over them. He who is able to master *these* variations, I mean in such an easy, provocative way that they glide past the hearer—as they should—like little scenes of a puppet show, may safely tour the world, for he will return with the golden laurels of the second Paganini–Liszt.

TRANSCRIPTIONS OF SCHUBERT LIEDER

THIS IS A fitting occasion to mention Franz Liszt's transcriptions of Franz Schubert's songs, which have found such favor with the public. Performed by Liszt, they are said to be highly effective, but no other than master hands will undertake to render them; they are perhaps the most difficult pieces ever written for the pianoforte. A witty fellow wondered whether a simplified edition could not be arranged; he was merely curious to know what would result, whether this might not be the pure Schubert song. Not always. Liszt has changed and added; the *way* he has done it testifies to the powerful nature of *his* conception, *his* playing; others will be of different opinion. It all amounts to the old question whether the reproductive artist may set himself above the creative one, whether he be allowed arbitrarily to modify the latter's works for his own purposes. The answer is easy. A bungler is ridiculous when he does it

[1] See below, p. 249.

badly; an intelligent artist may do it as long as he does not destroy the identity of the original. This type of transcription has introduced a new style in the school of piano playing.

FRANZ LISZT

I

STILL exhausted by a series of six concerts which he gave in Prague during an eight-days' stay there, Liszt arrived last Saturday [March 14, 1840] in Dresden. Perhaps he was never more eagerly expected anywhere than in the capital where pianoforte music and its performance are prized above all. On Monday he gave a concert; the hall presented a brilliant spectacle, filled with the most distinguished society, including several members of the royal family. All eyes were fixed on the door through which the artist was to enter. Many portraits of him were in circulation, and that by Kriehuber, who has most correctly rendered his Jovian profile, is excellent; but the youthful Jupiter himself, of course, interests us to quite a different degree. A great deal has been said about the prosaic nature of our present times, the stuffy atmosphere of courts and capitals, of railroad civilization, etc.; but let the right man appear, and we listen reverently to his every manifestation. How much more to this artist, whose miraculous performances were famous even twenty years ago; whose name we have been accustomed to hear mentioned with the very important—before whom, as before Paganini, all parties bowed and for a moment appeared to be reconciled. Indeed the whole audience excitedly acclaimed him at his entrance; whereupon he began to play. I had heard him before; but it is one thing when the artist is playing before a public, and another, when he is playing before a small group—even the artist himself changes. The beautiful illuminated hall, the glow of candlelight, the handsomely dressed audience—all this tends to elevate the frame of mind of the giver as well as that of the receiver. And now the daemon began to stir in him; first he played with the public as if to try it, then gave it something more profound, until he had enmeshed every member of the audience with his art and did with them as he willed. With the exception of Paganini no artist to a like degree possesses this power of subjecting the public, of lifting it, sustaining it, and letting it fall again. A Viennese writer has composed a poem on Liszt, consisting of nothing but adjectives attached to the single letters of his name. Intrinsically of bad taste, the poem nevertheless is applicable, for just as letters and concepts rise before us when turning the pages of a dictionary, so here there arise tones and emotions. Within a few seconds tenderness, boldness, exquisiteness, wildness succeed one another; the instrument glows and flashes under the master's hands. All this has already been described a hundred times, and the Viennese, especially, have tried to catch the eagle in every way—through pursuits, snares, pitchforks, and poems. But he must be heard—and also seen; for if Liszt played behind the screen, a great deal of poetry would be lost.

From beginning to end he alone played and accompanied.[1] Just as Mendelssohn is said to have once had the idea to compose an entire concert with overture, vocal pieces, and other appurtenances (one may safely publish this idea for the general benefit!), so does Liszt nearly always give his concerts unassisted. Only Madame Schroeder-Devrient—almost the only artist capable of asserting herself in such company—toward the close of the concert performed Schubert's *Erlking* and some of his smaller songs together with Liszt.

I am not sufficiently familiar with the Dresden public's barometer of applause to be able to decide what impression this extraordinary artist made there. The enthusiasm was considered immense; however the Viennese applauds more than any other German, and, in idolatry, prides himself on the torn gloves that he has sacrificed to Liszt. In North Germany, as I have mentioned before, things are different.

[1] Solo recitals were not customary at the time.

Early on Tuesday Liszt left for Leipzig. Our next review will treat of his appearance there.

II

Would that I could, ye distant strangers and the many among you who can scarcely hope to see this artist in person, and therefore search for every word that is spoken about him—would that I could give you a picture of this eminent man! But it is difficult. It would be easiest to talk about his external appearance. People have often tried to describe it; the artist's head is said to bear a resemblance to Schiller's, even to Napoleon's; and since all extraordinary beings appear to have a trait in common, i.e., that of energy and strength of will about their eyes and mouth, these comparisons are partly accurate. Particularly does he resemble Napoleon in his portraits as a young general—pale, lean, distinguished in profile, the expression of his entire person culminating in his head. His resemblance to the deceased Ludwig Schunke [1] is equally striking, and extends into their art to such a degree that, when listening to Liszt's playing, I often had the illusion of hearing something already heard before. But what is most difficult is, precisely, to talk about this art. It is no longer pianoforte playing of this kind or that; instead, it is generally the outward expression of a daring character whom Fortune has permitted to dominate and to triumph not with dangerous implements, but with the peaceful means of art. No matter how many important artists have passed before us in the last years; no matter how many artists equaling Liszt in many respects we ourselves possess, not one can match him in point of energy and boldness. People have been fond of placing Thalberg in the rank beside him and then drawing comparisons. But a look at both heads decides the question. I remember the remark of a Viennese draftsman who said not inaptly of his countryman's head that it resembled "that of a handsome young countess with a man's nose"; while

[1] Pianist, close friend of Schumann's; see p. 25.

of Liszt he observed that "he might sit to any painter as a Greek god." There is a similar difference in their art. Chopin stands nearer to Liszt as a player, for at least he loses nothing beside him in magic tenderness and grace; Paganini, nearest of all, and among women, Madame Malibran; [1] from the latter two Liszt himself acknowledges that he has learned the most.

Liszt is now probably thirty years old. That he was hailed as a prodigy even as a child; that he was early transplanted to foreign lands; that his name afterwards appeared here and there among the most distinguished, and again vanished for a considerable time, until finally Paganini appeared, inciting the youth to new endeavors; and that he suddenly re-appeared in Vienna two years ago, rousing the imperial city to enthusiasm— all this and more do we know. Since the establishment of our paper we have followed Liszt's career, concealing nothing that has been publicly said for or against his art, though by far the greater number of voices, especially those of all great artists, have sounded the praise of his extraordinary talent. Thus he recently came among us already decorated with the highest honors that can be bestowed upon an artist, and established in fame. To increase his reputation by adding new honors was difficult— indeed, it was easier to diminish them, for pedants and rascals are ever with us. This, too, was attempted here. Not by any fault of Liszt's the public had been made restless with previous announcements and rendered ill-humored by errors in the concert arrangements. A writer, notorious here for his lampoons, made use of this by anonymously agitating against the artist, saying that "he had come among us to satisfy his insatiable greed." Better not dwell on this vulgarity.

The first concert, on the 17th [March 1840], was a strange scene. People stood uncomfortably crowded together. One scarcely recognized the hall. The platform was also filled with listeners. In the midst of all—Liszt.

He began with the scherzo and finale of Beethoven's *Pastoral* Symphony. The selection was capricious enough, and for many

[1] Famous operatic contralto.

158

reasons unfortunate. At home, in a *tête-à-tête*, this extremely careful transcription might lead one almost to forget the orchestra. But in a large hall, in the place where we have been accustomed to hear the symphony itself performed frequently and perfectly by the orchestra, the weakness of the pianoforte was all the more striking; particularly since the transcription attempts to reproduce the masses in all their fullness.

A simpler arrangement, a mere indication, would perhaps have been much more effective here. Of course one could nevertheless recognize the master of the instrument. People were satisfied; they had at least seen him shake his mane. To sustain the figure, the lion presently began to show his power. This was in a fantasy on themes by Pacini, which he played in a most remarkable fashion. But I would sacrifice all the astonishing, audacious *bravura* that he displayed here for the sake of the magical tenderness that he expressed in the following étude. With the sole exception of Chopin, as I have already said, I know no one who could equal it. He closed with the well-known chromatic galop; and as the clapping refused to cease, he added his famous *Bravura* Waltz.

Fatigue and indisposition prevented the artist from giving the concert promised for the next day. In the meanwhile a musical festival was prepared for him that will never be forgotten by Liszt himself nor by anyone present. The host (F. Mendelssohn) had chosen for performance only compositions unknown to his guest: Franz Schubert's symphony [in C major]; his own psalm, *As the Hart Pants;* the overture *A Calm Sea and Prosperous Voyage;* three choruses from *St. Paul;* and in conclusion the Concerto for Three Pianos in D minor by Sebastian Bach. The last was played by Liszt, Mendelssohn, and Hiller. It all seemed to spring from the moment, without preparation. We passed three happy hours of music, such as one sometimes does not meet with in years. At the end Liszt played alone, and wonderfully enough. The assembly broke up amid the most joyful excitement, and the joy and rapture that mirrored themselves in all eyes ought to serve the host as thanks for the homage which, on that evening, he paid to the famous artistic talent of another.

Liszt's most amazing performance was yet to come—Weber's *Concertstück*, which he played at his second concert. As virtuoso and audience seemed to be in the most animated mood possible on that evening, the enthusiasm during and after his playing exceeded everything hitherto known here. Beginning the piece with a force and grandeur of expression that made one think of an attack on a battlefield, he carried this on with continually increasing power up to the passage where the player, as it were, places himself at the head of the orchestra, leading it forward in triumph. Here indeed he resembled that great commander to whom he has been compared in personal appearance, and the tempestuous applause that greeted him was not unlike an adoring *Vive l'Empereur!* He then played a fantasy on themes from the *Huguenots*, Schubert's *Ave Maria*, and *Serenade*, and, at the request of the audience, the *Erlking*. But the *Concertstück* was and remained his crowning performance.

I do not know who originated the idea of having a beloved primadonna present him with a wreath of flowers at the close of the concert. But the flowers were certainly not undeserved; and how narrow and mean must be the man who would wish to censure so friendly an attention, as was done in one of the papers here! The artist has put his life into the joys which he provided for you; he spares you the knowledge of the pains his art costs him; he gives you the best he has—the flowering of his being; and are we to grudge him even a simple wreath? But Liszt left no debts unpaid. With visible delight in the fiery reception he had received at his second concert, he declared himself at once ready to give a third for the benefit of any charitable institution, the selection of which he left to the decision of others. So, for the third time, he played again last Monday for the benefit of the pension fund for aged or invalid musicians, though he had given a concert for the poor in Dresden the day before. The hall was full to capacity; the object

Montag, den 30. März 1840.

CONCERT

im Saale des Gewandhauses

zum Besten des Institutfonds

für alte und kranke Musiker

gegeben von

FRANZ LISZT.

Erster Theil.

Ouverture zu Coriolan, von L. v. Beethoven.

Arie aus Sargin, von Paer, gesungen von Fräulein Louise Schlegel.

Concert für das Pianoforte, von Felix Mendelssohn-Bartholdy, (Nº 2. D moll) vorgetragen vom Concertgeber.

Zweiter Theil.

Ouverture: „die Hebriden," von Felix Mendelssohn-Bartholdy.

Zwei Lieder, Zwiegesang, von L. Spohr, und Ungeduld, von Fr. Schubert, gesungen von Mad. Bünau-Grabau.

Etuden, von Ferdinand Hiller, vorgetragen vom Concertgeber.

Carnavalsscenen, von R. Schumann, vorgetragen vom Concertgeber.

Op. 9. 1. *Préambule*. 2. *Andantino* (Eusebius). 3. *Agitato* (Florestan). 4. *Valse* (la Coquette). 5. *Replique*. 6. *Notturno* (Chopin). 7. *Scherzo* (Pantalon et Colombine). 8. *Reconnaissance*. 9. *Promenade*. 10. *Finale*.

Arie aus Titus, von Mozart, gesungen von Fräulein Schloss.

Hexameron. Variationen für das Pianoforte, über ein Thema von Bellini, vorgetragen vom Concertgeber.

1. *Introduction*, von Liszt. 2. *Erste Variation*, von Thalberg. 3. *Zweite Variation*, von Liszt. 4. *Dritte Variation*, von Herz. 5. *Vierte Variation*, von Pixis. 6. *Finale*, von Liszt.

Einlassbillets à 1 **Thaler** 8 **Gr.** sind in den Musikalienhandlungen der Herren Breitkopf & Härtel, Wilh. Härtel, Friedr. Hofmeister und Friedr. Kistner zu haben. An der Casse kostet das Billet 2 **Thaler.**

Der Saal wird nicht früher, als um 6 Uhr geöffnet

Anfang um 7 Uhr.

Program of Liszt's third concert in Leipzig.

of the concert, the program, the assistance of our fairest singers, and, above all, Liszt himself, had created the highest interest in the concert. Still fatigued with his journey and from his frequent playing on the preceding days, Liszt arrived in the morning and went at once to the rehearsal, so that he had little time to himself before the actual concert.

He allowed himself no respite. I would not leave this unmentioned: a man is not a god; and the visible effort with which Liszt played on that evening was but a natural consequence of so many preceding ones. With the most friendly intentions he had selected three pieces by composers residing here—Mendelssohn, Hiller, and myself; Mendelssohn's latest concerto, études by Hiller, and several numbers from an early work of mine, entitled *Carnaval*. To the astonishment of many timid virtuosos I must state that Liszt played these compositions almost at sight. He was slightly familiar with the études and the *Carnaval*, but he had never seen Mendelssohn's concerto until a few days before the concert. He was, however, so continuously occupied that he had been unable to find time, at such short notice, for thorough study. He met my doubt as to whether such rhapsodic carnival descriptions would make any impression on the general public with the decided assurance that he hoped they would. And yet I think he was mistaken. Let me make a few observations regarding this composition, which owed its origin to pure chance. The name of a city in which a musical friend of mine lived consisted of letters belonging to the scale which are also contained in my name,[1] and this suggested one of those musical games that are no longer new, since Bach provided the model. One piece after the other was completed during the carnival season of 1835, in a serious mood, by the way, and under peculiar circumstances. I afterwards gave titles to the numbers, and named the entire collection *Carnaval*. Though some of it may attract certain persons, its musical moods change too rapidly to be easily followed by the general public which does not care to be startled at every other

[1] ASCH: see Schauffler, Florestan, p. 290.

minute. My amiable friend did not consider this, as I have said, and though he played the work with such great sympathy and genius that it could not fail to strike a few, the audience as a whole was unmoved.[1] It was different with Hiller's études which have a more customary form; one in D-flat major, another in E minor, both very tender yet characteristic, found a warm welcome. Mendelssohn's concerto, with its quiet, masterful clarity, was already well known through its composer. As I have already observed, Liszt played these pieces almost at sight; no one will be quite able to imitate him in this. He displayed his virtuosity in its fullest force, however, in the closing piece, the *Hexameron*, a cyclus of variations by Thalberg, Pixis, Herz, and Liszt himself. It was amazing that he found the strength to repeat, to the delight of the audience, half of the *Hexameron*, and then his own galop. How I hoped that he would give us some of Chopin's compositions, which he plays incomparably, with the greatest love! But in his own room he generously plays whatever music one requests of him. How often have I thus listened to him with wonder!

He left us Tuesday evening.

[1] Liszt's report: "The musicians, as well as the so-called musical experts, with few exceptions, still wore a thick mask over their ears, which prevented them from comprehending this piece, so charming, so bejewelled, and, through artistic imagination, so variously and harmoniously put together."

Hector Berlioz

SYMPHONIE FANTASTIQUE

An Episode in the Life of an Artist, Opus 4

This review was written in 1835, in the first year of Schumann's activity as a regular music critic. By far the longest of his articles, it was obviously written in order to establish the author as a learned musicologist, as able to serve scientific analysis and footnotes to his readers as any of the schoolmasters he despised. It is remarkable that Schumann, despite all this academic equipment, wrote with his accustomed freshness and vigor.

THE VARIOUS MATTERS for reflection presented in this symphony could so easily become involved during the following, that I prefer to treat them under separate headings, no matter how interdependent for their meanings they may be. These four headings will represent the four points of view from which a work of musical art can be surveyed: that of *form* (the whole, the separate movements, the section, the phrase); that of musical *composition* (harmony, melody, texture, style, workmanship); that of the *special idea* which the artist intended to represent, and that of *spirit*, which governs form, idea, material.

Form is the vessel of the spirit. Greater spaces require greater minds to fill them. By the word "symphony" we designate the largest proportions as yet attained in instrumental music.

We are accustomed to judge a thing from the name it bears; we make certain demands upon a "fantasy," others upon a "sonata."

Talents of the second order satisfy us when they master the

traditional form; we approve of those of the first order when they enlarge it. Genius alone may act in freedom.

After *Beethoven's* Ninth Symphony, outwardly the greatest instrumental work, limit and proportion appeared to be exhausted.

And here I must cite:—Ferdinand *Ries,* whose remarkable originality was only overshadowed by that of Beethoven; Franz *Schubert,* the imaginative painter, whose pencil was steeped now in moonbeams, now in the full glow of the sun, and who, after Beethoven's nine muses, might have borne to us a tenth; [1] *Spohr,* whose tender language did not echo loudly enough in the great vault of the symphony, where he should have spoken; *Kalliwoda,* the cheerful, harmonious human being, whose later symphonies, with a more labored foundation, did not reach the imaginative heights of his first. Of recent writers, we know and esteem *Maurer, Schneider, Moscheles, Müller, Hesse, Lachner,* and *Mendelssohn,*—whose name we have intentionally kept to the last.

None of the preceding, who, with the exception of Franz Schubert, still live among us, had ventured to make any essential alterations in the old form, if we except certain experiments such as those in Spohr's latest symphony. Mendelssohn, an important artist in point of production as well as of thought, saw, perhaps, that nothing was to be gained on this road and struck into a new path, in which, however, Beethoven had preceded him with his great *Leonore* Overture. With his concert overtures, in which the idea of the symphony is compressed within a smaller space, he won the crown and sceptre of all instrumental composers of the day. It was to be feared that from now on the name of the symphony would belong entirely to history.

Foreign countries had remained silent before all this. Cherubini had worked for years at a symphony, but he himself, perhaps too soon and too modestly, declared his inability to compose one. The rest of France and Italy wrote operas.

[1] The symphony in C had not yet come to light when this was written. [Schumann]

Meanwhile, in an obscure corner of the northern coast of France, a young medical student dreams of new things. Four movements are too few for him. He takes five as if for a play. At first (not for the last-mentioned reason, which is no reason at all, since Beethoven's Ninth Symphony has four movements, but for another) I took Berlioz's symphony to be a consequence of Beethoven's; but it was played at the Paris *Conservatoire* in 1820, and Beethoven's was only published afterwards, so that any idea of imitativeness is out of the question. Now, courage, and to the symphony itself!

If we look at the five movements in their relation to each other, we shall find the old order of succession present up to the two last, which—though two scenes from a dream—seem to form a whole. The first movement begins with an adagio, followed by an allegro; the second takes the place of the scherzo; the third that of the middle adagio; the two last provide the allegro finale movement. All of them also cohere in point of tonality, the introductory largo being in C minor, the allegro in C major, the scherzo in A major, the adagio in F major, the last movements in G minor and C major.

So far everything goes smoothly. If only I might succeed in giving my reader, whom I would like to lead up and downstairs through this fabulous edifice, a picture of its various chambers!

The slow introduction to the first allegro distinguishes itself but little from those of other symphonies (I speak here of forms only), if at all, though a certain orderliness is apparent after one has made several attempts to alter the relative positions of the longer sections. There are really two variations on a theme, with free episodes. The principal theme extends to bar 2, page 2; [1] the episode to bar 5, page 3; the first·variation to bar 6, page 5; the episode to bar 8, page 6. Second variation on the sustained basses (at least I find the intervals of the theme in the horn *obligato*, though only as reminiscences) to bar 1, page 7. Then a striving towards the allegro. Preliminary

[1] I refer here to Liszt's piano transcription of the symphony. [Schumann]

chords. We pass from the antechamber to the inner room. Allegro. He who stops at details will not progress but lose his way. Run rapidly over the whole to page 9, the first *animato*. Three ideas were placed closely together here; the first, which Berlioz calls *la double idée fixe* for reasons to be explained hereafter, goes up to the words *sempre dolce e ardamente;* the second, borrowed from the adagio, to the first *sf*, until, on page 9, the last one joins in up to the *animato*. What follows is to be taken as a whole up to the *rinforzando* of the basses on page 10, nor should the passage from *ritenuto il tempo* up to the *animato* on page 9 be overlooked. With the *rinforzando* we arrive at a singularly luminous spot (the second subject proper), whence we obtain a momentary glimpse of what has preceded it. The first part ends and is repeated. From here on it seems as though the sections were intended to move in clearer succession, but with the progress of the music they become now longer, now shorter, from the beginning of the second part to the *con fuoco*, page 12, and from there to the "sec.," page 13. A pause. A horn in the far distance. Something familiar seems to resound, up to the first *pp*, page 14. From now on the clues grow more difficult and mysterious. Two thoughts, one four, one nine measures long. Passages of two measures each. Free curves and turns. The second theme, more and more compressed, afterwards appears in full splendor up to the *pp*, page 16. Third thought of the first theme, descending to ever lower positions. Darkness. Bit by bit the silhouettes come to life and take form, up to the *disperato*, page 17. The first form of the principal theme, in the most oblique refractions, up to page 19. And now the whole first theme with immense pomp, to the *animato*, page 20. Completely fantastic forms; reminiscent only once, as though broken, of the older ones. Evanescence.

I believe that Berlioz, when a young student of medicine, could never have dissected the head of a handsome murderer with greater distaste than that which I feel in analyzing his first movement. And has my dissection in any way been useful to my readers? My intention was threefold: first, to demonstrate to those to whom the symphony is wholly unknown how little in music can be clarified with a piece of analytic criticism; second, to point out a few high spots to those who had superficially looked the score over, and then possibly laid it aside because they did not quite see their way about in it; and last, to prove to those who know the work, yet do not recognize its merit, that, in spite of an apparent formlessness, there is an inherent correct symmetrical order corresponding to the great dimensions of the work—and this besides the inner connection of thought. For the very singularity of this new form, this new expression, provides the basis for unhappy misunderstanding. Too many persons lay stress on details when they first hear a work, with results similar to those which sometimes come from the reading of a difficult manuscript. In either case the man who adheres too closely to the meaning of each word takes more time and obtains fewer results than he who quickly scans the whole and is thus able to grasp its meaning and its contents. Besides, nothing excites irritation and contradiction quite so readily as a new form bearing an old name. If, for example, a composition written in 5-4 time were styled a march, or one in twelve short consecutive movements a symphony, the composer would certainly find everyone prejudiced against him, although it stands to reason that we should never fail to examine what we have before us. Therefore the more singular and complex a work appears to be, the more careful one ought to be before arriving at a judgment. Have we not had experience enough with Beethoven? Were not his last works in particular found at first to be similarly unintelligible in regard to construction and form, in which they are so inexhaustibly inventive—and even in regard to their spirit, although this certainly could not be denied to them. Now if we take the entire first allegro as a whole, without letting ourselves be perturbed by small, sometimes sharp jutting corners, the following form will become distinct:

FIRST THEME.
(G major)
Middle section,   Middle section,
on a second theme.   on the second theme.

First theme.   First theme.
(C major)....................................(C major)
Commencement.   Coda.
(C major)....(G major; E minor)....(E minor; G major)....(C major)

Which we compare with the older model:

MIDDLE PERIOD.
(A minor)

Second theme.   First theme.
(G major)......................(C major)
First theme.   Second theme.
(C major)....working out of both themes....(C major)

We do not know in what respect the earlier form may be
considered superior to the later one in variety and unity of
treatment, but we wish we possessed the magnificent imagination necessary to the composing of either one. Something remains to be said in regard to the structure of the single phrase.
Recent times can scarcely boast of any other work in which
symmetrical proportions of measure and rhythm are more
freely united and applied with asymmetrical ones than in this
work. Scarcely ever does the latter part of a period correspond
with the former, the answer with the question. This is so peculiar to Berlioz, so natural to his southern character, and so
strange to us northerners, that the first uneasy reaction, the
complaints of obscurity, are both explicable and excusable.
Only by seeing and hearing for ourselves can we become convinced of the boldness with which all this has been accomplished, and perceive, too, that nothing could be added to or
taken from, without depriving the idea of its sharp incisiveness,
its strength. It seems as though music itself sought to return to
its origins where the laws of downbeat did not yet oppress it,
and spontaneously to aspire to a free beat, a higher poetical
measure—such as are found in the Greek choruses, the language
of the Bible, the prose of Jean Paul. We will not enlarge fur-

ther on this, but remind our readers of the remarks made, many years ago, prophetically, by the childlike poet, Ernst Wagner. "He to whom it will be given to cover and make imperceptible the tyranny of beat in music, will, at least apparently, set this art *free;* he who then bestows *consciousness* upon her, will equip her with the power of presenting a beautiful Idea, and, from this moment, she will be the *first* of all fine arts."

It would lead us too far, and to no end, were we similarly to analyze the other movements of the symphony. The second moves in varied windings like the dance it represents; the third, which is also the loveliest, moves ethereally up and down, as if in a semicircle; the last two have no central point whatsoever and strive unremittingly towards their end. In spite of the outward formlessness of this work we must recognize its intellectual coherence, and perhaps recall the somewhat oblique judgment concerning Jean Paul, whom someone called a bad logician and a great philosopher.

So far we have concerned ourselves only with the garment; but now we turn to the material from which it was woven—to the *musical composition.*

And here I must at once observe that my judgment is formed only from the piano score, in which, however, the instrumentation has been indicated at the most salient points. And even if this were not so, everything appears to me invented and conceived so thoroughly in the character of the orchestra, each instrument so rightly in its place, I might say exploited in its primordial sonority, that a good musician might be able to reconstruct a tolerable score, save, of course, for those new combinations and orchestral effects of which Berlioz is said to be so productive.

If ever I found a judgment unjust, it is the summary of M. Fétis: *"Je vis qu'il manquait d'idées mélodiques et harmoniques."*

He has denied everything to Berlioz: imagination, invention, originality. Yet, how could he have denied him wealth of melody and harmony? I have not the least intention, however, of arguing against this otherwise brilliantly and wittily written review since I recognize neither personalism nor injustice in it, but only complete blindness, entire want of feeling for this kind of music. Nor am I asking my reader to believe anything which he cannot discover for himself! Though brief extracts from a work are often prejudicial, I will nevertheless attempt to make my meaning clearer with a few examples.

[1] As to the *harmonic* value of our symphony, we recognize in it the eighteen-year-old awkward composer who is not over-concerned with etiquette and rushes directly towards his main objective. If Berlioz, for instance, wants to get from G to D-flat, he does so without ceremony (example 1), see page 16 of the symphony. Even though one rightfully may shake one's head over such conduct, reasonable musical people who heard the symphony in Paris declare that the passage could not be otherwise; indeed, someone made the notable remark concerning Berlioz's music *"que cela est fort beau, quoique ce ne soit pas de la musique."* Though this was intended as a witticism, there is some truth in it. Besides such peculiar passages are quite exceptional.[1] I will even maintain that in spite of the manifold combinations into which Berlioz works up small material, his harmony is distinguished by a sturdiness and concision of a kind which we find—though certainly more complexly—in Beethoven.

Or does he, perhaps, deviate too much from the principal key? Take the first movement: First part;[2] nothing but C minor; then he faithfully brings in the same intervals of the first thought in E-flat major;[3] after that, he rests a long while on A-flat,[4] and arrives easily at C major. It may be seen from the outline I have given above that the allegro is built on the simple C major, G major, and E minor. And so throughout. The bright A major sharply shines throughout the entire sec-

[1] See p. 61 of the score, bars 1 to 2.
[2] P. 1-3, b. 5.
[3] P. 3, b. 6.
[4] P. 6, b. 4. [Schumann]

ond movement; in the third we find the idyllic F major, with its sister-tones of C and B-flat major. In the fourth we have G minor with B flat and E flat major; only in the last movement, in spite of the predominating C, there is hectic confusion, as befits infernal weddings. Yet, from time to time, one does meet flat and common harmonies,[1] or defective ones—at least such that the old rules forbid,[2] some of which, however, sound magnificently; unclear and vague ones,[3] or some that sound badly, tormented, and distorted.[4] May the time that would sanction such passages as beautiful never come! Berlioz, however, constitutes a special case. Let someone attempt to change or improve any passage in a way which would be child's play to any practiced harmonist and see how insipid the improvements will appear! For an entirely individual, indestructible energy marks the first outbreaks of a strong, youthful temperament. No matter how coarsely it expresses itself, its effect is the greater, the less one seeks through criticism to impose the conventions of art upon it. It is vain to seek to refine it by art or to confine it forcibly within bounds until it has learned to use its own creative means more prudently and to find its aim and its path from within. Berlioz does not try to be pleasing and elegant; what he hates, he grasps fiercely by the hair; what he loves, he almost crushes in his fervor—you cannot measure him

[1] P. 2, b. 6, 7; p. 6, b. 1-3; p. 8, b. 1-8; p. 21, last staff, b. 1-4. In the second movement, p. 35, st. 5, b. 1-18.

[2] In the first measure, p. 1, the B (probably an error of print); p. 3, b. 2-4; p. 9, b. 8, 9, b. 15-19; p. 10, b. 11-14; p. 20, b. 8-18; p. 37, b. 11-14, 28-29; p. 48, st. 5, b. 2, 3; p. 57, st. 5, b. 3; p. 62, b. 9-14; p. 78, st. 5, b. 1-3, and what follows; p. 82, st. 4, b. 1, 2, and what follows; p. 83, b. 13-17; p. 86, b. 11-13; p. 87, b. 5, 6. I repeat that I only judge from the pianoforte score; in the full one much may look different.

[3] P. 20, b. 3. Probably the harmonies are:

6⌒7	6⌒6♯	6♭⌒6♮	6⌒6♯
3♯—	3—	3♭—	3—
D♯,	E,	F,	F♯, etc.

p. 62, st. 5, b. 1, 2; p. 65, st. 4; p. 3, perhaps a jest of Liszt's who wished to imitate the cessation of the cymbals; p. 79, b. 8-10; p. 81, b. 6 and ff.; p. 88, b. 1-3, and other places.

[4] P. 2, st. 4; p. 5, b. 1; p. 9, b. 15-19; p. 17, from b. 7 onward for a while; p. 30, st. 4, b. 6, 7; p. 28, b. 12-19; p. 88, b. 1-3 and others. [Schumann]

by degrees: for once let us indulge the fiery youth, who should
not be measured with the retailer's yardstick! Let us also point
out the many tender and beautiful original passages that balance what is coarse and bizarre: for instance, the whole harmonic formation throughout the first song theme,[1] and its repetition in E♭.[2] The A♭, held for fourteen measures in the basses,
is highly effective [3] as is the organ point in the middle parts.[4]
The chromatic heavily ascending and descending chords of the
sixth,[5] though meaningless in themselves, must nevertheless
sound impressive in this passage. It is not possible to judge
from the piano score the progressions where, between imitations of bass (or tenor) and soprano,[6] we distinguish horrible
octaves, and false relations come out; if the octaves are well
covered, these passages must pierce to the bone.

The harmonic foundation of the second movement is, with
few exceptions, simple and less deep. The third may, on purely
harmonic grounds, be measured with any other symphonic
masterwork; here every tone lives. In the fourth all is interesting and couched in the most concise and pithy style. The fifth
whirls and whips about too chaotically; except for certain new
passages [7] it is ugly, crass, and repulsive.

[2] Though Berlioz neglects the parts for the sake of the
whole, he often handles the more *intricate, finely modelled detail* with adroitness. He does not squeeze out his themes to the
last drop, nor does he embitter our pleasure in a good idea by
tiresome thematic treatment, as so many others do. In fact
he indicates that he might have worked things out more rigor-
ously, had he chosen and had it been fitting—sketches, in the

---

[1] P. 1, from b. 3 on.
[2] P. 3, b. 6.
[3] P. 6, b. 4.
[4] P. 11, b. 10.
[5] P. 12, b. 13.
[6] P. 17, b. 7.
[7] P. 76, from st. 4 on; p. 80, where the tone E♭ is held out in the middle
parts through twenty-nine bars; p. 81, b. 20, the organ point on the dominant;
p. 82, b. 11, where I vainly sought to eliminate the unpleasant fifth on st. 4,
from b. 1-2. [Schumann]

concise, sparkling manner of Beethoven. He often expresses his loveliest thoughts only once—as it were *en passant* (example 2).[1]

[3] Neither significant in itself nor suited to contrapuntal treatment, the principal motif of the symphony (example 3) grows on us more and more through its later positions. From the beginning of the second movement it gains interest and continues to do so [2] (example 2) until it winds through screaming chords into C major.[3] In the second part it develops into a trio, note by note, with a new rhythm and new harmonies.[4] Towards the close it comes in again, but faintly and haltingly.[5] In the third movement it appears as a recitative, interrupted by the orchestra [6] where it takes on the expression of the most dreadful passion up to the shrill A♭ whereupon it seems to collapse as in a swoon. Later [7] it appears softened, calmed, led by the principal theme. In the *Marche du supplice* it strives to speak again, but is cut off by the *coup fatal*.[8] In the vision, it appears upon a common C and E♭ clarinet,[9] withered, degraded, and dirty. Berlioz did this intentionally.

The second theme of the first movement seems to flow directly from the first; [10] they are so intricately interwoven that it is difficult to indicate the actual beginning and close of the section until finally the new thought emerges (example 4), to reappear soon, and almost imperceptibly, in the bass.[11] He takes it up later, and repeats its outline with the greatest deftness (example 5); in this last example his method of developing material is particularly evident. With equal refinement he later

[1] P. 3, b. 2; p. 14, st. 4, b. 6-18; p. 16, st. 6, b. 1-8; p. 19, st. 5, b. 1-15; p. 40, st. 4, b. 1-16.
[2] P. 16, st. 6, b. 3.
[3] P. 19, b. 7.
[4] p. 29, b. 1.
[5] P. 35, st. 5.
[6] P. 43, last measure.
[7] P. 49, b. 3, 13.
[8] P. 63, b. 4.
[9] P. 67, b. 1; p. 68, b. 1.
[10] P. 10, st. 5, b. 3.
[11] P. 11, b. 5; p. 12, b. 7. [Schumann]

completes the design of a thought which appeared to have been
entirely forgotten.[1]

The motives of the second movement are less artistically interwoven; yet the theme in the basses appears to excellent advantage;[2] his development of a single measure of this theme
is particularly fine.[3]

In the course of the third movement charming figures vary
the monotonous main pattern;[4] Beethoven himself could
scarcely have worked things out more meticulously. The whole
movement is full of subtle cross references. Once he jumps
from C to the major seventh below; later he makes excellent
use of this insignificant stroke (example 6).

In the fourth movement he very beautifully provides the
principal theme with a counterpoint (example 7); and the
careful way in which he transposes it in E♭ major (example 8)
and G minor (example 9) deserves special mention.[5]

In the last movement he brings the *Dies Irae* first in whole
notes, then in half notes, then in eighths;[6] at certain intervals
the bells accompany it with strokes on the tonic and dominant.
The following double fugue (example 10) which he modestly
terms *fugato*, although not by Bach, is nevertheless regular and
clear in structure. The *Dies Irae* and the *Ronde du sabbat* are
well interwoven (example 11). Only the theme of the last does
not suffice, and the new accompaniment is too cheap and frivolous, composed of rising and descending thirds. From the third
page before the last onward everything goes head over heels,
as often mentioned before; the *Dies Irae* once more begins,
pianissimo, at this point.[7] Lacking the full score, the last pages
can only be called poor.

[4] If, as M. Fétis declares, not even Berlioz's warmest

[1] P. 9, b. 19; p. 16, b. 3.
[2] P. 31, b. 10; p. 37, b. 1.
[3] P. 28, b. 10.
[4] P. 39, b. 4; p. 42, b. 1; p. 47, b. 1.
[5] P. 87, b. 8.
[6] P. 71, st. 4, b. 7; p. 72, b. 6, also b. 16.
[7] P. 55, b. 15; p. 57, b. 12; p. 58, b. 5; p. 60, b. 1, 10, and then, in the
inversion, p. 61, b. 3. [Schumann]

friends dare break a lance for him in regard to *melody,* then I must be counted among his enemies. But do not think of the Italian kind, the kind which we know perfectly even before it begins.

It is true that the often cited principal melody of the whole symphony has something flat about it. Berlioz praises it rather too much when, in the program, he speaks of "its noble and reticent character," (*un certain caractère passionné, mais noble et timide*). However, we must remember that he did not intend to present a great thought here, but rather a haunting idea which for days obstinately pursues one. Monotony, insanity, could scarcely have been achieved better. In the review I have mentioned we are told that the principal melody of the second movement is vulgar and trivial; but there Berlioz leads us into a ballroom (as Beethoven does in the last movement of the A major Symphony); nothing more nor less. It is much the same with the opening melody (example 12) of the third movement, which M. Fétis, I believe, called gloomy and tasteless. Only wander about a little in the Alps and other regions of the shepherds and listen to the shawms and Alpine horns; it sounds exactly like them. All the melodies of the symphony are equally natural and original. In some episodes they leave what is merely characteristic behind them and attain a universal, loftier beauty. What, for instance, can be said against the first song with which the symphony begins? Does it, perhaps, exceed the limits of an octave by more than a single step? Does it not contain enough melancholy? What objection to the sorrowful oboe tune in one of the former examples? Does it take forbidden leaps? But who wants to point to every little matter! If I were to reproach Berlioz for anything, it would be for his neglected middle parts; but what prevents me from this is a peculiar circumstance, such as I have remarked in the case of few other composers. His melodies are distinguished by such intensity of almost every tone that, like some old folk songs, they will scarcely bear any harmonic accompaniment; indeed would even lose fullness of tone through it. On this account Berlioz generally harmonizes them with a sustained ground bass or with the chords of the surrounding upper and lower fifths.[1] To be sure, his melodies are not to be listened to with the ears alone else they will pass by unheeded by those who do not know how to round them out from within, that is to say, not with half a voice but wholeheartedly. For those who do, however, they will take on a significance which appears to root itself ever deeper, the oftener they repeat them.

[5] Not to omit anything, here I will add a few remarks on the symphony as an *orchestral work*, and on *Franz Liszt's pianoforte arrangement* of it.

Born a virtuoso in respect to the orchestra, Berlioz demands inordinate things both of the individual executants and of the ensemble—more than Beethoven, more than all others. But it is not greater technical proficiency that he asks of the instrumentalist. He demands sympathy, study, love. The individual must subordinate himself to serve the whole, and this in turn must subject itself to the will of the leaders. Nothing will be achieved with three or four rehearsals. As orchestral music the symphony might be thought to hold the same place as is held by the Chopin concertos in the realm of pianoforte playing, even though the works do not compare with one another. Even Berlioz' opponent, M. Fétis, has done full justice to his instinct for orchestration. I have already stated that the instrumentation of solo passages may be inferred from the piano score alone. Yet it would be difficult for the most lively imagination to form a complete idea of his great and varied effects, contrasts, and combinations. He despises nothing that is tone, sound, or clangor; he makes use of muffled kettledrums, harps, muted horns, English horn, and even bells. Florestan trusts Berlioz may one day order the *tutti* to whistle together—though he might then as well write pauses, for it would be hardly possible for the musicians to contract their lips without laughing—and in

---

[1] The first, for instance, p. 19, b. 7; p. 47, b. 1; the second, in the principal melody of the "Ball," where the real ground harmonies are A, D, E, A, and then in the "March," p. 47, b. 1. [Schumann]

future scores add warbling nightingales and accidental thunderstorms. Enough! All this must be heard before it can be judged. Experience alone will teach us whether the composer has the stuff in him to justify such expectations, and whether the net income of pleasure will proportionally increase. It is doubtful whether Berlioz could accomplish as much with small means. Let us be satisfied with what he has given us.

[6] *Liszt's pianoforte arrangement* deserves an extended description; we will, however, reserve that, as well as certain remarks on the possible symphonic treatment of the pianoforte, for the future.[1] Liszt has worked out his arrangement with so much industry and enthusiasm that it may be regarded as an original work, a *résumé* of his profound studies, a practical pianoforte school in score playing. The art of interpretation, so wholly different from the detail playing of the virtuoso; the many kinds of touch that it demands; the effective use of the pedal; the clear interweaving of separate parts; the grasp of the orchestral masses; in short, the understanding of the means and possibilities yet hidden in the pianoforte are and could only have been the work of a master, a genius of interpretation, such as Liszt most eminently is. Under such circumstances, the piano score need not fear close comparison with orchestral performances. Recently Liszt himself publicly performed this score in Paris as an introduction to a later symphony by Berlioz, *Le Retour à la vie*, a melologue in continuation of the *Fantastique*.

And now let us give a backward glance over the way so far trodden by us. According to our first plan we intended to treat form, musical composition, idea, and spirit in separate sections. We saw that the form of the whole deviated little from the established one; that the various parts moved mostly in novel figures; that the sections and phrases differed from others. In musical composition we observed the harmonic style, the intelligently elaborated detail, the cross references and special forms, the originality of the melodies; and we gave a glance at the instrumentation and the pianoforte arrangement. We will close with a few remarks on the idea and spirit of the work.

[1] See pp. 63-64.

In a program Berlioz himself has indicated the associations which he would like us to entertain while listening to this symphony. It is in brief as follows:

The composer intended to describe in music a few moments in the life of an artist. It seems necessary that the scheme of an instrumental drama be explained beforehand by words. The following program may be likened to the introductory spoken text preceding each musical number in an opera. *First movement—Dreams, sufferings.* The composer imagines a young musician, tormented by the moral sickness which a famous author has characterized by the expression *la vague des passions,* who for the first time sees in a woman the living image of his ideal. By a remarkable freak of fortune the beloved image never appears to him unaccompanied by a musical thought, in which he finds a certain passionate, shy, and distinguished character, the character of the girl herself; this melody and this image haunt him continually like a dual obsession. A dreamy melancholy, interrupted only by a few soft tones of joy, and in the end rising to the heights of loving frenzy, pain, jealousy, inner fervor, the tears of first love, constitute the content of the first movement. *Second movement—A ball.* Amid the joy of a festival the artist stands and gazes, in an exalted mood, on the beauties of nature; but everywhere, in the city, in the country, the beloved image follows him and troubles his spirits. *Third movement—Scene in the country.* One evening he hears the chant of two shepherds. This dialogue, the place, the soft rustling of the leaves, a glimmer of hope for a response of love, all unite to still his troubled heart and to give his thoughts a happier trend. For, perhaps, he will not remain alone much longer. But what if this thought should prove a fond illusion! The adagio expresses alternate hope and pain, light and darkness. At the close, one of the shepherds repeats his chant; the other does not reply. Thunder in the distance—loneliness—deep silence. *Fourth movement—The march to the scaffold.* The artist, now aware that his love is not returned, poisons himself with opium. Too weak to kill him, the drug plunges him into a sleep filled with frightening visions. He dreams that he has murdered her, and that, condemned to death, he witnesses his own execution. The procession begins to move; a march now somber and wild, now resplendent and solemn, accompanies it. There is a muffled sound of footsteps; brutal noise of the crowd. At the end of the march the fixed idea appears, like a last thought of the beloved one; but, cut short by the blow of the axe, only partially. *Fifth movement—Dream of a witches' sabbath.* He sees himself amid hideous grotesques, witches, malformed creatures of all sorts, gathered together for his funeral. Lamentations, howls, laughter, cries of pain. The beloved melody resounds once more, but as a common dirty dance theme; it is *she* who arrives. Joyous roars at her advent. Demoniac orgies. Death bells. The *Dies Irae* in a parody.

Such is the program. All Germany sniffed: to our minds such indications have something undignified and charlatanic about them! In any case the five principal titles would have sufficed; the more exact circumstances, although interesting on account of the personality of the composer who experienced the events of his own symphony, would have spread by word of mouth. In brief the sensitive German, averse to the subjective as he is, does not wish to be led so rudely in his thoughts; he was already sufficiently offended that Beethoven in the *Pastoral* Symphony did not trust him enough to divine its character without assistance. It seems as if men stand somewhat in awe of the workshop of genius; they do not care to know the causes, tools, and mysteries of creation; just as Nature herself seems to exhibit a certain delicacy in covering her roots with earth. Therefore let the artist also lock the door upon himself and his griefs; we should gain too deep an insight if every work revealed to us the causes of its existence.

But Berlioz wrote for his own Frenchmen, who are not overly impressed by modesty. I can imagine them reading the program as they listen, and applauding their countryman who so accurately pictured the whole. By itself, music does not mean anything to them. Whether a listener, unaware of the composer's intention, would see pictures in his mind similar to those which Berlioz has indicated, I cannot decide, as I read the program before I heard the work. Once the eye is directed to a certain point, the ear can no longer judge independently. And if anyone asks whether music is capable of accomplishing that which Berlioz has demanded of it in his symphony, let them attempt to associate it with other or antithetic pictures. I confess that the program at first spoiled my enjoyment, my freedom; but as this faded into the background and my own imagination began to work, I found more than was set down, and almost everywhere in the music a vital, glowing tone. Many are too conservative in their approach to the difficult question as to how far instrumental music may go in the presentation of thoughts and events. People certainly err if they suppose that composers deliberately take pen and paper with the purpose of sketching, painting, expressing this or that. Yet we must not too lightly estimate outward influences and impressions. Unconsciously an idea sometimes develops simultaneously with the musical image; the eye is awake as well as the ear; and this ever-busy organ frequently follows certain outlines amidst all the sounds and tones which, keeping pace with the music, may take form and crystallize. The greater the number of elements cognate in music, which the thought or picture created in tones contains, the more poetic and plastic the expression of the composition. And the more imaginatively or keenly the musician grasps these, the more his work will uplift and move us. Why should not the thought of immortality have seized Beethoven during his improvisations? Why should not the memory of a great fallen hero have excited a composition in him? Why could not the memory of bygone happy days have inspired another? Shall we be ungrateful to Shakespeare, who has inspired in a young tone poet a work not unworthy of himself—ungrateful to Nature, denying that we borrow of her beauty and nobility wherewith to grace our works? Italy, the Alps, the sight of the ocean, spring, twilight—has music indeed not told us anything of these?

In fact smaller, specific pictures can lend music so charming yet stable a character that one is surprised at her ability thus to express herself. A composer once told me how during the process of notation he had been continually haunted by the image of a butterfly floating down a brook on a leaf; this had lent his composition exactly the tenderness and simplicity which such objects might in reality possess. Franz Schubert was a master of this type of *genre* painting. I cannot resist relating from my own experience how once, while I was playing a Schubert march, the friend with whom I was playing gave the following answer to my question whether he had not seen certain very special forms before him: "Yes! I felt I was in Seville more than a hundred years ago, amid promenading Dons and Donnas, with their trains, pointed shoes, daggers, etc." Strange to say, our visions were alike, even to the name of the city. May my readers forgive me for citing this modest instance.

We leave the question open whether the program to Berlioz' symphony contains poetic elements. What concerns us here is whether this music, without text or explanation, can stand alone, and principally whether it is informed with spirit. I think I have already answered the first question; as to the second, no one can deny spirit to Berlioz, not even in those passages where he has obviously failed. And if we were to take umbrage at the taste of the day which tolerated a burlesque of the *Dies Irae,* we would only be repeating what for years has been written and said against Byron, Heine, Victor Hugo, Grabbe, and others. For a few moments in an eternity, Poetry has veiled herself in irony in order to hide her grief-stricken countenance. Perhaps the friendly hand of a genius may one day unveil it.

Much of good and evil might still be weighed; but enough for today. Should these lines help once for all to induce Berlioz to moderate his eccentric trend; should they aid in obtaining complete recognition of his symphony, not as the masterpiece of a master but as a work outstanding in its originality; should they inspire German artists (to whom Berlioz offers a brotherly hand—a strong hand, ready to fight with them against mediocrity) to fresher productivity, the purpose of their publication will have been achieved.

etc.

3) Clar. et Bassons.

4)

5) Violoncelli.

Violini.

pp

185

etc.

diminuendo

etc.

9)

Instruments à cordes.

OVERTURE TO WAVERLEY, OPUS 1

BERLIOZ seeks new laurels [1]—this raging bacchant, the terror
of the Philistines, to whom he appears as a shaggy monster
with rapacious eyes. But where do we find him today? Beside

[1] Schumann in this review contrasts the music of Berlioz with that of
W. Sterndale Bennett to whom Eusebius "here offers a wreath of violets."

the blazing hearth in the house of a Scottish laird, among hunters, hounds, and laughing country lasses! An overture to *Waverley* lies before me, an overture to that novel by Sir Walter Scott which, in its unhurried movement, its romantic freshness, its genuinely English flavor, remains closest to our hearts of all the newer foreign novels. It is to this that Berlioz has written a piece of music. People will ask to which chapter, which scene, wherefore, and to what end? For critics always wish to know what the composer himself cannot tell them, and critics sometimes scarcely understand a tenth part of what they are talking about. Good heavens! Will the day ever come when we shall no longer be asked what was the intention of our compositions? Pick out the fifths and leave us in peace! However, we find a hint in the motto printed on the title page of the overture:

> *Dreams of love and ladies' charms*
> *Give place to honour and to arms.*

This gives us a clue; at the moment I wish for nothing more than that an orchestra would begin the overture while all my readers sat about and judged the matter for themselves. It would be an easy thing to sketch the overture, either poetically, by a description of the various pictures which it evokes, or by an analysis of the mechanism of the work. Something is to be said for both these ways of interpreting music; the first, at least, does not incur the danger of that dryness into which the second needs must fall. In short, Berlioz' music must be *heard;* even an examination of the score is not sufficient for its understanding, and it is labor lost to make it out at the piano. He appears to get results in spots by mere tone effects; by groups of chords which are thrown off; sometimes by strange veilings of tone which even the experienced ear is unable to distinguish from the mere aspect of written notes. Under careful scrutiny certain thoughts, taken by themselves, often appear commonplace, even trivial. But the whole exercises an irresistible charm on me despite much that is repellent and unusual to a German ear. In every one of his works, Berlioz shows himself different: in each one he ventures on new ground; it is hard to know whether we should term him a genius or a musical adventurer. He dazzles like a flash of lightning, but he leaves behind him the smell of brimstone; he sets great sentences and truths before us, and directly after, he begins stammering like an apprentice. Many not yet past the first beginnings of musical training and feeling (and the majority never gets beyond this!) must look upon him as a madman; particularly professional musicians who spend nine-tenths of their lives amidst the commonplace; [1] all the more to them, since he makes demands as no one hitherto had done. Therefore the opposition to his compositions; therefore the passage of years before any of them can fight its way through to the clarity of a perfect performance. The *Waverley* Overture will meanwhile more easily make its way; *Waverley* and the figure of the hero are well known, and its motto, in particular, speaks of "dreams of love which give place to honor and to arms." What can be clearer? It is to be desired that the overture be printed and performed in Germany; only small talents, unlikely to develop even by listening to finer things, could be injured by such music. Let me further mention the singular fact that this overture bears a distant resemblance to Mendelssohn's *Calm Sea*. A note on the title page of the overture, which is numbered opus 1, should not be overlooked. Berlioz therein remarks that he has destroyed the work which he formerly published and numbered as his first, *Eight Scenes from Faust*, and that he now wishes the *Waverley* Overture to be considered as his first. But who can guarantee that his second opus 1 may not eventually also cease to interest him? Therefore let everyone now hasten to make its acquaintance; for in spite of all its youthful shortcomings it is, in grandeur and originality of invention, the most remarkable creation in

---

[1] I have often been obliged to learn that the greatest limitations are to be found precisely among professional musicians; on the other hand, a certain solidity is rarely wanting among them. [Schumann]

the domain of instrumental music that France has lately produced.

OVERTURE TO LES FRANCS-JUGES, OPUS 3

THE CHOICE of subjects which Berlioz adopts as the setting for his music in itself deserves to be called creative. He has composed pieces on Goethe's *Faust;* Moore's Poems; *King Lear* and *The Tempest* by Shakespeare; *Childe Harold* and *Sardanapalus* by Lord Byron.[1] I do not know whether the above is intended to serve as an independent concert overture or as introduction to a drama. The title, however, implies its content and character distinctly enough. It was written, as the reader may learn from an early biography of Berlioz, at a critical period of his life, and shows traces of it. Certainly the arrangement is little more than a miserable skeleton for which the composer might easily sue the arranger; however, no orchestral music exists which is more difficult to arrange than that by Berlioz. As far as we may judge the orchestration from the parts, however, we think the trouble of a German conductor in bringing the work out would be well rewarded, were it only to make the public aware of extremes of the French School, Auber and Berlioz. The one writes with the feather-lightness of a Scribe, the other with the awkwardness of a Polyphemus. Our worthy cantors will faint over these harmonies and scream about sansculottism. We certainly have no intention of comparing *Les Francs-Juges* with Mozart's overture to the *Marriage of Figaro.* In the firm conviction, however, that certain theorizing schoolmasters have done far more harm than our practical titans, and that protection of miserable mediocrity has done far more damage than praise of poetical extravagance, we challenge posterity once for all to bear witness that we never waited ten years, as has been the custom, before reviewing the compositions of Berlioz, but that we have maintained from the start that genius burned in this Frenchman.

[1] Schumann himself wrote music to Goethe's *Faust,* to Moore's *Paradise and the Peri,* and to Byron's *Manfred.*

BERLIOZ (1838)

BERLIOZ has harmed his own cause by publishing so few of his compositions, and by not being able to make up his mind to tour in Germany.[1] But while he has been so unfortunate as to be sometimes confounded with De Bériot—whom he resembles as little as mock turtle soup resembles lemonade—here and there at least, something is known about him, and Paganini is not his only admirer, although by no means his most obscure. The *Neue Zeitschrift für Musik* was the first journal that repeatedly drew public attention to Berlioz, and Leipzig was the first city where one of his compositions was performed. This was the overture *Les Francs-Juges;* a youthful work with the failings liable to occur in composing such a bold piece of music. Later it was played in other cities: Weimar, Bremen, and, if I am not mistaken, also in Berlin. In Vienna they laughed at it. Vienna, however, is the city where Beethoven lived; and there certainly is no place in the world where so little of Beethoven is played and so little spoken about him as in Vienna. They are afraid of everything new there; everything that leaves the beaten track. In music, too, they do not want a revolution.[2] *Florestan*

#

Berlioz, although he often sacrifices human beings at the altar or conducts himself as madly as an Indian fakir, is quite as sincere as is Haydn when, with his modest air, he offers us a cherry blossom. But far be it from us to seek to impose our faith with force.

[1] In the meantime [before 1854] Berlioz has made good in both respects. [Schumann]

[2] The political implication of this sentence is explained by Schumann's aversion to Metternich's reactionary regime in Vienna, which he visited in 1838.

Mendelssohn

[MEYERBEER AND MENDELSSOHN]

The following article contains a great part of Schumann's musical credo; and it is only for this reason—not because of any personal vanity—that in the footnote at the end Schumann published the praise which he had received from Friedrich Rochlitz, the old master of German musicology, renowned founder of the ALLGEMEINE MUSIKALISCHE ZEITUNG.

[*Les Huguenots*]

TODAY I feel like a brave young warrior, drawing his sword for the first time in behalf of a great cause. This little Leipzig, where several momentous affairs have already been decided,[1] appears to have been called upon to settle musical ones as well. The two most important compositions of today have been here performed in juxtaposition, perhaps for the first time: *Les Huguenots* by Meyerbeer and Mendelssohn's *St. Paul.* How to begin, where to end? There can be no question of competition, of preferring one to the other. Our readers know only too well to what aims these pages are devoted; too well that when Mendelssohn is the subject, there can be no question of Meyerbeer, so diametrically do their paths diverge; that, in order to characterize them both, we have only to attribute to the one what we cannot attribute to the other—granting the talent which they both possess. I am often compelled to hold my head, to ask whether everything behind it is in proper condition, when I reflect on Meyerbeer's success in healthy, musical Germany, when I hear otherwise worthy people, musicians even, who, incidentally, look upon Mendelssohn's quieter victories with pleasure, declaring that there is real value in the

[1] Schumann is alluding to the so-called "Battle of the Peoples" in October 1813, in which Napoleon was defeated.

former's music. Still elated by Schröder-Devrient's lofty performance of *Fidelio,* I went to hear the *Huguenots* for the first time. Who does not gladly hope? Had not Ries himself [1] written that some passages in the *Huguenots* might be placed beside some of Beethoven's, etc.? And what said others, what said I? I agreed entirely with Florestan who, shaking his fist at the opera house, let fall these words: "In *Il Crociato* I still counted Meyerbeer among the musicians; in *Robert le Diable* I began to waver; beginning with *Les Huguenots* I unhesitantly rank him among the performers in Franconi's circus." I cannot express the aversion which the whole work inspired in us; we turned away from it—we were weary and exhausted with anger. After repeated hearings I found much that was excusable, that impressed me more favorably. My final judgment nonetheless remained the same as heretofore, and I must shout incessantly to those who even remotely compare *Les Huguenots* with *Fidelio,* or any similar work, that they understand nothing of the matter—nothing, nothing! I certainly shall not attempt a conversion—one would not know where to begin and where to end.

An intelligent man has described this music and text accurately by saying that they play alternately in the brothel and in church. I am no moralist, but it enrages a good Protestant to hear his most cherished hymn shouted upon the boards, it enrages him to see the bloodiest drama in the whole history of his religion degraded to the level of a farce at a fair for the purpose of raising money and applause; indeed the whole opera irks him, beginning with the overture, with its ridiculously cheap holiness, to the ending, where we are all condemned to be burnt at the stake.[2] What can be the opera's next

---

[1] Beethoven's most famous pupil.

[2] It is only necessary to read the closing lines of the opera:—

> *"Par le fer et l'incendie*
> *Exterminons la race impie,*
> *Frappons, poursuivons l'hérétique!*
> *Dieu le veut, Dieu veut le sang,*
> *Oui, Dieu veut le sang!"* [Schumann]

step after *Les Huguenots* save the execution of criminals and the exhibition of gay harlots? Reflect on the whole, and what does it amount to? In the first act we have a masculine orgy, including—oh, how clever!—only one woman, but a veiled one! In the second a revel of bathing women, and, among them—as carrion for the Parisians—a man, he with bandaged eyes. In the third act the lewd tendency is mixed with the sacred; slaughter is prepared in the fourth, and in the fifth it is carried out in a church. Debauchery, murder, and prayer; this, and nothing else, makes *Les Huguenots*. It would be vain to seek for one pure, lasting idea, one spark of Christian feeling in it. Meyerbeer nails the heart to the skin and cries: "Look! there it is, for all to see!" Everything is artificial, everything pretense and hypocrisy. And then these heroes and heroines—two alone excepted: Marcel and St. Bris, who do not sink so low as the rest. There is Nevers, the perfect French debauchee[1] who loves Valentine, gives her up, and then takes her for his wife; Valentine herself, who loves Raoul, marries Nevers, swears she loves him,[2] and then in the end plights troth to Raoul; Raoul, who loves Valentine, rejects her, falls in love with the Queen, and finally takes Valentine to wife; finally the Queen, the queen of all these puppets! And people are pleased with this because it is gratifying to the eye and comes from Paris! And you respectable German girls, is it possible you do not hide your eyes? And the archfox of all composers rubs his hands with joy!

An entire book would be insufficient for the discussion of the music. Every measure is planned; something could be said about each. "To strike dumb or to titillate" is Meyerbeer's principal motto, nor does he fail to do both to the rabble. As for this interpolated choral which sets Frenchmen beside themselves, let me confess that were a student to bring me such a lesson in counterpoint, all I would ask him is never to make a worse one. How calculated and shallow, how consciously

[1] Words like *Je ris du Dieu de l'univers,* etc., are trifles in this text. [Schumann]

[2] *"D'aujourd'hui tout mon sang est à vous,"* etc. [Schumann]

superficial so that the mob cannot miss it, how crude Marcel's eternal vociferation of *Eine feste Burg*, etc.! Many people make much of the consecration of the swords in the fourth act. I acknowledge that there is much dramatic movement, some strikingly clever turns, and that the chorus especially is of great outward effect; situation, scenery, instrumentation are closely interwoven; and as the horrible is Meyerbeer's element, he has written this with fire and love. However, if we look at the melody from a musical point of view it is nothing but a revamped *Marseillaise*. Besides, who could fail to achieve an effect with such means at such a place? I do not blame the use of any means in the right place; but we must not exclaim "Glorious!" when a dozen trombones, trumpets, and ophicleides, and a hundred voices singing in unison can be heard in the distance. One Meyerbeerian trick I must mention here. He knows the public too well not to realize that an excess of noise in the end stupefies. How cleverly he averts this pitfall! After such explosions as those mentioned above, he gives us whole arias accompanied by a single instrument, as if he meant to say, "Behold what I can do with so little! Look, Germans, look!"

Unfortunately we cannot deny him a certain amount of wit; however we have not time to examine every detail. Meyerbeer's extreme externalism, his lack of originality and his eclecticism, are as well known as is his talent for dramatic treatment, preparation, polish, brilliancy, instrumental cleverness, also his considerable variety in forms. It is easy to trace in Meyerbeer Rossini, Mozart, Herold, Weber, Bellini, even Spohr; in short, all there is of music. But one thing belongs to him alone—that famous, unbearably bleating, obscene rhythm, which appears in almost every theme of his opera. I even began to point out the pages where this may be found (pages 6, 17, 59, 68, 77, 100, 117), but finally got enough of it. Only hatred could deny that the work contains some better elements, even a few nobler and grander emotions. Thus Marcel's battle song is impressive, the page's song charming; most of the third act is interesting through the lively presentation of popular scenes. The first part of the duet between Valentine and Marcel is effective through its characterization; the sextet and the jesting chorus through their comic treatment; the consecration of the swords through its originality; and above all, the immediately following duet between Raoul and Valentine through musical workmanship and flow of thought. But what does this amount to compared with the vulgarity, distortion, unnaturalness, indecency, unmusicality of the whole? Truly, may God be praised, we are at our goal, for nothing worse can come unless one turns the stage into a gallows; and on the extreme cry of terror from a talent tortured by the times there immediately follows the hope that betterment must be at hand.

[*St. Paul*]

LET US DEVOTE a few words to something nobler. Here you are tuned to faith and hope, and you learn once more to love mankind; here, after a wearying search, you may find rest under palm trees, where a verdant landscape lies at your feet. *St. Paul*, a work of the purest kind, breathes peace and serenity. We would, however, injure ourselves and harm the author if we even remotely sought to compare it with a work by Bach or Handel. The works resemble one another as all church music, all temples of God, all the madonnas of the painters resemble one another; but Bach and Handel were already adults when they wrote theirs, while Mendelssohn was yet almost a youth. This is the work of a young master, whose senses are still encircled by the Graces, who is still full of the joy of living and hope for the future; and it should not be compared with one of that sober epoch, with one of those divine masters who, with a long, holy life behind them, already looked beyond the clouds.

The outline of the action, the resumption of the choral (which we already find in the old oratorios), the treatment of the chorus and the soloists (now as active, now as contemplative masses and personages), the character of these personages

197

themselves—all this and other matters have been frequently discussed in these pages. The fact that the principal events are confined to the first part of the work to the detriment of the whole; that the subordinate figure of Stephen, although not overshadowing that of St. Paul, nevertheless diminishes our interest in him; that, in fine, the music figures Saul of Tarsus rather as a convert than as a converter; all this has been correctly pointed out; also that the oratorio is really very long and might easily have been divided into two parts. Mendelssohn's poetic conception of the appearance of the Lord invites artistic discussion; but I believe that an analysis is apt to spoil things; and that one could not more deeply insult the composer than by applying it here, in one of his most beautiful creations. I believe that the Lord God speaks in many tongues, and reveals His will to His chosen ones through choiring angels. I believe that a painter can express the presence of the Highest more poetically by means of cherub heads looking out from the border of the picture than by the form of an old man, the symbol of the Trinity, and so on. I would not know how beauty could offend where a realistic presentation is not possible. It has also been remarked that because of the rare ornamentation with which Mendelssohn adorned them, certain chorals in *St. Paul* have lost some of their simplicity. As if choral music were not as good a symbol of joyful trust in God as of supplicating prayer; as if there were no possible difference between "Sleepers, wake!" and "Out of the depths"; as if a work of art were not intended to satisfy other demands than those of a church congregation! And, finally, they have tried to classify *St. Paul*, not as a Protestant, but as a concert oratorio, though one clever person has struck the middle path, and baptized it a "Protestant concert oratorio." We see that certain objections—even well-founded ones—are possible, and we are very happy to acknowledge the vigilance of criticism. But oppose to these that which no one will deny to this oratorio: besides the inner core of deep religious feeling which expresses itself throughout, its masterly musical perfection, its prevailing lyricism of the most noble kind, the marriage of word and tone, of language and music, which cause the depths to wax eloquent—the charming grouping of figures, the grace that seems to have been breathed over the work, the freshness, the indelible colorfulness of the instrumentation, the perfectly articulate style, not to mention the masterly play with all forms of composition. These, I believe, ought to satisfy us. I have only one objection. The music of *St. Paul,* on the whole, is sustained in so clear and popular a vein, impresses so instantaneously yet lastingly, that the composer seems to have had the intention of writing for the masses. Admirable as this intention may be, it would, if continued, certainly deprive future compositions of something of that power and inspiration which we find in the works of those who yield themselves, regardless of consequences, without aim or limit, to their great subjects. Let us remember that Beethoven, who wrote a *Christ on the Mount of Olives,* also composed the *Missa Solemnis;* and let us trust that, as the youth Mendelssohn has written one oratorio, the man will achieve another.[1] Until then, let us be satisfied with this one, let us learn from it and enjoy it.

And now to a conclusive judgment on two men whose works most sharply illustrate the tendency and confusion of our day. From the bottom of my heart do I despise Meyerbeer's fame. His *Huguenots* is a comprehensive list of all the defects and some few advantages of his age.

And then let us honor and love this Mendelssohn-Paul. He is the prophet of a glorious future, in which his works, and not the narrow applause of his contemporaries, shall ennoble him. *His* road leads to happiness, the other, to evil.[2]

[1] Mendelssohn fulfilled this prophecy in his *Elijah.* [Schumann]

[2] At the time of its publication, the above article generated a great many attacks on its author, especially in Paris and Hamburg papers; but at the same time it won him praise from a very distinguished man—Fr. Rochlitz [who wrote in a letter]: "For years I have read nothing, absolutely nothing, about music that has so truly pleased me as this. Clear, decided, firmly grounded, these views will be valuable wherever Justice and Reason reign . . ." [Schumann]

A MIDSUMMER NIGHT'S DREAM

(A letter)

THE FIRST person to hear something about the *Midsummer Night's Dream* from me is naturally you yourself, dear friend. We finally saw it yesterday, for the first time in almost three hundred years; and that the theater manager enlivened a winter evening with it displayed good sense since in the real summertime one's taste would naturally be more for the *Winter's Tale*—for obvious reasons. Many people, I can assure you, went to see Shakespeare only to hear Mendelssohn; the case was the reverse with me. For I know very well that Mendelssohn is not like those inferior actors who put on grand airs when they are accidentally associated with the great. His music (with the exception of the overture) does not claim to be more than an accompaniment, a conciliation, a bridge between Bottom and Oberon, without which it would be almost impossible for us to enter fairyland—a rôle which the music certainly must also have played in Shakespeare's time. Those who expected more from this music must have been greatly disappointed. It remains even more in the background than does that for *Antigone*, where the choruses have compelled the composer to richer expression. This music is not involved in the action, in the love relations of the four young people. Only once, in eloquent accents, does it evoke Hermia's search for her beloved; this is an excellent number. For the rest, the music only accompanies the fairy motifs of the play. Here Mendelssohn is in his element, in his very own, as you well know. The world has long been of one opinion regarding the overture—though, of course, transformed Bottoms are to be found everywhere. There is cast a bloom of youth over it as scarcely over any other work by this composer; in a happy moment the finished master accomplished his first and highest flight. It seemed almost touching to hear fragments from the overture in some of his more recent compositions; but I could not wholly approve

of the finale which almost literally repeats the close of the overture. The composer's intention in thus rounding off the whole
is clear, but it seems to me too intellectual an achievement. He
should have endowed this scene with his freshest tones; here
where music could have achieved the greatest effect, I would
have expected something original, fire-new. Imagine the scene
where the elves, climbing into the house through every niche
and fissure, dance their rounds, Puck at their head:

> *I am sent with broom before,*
> *To sweep the dust behind the door.*

while Oberon scatters his blessings:

> *With this field-dew consecrate,*
> *Every fairy take his gait;—*
> *And each several chamber bless,*
> *Through this palace with sweet peace.*

Nothing more perfect for adaptation to music could have
been invented. If only Mendelssohn would be willing to compose something quite new for this passage! So it seemed to me
that the greatest effect of the play was also wanting at the end.
Though we well remembered the many charming preceding
musical numbers; though Bottom's ass's head no doubt continues to amuse many persons today; though many will never
forget the magic of the green forest night and the confusion
reigning in it, yet the whole impression was rather that of a
curiosity than of anything else. Otherwise, you may believe me,
the music is as fine and witty as can be. From the first entrance
of Puck and the elves, the instruments chatter and jest as if the
elves themselves were playing; we hear quite new tones here.
The fairy song immediately following with the concluding
words,

> *So, good night, with lullaby,*

is very charming, and the same holds true for all the other
numbers involving the elves. There is also a march (the first,

I believe, that Mendelssohn ever wrote) before the close of the last part.[1] At moments it resembles the march in Spohr's *Consecration of Tones*, and might have been more original; nevertheless it contains a very delightful middle section . . .

OVERTURE TO THE LEGEND OF THE FAIR MELUSINE

(Heard for the first time in Leipzig Concerts, December 1835)

NOTHING worries people more than their inability to decide which among the overtures of Mendelssohn is the loveliest, indeed the best. A decision among the first three was already difficult—and here comes a fourth! Florestan divides the parties into the Midsummer Night's Dreamers (the strongest by far), the Fingallians (not the weakest, especially among the fair sex), and so on. The Melusinians must be called the smallest party, as this overture has not yet been heard in Germany outside of Leipzig, and since audiences in England, where the Philharmonic Society as the owner of the score gave the first performance, can only be used as reserves in an emergency.

There are works of such delicate structure that the most boorish criticism will approach it timidly and make an obeisance before it. Just as this was the case with the *Midsummer Night's Dream* overture—at least I can only remember having read poetic reviews (excuse the contradiction in terms) of it—so is it now the case with the legend of the fair Melusine.

In order to understand the overture it is not necessary to read the long-spun-out, though very imaginative tale by Tieck, but simply to know that the charming Melusine was deeply in love with the handsome knight Lusignan, and married him under the condition that on certain days of the year he would leave her alone. Lusignan finally breaks his word—Melusine was a mermaid, half fish, half woman. This material has been exploited on several previous occasions in words as well as in music. But it is as inadmissible to seek crude historical connections in this overture as it was in that to the *Midsummer*

---

[1] The famous wedding march.

Night's Dream.[1] Poetically as Mendelssohn always conceives a subject, in this overture he merely sketches the characters of the proud, knightly Lusignan and the seductive and yielding Melusine; but the watery waves seem to rise into their embraces, now covering, now separating them. Everyone will think of the gay pictures so favored by youthful fantasy—those legends of life in the marine abysses full of darting fish with golden scales, of pearls in open shells, of buried treasures which the sea has stolen from men, of emerald castles towering one over the other, and so on. What distinguishes this overture from the preceding ones is, I think, that, quite in the vein of a fairy tale, it murmurs of old legends, but does not represent them. At first sight, therefore, its surface appears somewhat cold and mute. But the life and motion of the depths may be far more clearly described in tones than in words, for which reason this overture (we confess) is much better than is our description of it.

What one may say about the musical composition after two hearings and a few casual glances at the score confines itself to what goes almost without saying—that it has been written by a master of form and means. The whole begins and ends with an enchanting water-like motif, ebbing and flowing with such effect that we seem to be carried from the battleground of violent passions to the sublime, earth-embracing ocean, especially where the motif modulates from A flat through G to C. The rhythm of the knightly theme in F minor would gain in dignity and significance were it taken in slower tempo. How tenderly and endearingly the melody in A-flat, behind which we seem to see Melusine, lingers in our memory! Of the instrumental details we still hear the fine B-flat of the trumpet (near the beginning), adding the seventh to the chord—a tone from primeval times.

At first we fancied that the overture was written in 6-8 time,

---

[1] To the question of an inquisitive person who once asked Mendelssohn what he really meant by the overture to *Melusine* the composer promptly gave the answer: "Hm—a *mésalliance!*" [Schumann]

a misapprehension probably caused by the too rapid tempo of the first performance, which took place in the absence of the composer. The 6-4 time which we found in the score has a less passionate, more fantastic cast, and quiets the player; yet it seemed entirely too broad and extended to us. This observation may seem insignificant, yet it arises from a feeling we could not repress, and we merely mention it here without upholding it as correct. But no matter what the time-signature, the overture remains what it is. 2 [1]

THIRD [SCOTTISH] SYMPHONY, OPUS 56

ALL WHO hitherto have sympathetically followed the brilliant course of this rare planet, F. Mendelssohn-Bartholdy, have awaited his new symphony with great eagerness. We looked forward to it as if it were his first performance in the domain of the symphony; for his First Symphony in C minor belongs to the period of early youth; his second, written for the London Philharmonic Society,[2] has not been published; and his symphonic cantata, *The Hymn of Praise,* cannot be regarded as a purely instrumental work. Except for an opera, all that was missing in the rich circle of his creations was a symphony; in all other categories he had already shown his fecundity.

We learn from a third party that the beginning of the new symphony was also written at an earlier period, during Mendelssohn's residence in Rome; its completion, however, is of quite recent date. This is interesting to know in view of its very special character. Just as the sight of a yellowed page, unexpectedly found in an old mislaid volume, conjures up a vanished time and shines in such brightness that we forget the present, so must many lovely reminiscences have risen to encircle the imagination of the master when among his papers he re-discovered these old melodies sung in lovely Italy—until, intentionally or unintentionally, this tender tone picture revealed itself; a picture that—like those of Italian travel in Jean

[1] Meaning Florestan and Eusebius in conjunction.
[2] The so-called *Reformation* Symphony.

Paul's *Titan*—makes us forget for a while our unhappiness at never having seen that blessed land. And so it has been often said that a special folk tone breathes from this symphony—only a wholly unimaginative person could fail to observe it. This peculiarly charming color is the quality that will assure to Mendelssohn's symphony, as it has assured to Franz Schubert's, a special place in symphonic literature. We do not find in it the traditional instrumental pathos and massive breadth, nor is it a challenge to Beethoven; rather it approaches, mainly in character, the Schubert symphony—with the distinction that while Schubert's suggests rather a wild, gipsy-like type of existence, Mendelssohn's places us under Italian skies. With this we mean that the later one is of a graciously civilized character, speaking a more familiar language; however we must allow Schubert's symphony other superiorities, that of richer imaginativeness in particular.

In point of plan Mendelssohn's symphony is distinguished by its intimate connection of all four movements. Even the melodic treatment of the principal themes in the four different ones is unified; this fact will become plain on even cursory examination. More than any other symphony it forms a closely interwoven whole: character, key, and rhythm vary little from one another in the different movements. The composer, as he explains in a prefatory remark, even wishes that the four movements should be played with but a slight pause between them.

In regard to the purely musical side of the composition, no one will think of doubting its perfect finish. It stands beside its composer's overtures in tenderness and beauty of construction as a whole, and in the detail of the numbers that unite it; nor is it less rich than these in charming instrumental effects. And every page of the score proves how skillfully Mendelssohn retrieves one of his former ideas, how delicately he ornaments a return to the theme, so that it comes to us as in a new light, how rich and interesting he can render his details without overloading them or making a display of pedantic learning.

The effect of the symphony on the public will partly depend on the greater or lesser virtuosity of the orchestra. This is, of course, always the case, but here it is doubly so since the work depends less on the power of the orchestral masses than on a delicately polished use of the separate instruments. Above all, the work demands fine winds. Most irresistible is the scherzo; a more brilliant one has scarcely been written in modern times. In it the instruments speak like human beings.

As the pianoforte arrangement is by the composer himself, it is the truest reflection imaginable of the work. In spite of this, it frequently lets divine but half the charm of the orchestral effects in the symphony.

The ending of the whole symphony will arouse contending opinions. Many will expect it to be in the style of a last movement, while actually it closes the circle with a reminiscence of the beginning of the first. We consider it most poetic; it is like an evening corresponding to a lovely morning.

FORTY-SECOND PSALM, OPUS 42

AN EVENT of paramount importance was the new psalm, *As the Hart Pants*, by Mendelssohn. The great difference between this and the master's earlier sacred music might have been observed at a concert for the benefit of the poor where the performance of an older psalm by Mendelssohn preceded that of this new one. Though Mendelssohn has long been recognized as the most finished artist-nature of our day, a master of all styles, whether of church or concert hall, original in his *Lied* and chorus effects, we believe that in this Forty-Second Psalm he has reached the highest summit attainable to him as composer of sacred music or, for that matter, to modern church music in general. The grace, the art of workmanship which this style requires has been fully revealed here, the subtlety and purity in the treatment of details, the force and inwardness of the masses, and, above all, the spirit of the work—since I must use the word —delights us. It proves what art is to him, and what, through him, it is to us.

SECOND PIANO CONCERTO IN D MINOR, OPUS 40

WE VOTE a special thanks to recent concerto writers because at the end they no longer bore us with trills, particularly with octave jumps. The old *cadenza*, into which the former virtuosos crammed every possible difficulty, had a far more sensible reason for its existence, and might possibly be revived with success. Could not the scherzo, so familiar to us in the symphony and sonata, also be introduced with effect into the concerto? This should produce a charming battle between the piano and the separate orchestral voices; but a change, if only a slight one, in the whole form of the concerto would then become necessary. Mendelssohn would probably be most able to manage it.

And now we have a report to make concerning the latter's second concerto. Indeed he remains what he always was—he still takes things in his stride; no lips smile more charmingly than his. Virtuosos will find it difficult to display their astonishing proficiency in this concerto, for it gives them almost nothing to do which they have not done and played a hundred times before. We have often heard this complaint from their lips. There is *some* justice in it; opportunities for displaying *bravura* through the novelty and brilliancy of passage work should not be missing in a concerto. But *music* should be the prime consideration; and the composer who always gives us this in the richest measure will ever deserve our greatest homage. Music is the outflow of a noble soul, unconcerned whether it flows in the presence of hundreds or for itself in solitude; but always let it be that soul which expresses itself! This is why Mendelssohn's compositions are so irresistible when played by himself; the fingers are mere messengers and might as well remain concealed; his intention is that the ear alone shall receive and the heart then make its decision. I often think Mozart must have played in this manner. Although Mendelssohn deserves praise inasmuch as he *always* gives us music to hear, we cannot deny that he frequently provides it more casually in one work, more emphatically in another. This present concerto is among his most casual productions. Unless I am greatly mistaken, he must have written it in a few days, perhaps in a few hours. It is as though a tree had been shaken, and the ripe, sweet fruit had promptly fallen. People will ask how it compares to his first concerto. They are alike and not alike; alike because both were written by a finished master; unlike because this one was written ten years after the other. Here and there we have vistas of Sebastian Bach in the line of the harmony. Melody, form, instrumentation, on the other hand, are Mendelssohn's own. Let us then rejoice in the felicitous casual gift; the piece resembles some of those works known to us from the old masters which they composed while resting from their greater creations. Our younger master will certainly not forget that his predecessors then often suddenly brought forth some mighty work. The D minor concerto of Mozart, the G major of Beethoven, remain a proof of this.

SERENADE AND ALLEGRO FOR PIANOFORTE, WITH ORCHESTRAL ACCOMPANIMENT, OPUS 43

I AM ASSISTED by the memory of having heard this piece played by the master himself in one of his happiest moods. By itself, the pianoforte part allows us to surmise but half of the charms which it fully discloses when accompanied by the orchestra. The title suggests what we may expect—a serenade—evening music, followed by a fresh and healthy allegro. Who can tell for whom the first was destined? Certainly not for a beloved, as it is not sufficiently intimate and secret in character; neither for some great man—nothing points to that. I think it is a homage paid to evening itself, a greeting to existence, possibly inspired in the composer by a lovely moonlight night; and when we take into consideration the fact that from his lodgings he could look directly into the little study of the cantor Sebastian Bach, the piece seems perfectly comprehensible. But why so many words about such music? What boots it to dissect grace, to weigh moonlight: He who understands the poet's language will also understand this one; and though we have lately been informed by someone in Jena [1] that Mendelssohn's imagination often fails to attain the proper height, why, go hang thyself, hop-o'-my-thumb from Jena, if this lovely earth appears too low to thee!

[PIANO SONATA IN E MAJOR, OPUS 6]

THE DAVIDITES have expressed themselves in various issues on the newly published sonatas. They would scarcely be able to close this chain with more precious diamond clasps than are the above sonatas; [2] that is to say, these are the best things that have appeared since Beethoven, Weber, Hummel, and Moscheles in this their most highly prized genre of pianoforte music. After having at last worked oneself through the heap of rubbish which much to one's discomfort piles up around one, things such as these rise behind the music rack like palmy oases in the desert.

We could review these works from memory (because of this solemn close, we don the plural crown of "we") for we have known them by heart for many years. We need scarcely remind our readers that they have been in print for eight years and probably were composed years before that; meanwhile wondering whether it would not be better to wait for the same length of time before reviewing any new composition. In that case it would be surprising to find how few things remained to be reviewed; how slender our musical journals would turn out to be; and how intelligent everybody would have become. Only what possesses spirit and poetry continues to vibrate for the future—the longer and more steadily, the deeper and stronger are the strings which have been stirred. And though the David-ites have considered most of Mendelssohn's youthful works as merely preparatory to his masterpieces, the overtures, yet many of these, in spots, exhibit so much original poetry that on their strength alone the great future of this composer might with certainty have been foretold.

[1] K. Banck, see p. 124.

[2] In addition to this sonata those of Schubert discussed on p. 112.

Nor is it more than an image when they picture him touching Beethoven with his right hand, while looking up to him as to a saint, and being guided at the other by Carl Maria von Weber (with whom it would be more possible to be on a human footing); not more than an image when they see him wakening from the loveliest of his dreams—the "Midsummer Night's Dream"—and thus address him: "You no longer have need of us; trust your own wings." Nevertheless we have said it and here it stands.

If, indeed, much in this sonata is reminiscent, for example in the first movement reminiscent of the sadly reflective movement in Beethoven's last A major sonata; if the last movement generally recalls Weber—it is not because of weak dependence but because of spiritual affinity. On the other hand, how it grows, burgeons, bursts forth! How green and matinal is everything, as in a vernal landscape! It is not the foreign, the novel, which touches and attracts us here, but the beloved and familiar. Nothing seeks to impose on us or to astonish us; the right words are merely imparted to our feelings in such a way that we seem to have found them ourselves. But only see for yourselves!

SIX SONGS WITHOUT WORDS, SECOND BOOK, OPUS 30

WHO OF US in the twilight hour has not sat at his upright piano (a grand piano would serve a statelier occasion), and in the midst of improvising has not unconsciously begun to sing a quiet melody? Should one happen to be able to *play* the cantilena along with the accompaniment, above all, should one happen to be a Mendelssohn, the loveliest "song without words" would result. Or, still easier: to choose a text and then, eliminating the words, give in this form one's compositions to the world. However, this would not be fair; indeed, a form of deception, unless one intended therewith to test the definiteness with which music can express feelings, and hoped to persuade the poet whose words have been suppressed to provide a new text to the musical setting of his poem. Should this new text coincide with the old one, it would be one more proof for the dependability of musical expression. But to our songs! They meet our eye as clearly as does sunlight in point of purity and loveliness of feeling. The first almost equals the one in E major in the first volume though the earlier piece is closer to the flow from the original source. Florestan said: "He who has sung such a song may expect a long life before and after death; I believe I like it best of all." The second reminds me of Goethe's *Hunter's Evening Song*—

> *Im Felde schleich' ich still und wild,*
> *Gespannt mein Feuerrohr*

and its delicate gossamer structure equals the poet's. The third seems to me of less consequence, almost like a carol in a La Fontaine family scene ... but it is pure, unadulterated wine that passes round the board, even though it is not of the rarest and the strongest. I think the fourth very charming, a little melancholy and introspective, but hope and home speak from the distance. There is something undecided in the form, character, and rhythm of the next, and its effect is similarly undecided. The last, a Venetian barcarolle, softly and quietly rounds off the whole. So enjoy once more the gifts of this noble spirit!

SIX SONGS WITHOUT WORDS, THIRD BOOK, OPUS 38

WE ARE CONTENT to give this volume a "review without words." No one doubts the identity of a rosebush that spreads bloom and perfume around it, or of an eye that gazes happily toward the moon. These later songs differ little from the earlier ones, and like those stand halfway between a painting and a poem. Colors or words could easily be added to them did not the music speak eloquently enough by itself. They are all the children of a fertile imagination; nevertheless even the most devoted of mothers may consciously or unconsciously prefer one child to another, and to the full awareness of outsiders. Thus I might be led to believe that the composer preferred first the second song, then the Duet at the close, and then the fifth, which is more passionate—if one can speak thus of the rare agitations of a noble heart. I am least satisfied with the fourth, although it is definitely the most agreeable. More prosaic in nature, it seems to rest on soft pillows rather than out-of-doors among blossoms and songbirds. The "Duet" makes me feel sad that the rich German language possesses no simple expression for this word; a pair of lovers converse here, softly, intimately, and trustfully.

SIX SONGS WITHOUT WORDS, FOURTH BOOK, OPUS 53

AT LAST another book of genuine *Songs without Words*. They differ little from Mendelssohn's earlier ones save in their greater simplicity and, in the melodic sense, in their lighter, often popular tunes. This remark applies especially to the number which the composer has himself entitled "Folk Song"; it springs from the same source from which Eichendorff, for instance, drew his most admirable poems . . . We can never have too many of these. This popular vein, which is beginning to show itself in many compositions by our younger artists, excites bright hopes for the immediate future—an open eye might have perceived intimations of it in Beethoven's last works—though this may appear strange to many people. The third song, in G minor, is also popular in tone, but unlike that of a chorus; it sounds more like a four-part song. Let it also be noticed that in his *Songs without Words* Mendelssohn has progressed from the simple *Lied* through the duet to the polyphonic and choral style. This is often the case with the truly inventive artist; at the very time when one is inclined to believe that he cannot make further progress, quite unexpectedly he has already taken a step forward and won new ground. It cannot be denied that some other things in this fourth book remind us of older pieces from the earlier volumes; certain turns and repeated figures even threaten to become mannerisms. This, however, is a reproach that a hundred other artists would gladly purchase with sacrifices—I mean the reproach of being so recognizable from a certain turn that everyone could take his oath upon it. Therefore let us joyfully look forward to many new collections!

THREE CAPRICES, OPUS 33

IT SOMETIMES SEEMS as though this artist, to whom chance gave
the right name at baptism, had taken a few measures, even
chords, from his *Midsummer Night's Dream,* and enlarged and
elaborated them into separate works, as a painter might use
his madonna for all kinds of angels' heads. In that "Dream"
the composer's dearest wishes all converge in his goal; it is the
result of his very nature; and we all know how beautiful and
significant it is. Two of the above caprices must have belonged
to an earlier period, the middle one alone to his latest; the
former might have been written by other masters, but every
page of the second one is, as it were initialed in capital letters with F. M. B. I am fondest of all of this one, and take it
for a genie which has secretly stolen to earth. There is no strain
nor bluster in it; no haunting ghost, not even a mocking elf;
everywhere one steps on solid earth, on flowering German
earth; it is one of Walt's cross country summer flights in Jean
Paul. Even though I am almost convinced that no one can play
this piece with such inimitable grace as its composer, and am
in agreement with Eusebius who says that the composer could
with it make the most faithful of girls unfaithful for a few moments, I still feel that this shimmering gossamer web, this
vibrant coloring, this greatest sensitivity of gesture, cannot
elude any player. How different are the other capriccios! They
scarcely bear any relationship to this one. In the last, especially,
I seem to detect a speechless, restrained wrath which seems
painfully self-contained until the close, and then bursts forth
from the deeps within. Why? Who can tell? We are wild at
times, not angry with only this or that; we would like to hit out
right and left "with the gentlest fist" [Jean Paul] at things in
general; knock our own selves out of the world, perhaps, were
it not just barely tolerable. The caprice may affect others differently, but this, let it be said, is the effect it has on me. Concerning the first one, however, there can be no disagreement
that it suggests a gentle grief which asks and receives mitiga-

tion from the music into which it is immersed. We will reveal no more. Let the reader turn to the score itself.

PRELUDES AND FUGUES FOR THE PIANOFORTE, OPUS 35

A HOTHEAD (now in Paris) used to define the fugue as "a composition in which one voice becomes a fugitive from the other (*fuga a fugere*) and the listener a fugitive from them all"! For this reason he began to speak loudly, or oftener yet to scold, whenever he met with such music at concerts. But at bottom he understood very little of the matter, and moreover resembled the fox in the fable—i.e., he could not write a fugue himself, however much he secretly wished to do so. How differently, on the other hand, do those define fugues who *can* compose them: cantors, graduate music students, *et al!* According to these, Beethoven never did nor could write fugues; even Bach took liberties with them at which we are supposed to shrug our shoulders; Marpurg remains the only true guide; and so on. Others, again, think otherwise; I, for instance, who can luxuriate for hours in Beethoven's, Bach's, and Handel's fugues, always insisted that none could be composed today except watery ones, lukewarm ones, miserable and patchwork ones; until, finally, these by Mendelssohn somewhat calmed me. But true equestrians of the fugue greatly deceive themselves if they fancy that Mendelssohn's contain any of their splendid old artifices, such as *imitationes per augmentationem duplicem, triplicem,* etc., or *cancricantes motu contrario,* etc.—so too will romantic extravagants, should they hope to find undreamt-of phoenixes arising in them from the ashes of the old form. Yet if they have feeling for sound, natural music, they will find much of it here. It is not my present purpose to praise blindly, for I know right well that Bach wrote, nay created, fugues of quite another sort. But were he now to arise from the grave he would certainly—after perhaps having laid about him right and left because of the general condition of music—rejoice that a few composers at least still are gathering flowers from the field where he had planted such giant oak forests. In a word, these fugues have much of Sebastian and might deceive the sharp-sighted reviewer, were it not for the melody, the finer bloom, which we recognize as modern; and here and there those little touches peculiar to Mendelssohn, which identify him among a hundred other composers. Whether reviewers agree or not, it remains certain that the artist did not write them for pastime, but rather to call the attention of pianoforte players once more to this masterly old form and to accustom them to it again. That he has chosen the right means for succeeding in this—avoiding all useless imitations and small artificialities, allowing the melody of the cantilena to predominate while holding fast to the Bach form—is very much like him.

Whether the mold, however, might not be advantageously transformed without losing the true fugue character, is a question which will elicit answers from many persons. Beethoven in his day shook that mold; but he was too largely engaged otherwise, too busily occupied in raising the cupolas of other cathedrals to find time to lay the cornerstone of a new fugue form. Reicha also made an effort, but his creative powers lagged far in the wake of his good intentions; nonetheless his often peculiar ideas should not be entirely ignored. However, the best fugue will always be that which the public takes for— a Strauss waltz; in other words, where the artistic roots are covered as are those of a flower, permitting us to perceive the blossom only. I know—the case is real—of a by no means contemptible connoisseur of music who mistook a Bach fugue for a Chopin étude—to the honor of both; and many a young girl might imagine the last part of a Mendelssohnian fugue, that, for instance, of the second one, to be a song without words (in the first, the entrance of the parts would puzzle her); while the grace and softness of the forms would make her forget the sacrosanct place where, and the abhorrent name under which they were presented to her. In short, these are not fugues worked out merely by the head according to formula, but pieces of music sprung from the spirit, and carried out in poet fashion. But since the fugue provides an equally happy medium

215

for dignity as well as for vivacity and gaiety, the collection also contains some instances of that brief, rapid kind of which Bach with his master hand had brought forth so many specimens. Everyone will pick them out; these in especial betray the polished, intelligent artist who plays with fetters as though they were garlands. To mention the preludes: perhaps the majority, like many of Bach's, do not seem to have been originally connected with the fugues, but rather to have been subsequently prefixed to them. Most players will prefer them to the fugues since, even when they are played separately, their effect is complete; the very first, in particular, charms us at once from beginning to end. As to the others, we refer our readers to them. The work speaks for itself, even without the composer's name. *Jeanquirit* [1]

SONATA FOR PIANO AND CELLO, OPUS 45

AMONG SONATAS by outstanding musicians we have to mention one by Mendelssohn-Bartholdy.

Let us cast a cursory glance at Mendelssohn's work. A smile hovers round his mouth, but it is that of delight in his art, of quiet self-sufficiency in an intimate circle; and how beneficent is this glimpse of inner wealth, of peace, of inner grace! The sonata is one of his latest works; would that without running the risk of being called petty I could express in words the difference between present and past in his works. It seems to me as if everything in it today is striving to become even more musical, more refined, transfigured; and, if one will not mistake my expression, more like Mozart. In the first bloom of youth he still worked partly under the influence of Bach and Beethoven, even though already a master of form and polyphony. In his overtures he allowed himself to be influenced by foreign poetry or drew from nature; and though he always did so as musician and poet, voices here and there nonetheless warned against this tendency lest it become exclusive with him. But this sonata

[1] Stephen Heller, pianist and composer. Despite this signature the article is by Schumann.

is again of the purest, most self-sufficing music; as fine and clear and original a sonata as has ever proceeded from the greatest of master hands; especially fitting for the most refined family circles; to be played after the reading of a Byron or Goethe poem. We may be excused from saying more regarding its form and style; the sonata will be found to speak better and more emphatically for itself.

FIRST PIANO TRIO IN D MINOR, OPUS 49

IT IS NECESSARY to say but little of Mendelssohn's trio since already it must be in everyone's hands. It is the master trio of today as in their day were those of Beethoven in B-flat and D; as was that of Franz Schubert in E-flat; indeed a lovely composition which years from hence will still delight grand- and great-grandchildren. The storm of the last few years is gradually beginning to subside, and—let us confess it—has already cast many a pearl upon the beach. Though Mendelssohn was perhaps less shaken by it than others, he nonetheless remains the child of his epoch. He also had to struggle; also had to listen to the nonsensical jabber of the narrow-minded: "The real springtime of music lies behind us"; and he has raised himself so high that we can indeed say he is the Mozart of the nineteenth century; the most brilliant among musicians; the one who has most clearly recognized the contradictions of the time, and the first to reconcile them. Nor will he be the last composer. After Mozart came Beethoven; this modern Mozart will be followed by a newer Beethoven. Indeed, he may have already been born. And now, what more shall I say of this trio that has not also been said by everyone who has heard it? The happiest of all are those who heard it played by its creator. Though perhaps there may be bolder virtuosos, scarcely another than himself knows how to perform Mendelssohn's works with such enchanting freshness. Yet this should not deter others from playing the trio. Indeed, in comparison with others —for example, those by Schubert—it offers fewer difficulties; for these, in works of art of the first order, generally stand in precise relation to the effect; in fact, the greater the difficulties, the more intense the effect. I need scarcely mention that this trio is not written for the piano player alone; that the two others also must do their part and may depend upon delight and thanks. So let the new work have its effect everywhere, as it should have, and prove anew to us the artistic power of its creator. This now appears to be in fullest flower.

Mendelssohn as Conductor and Performer

It was part of Schumann's task to review the important concerts which took place in Leipzig. As most of these concerts centered around the figure of the director of the GEWAND-HAUS *Concerts, the more important parts of these reviews are reprinted here, following the chapter devoted to Mendelssohn's compositions.*

LETTERS OF AN ENTHUSIAST [1]

EUSEBIUS TO CHIARA

Do YOU REMEMBER how in the evening we sailed on the Brenta from Padua? The glowing Italian night closed the eyes of one after another of us. Suddenly at dawn a voice cried: "*Ecco, ecco, Signori, Venezia!*" And still, immense, the sea lay outspread before us—but from the farthest horizon there came a tintinnabulation as though the little waves were speaking to one another in a dream. Thus all breathes and weaves in the

[1] These letters might also be termed "Truth and Poetry." They refer to the first *Gewandhaus* Concerts, held under Mendelssohn's direction in October 1835. [Schumann]

Meeresstille; [1] we veritably drowse throughout it, and are more a thought than thinking. The Beethovenian chorus after Goethe [2] and the accented words sound almost rough beside these gossamer tones from the violins. Near the close a harmony detaches itself which makes us suspect that the seductive eye of a daughter of Nereus had gazed upon the poet to draw him down into the waves; but then for the first time a wave billows up, the whole sea becomes more loquacious; and now the sails and gay pennants flap, and so hallo—away, away! —"which of Meritis' [3] overtures do you like the best?" asked a simpleton near me—whereupon, embracing, the keys of E minor, B minor, and D major formed a triad of the Graces, and I could think of no better answer than the best one—"Every one of them." Meanwhile Meritis conducted as though he had composed the overture himself, and the orchestra played as though he had; however, a remark of Florestan's struck me. It was played, he said, much as he himself used to play when he came from the provinces to study with Master Raro. "The most severe crisis I ever met," he continued, "was this middle state between art and nature; just as I used to take everything vivaciously, so now I had to take everything slowly and clearly because of my lack of technique; and there resulted a paralysis, a stiffness sufficient to make me doubt my talent; luckily the crisis did not last long." I for my part was disturbed in the overture as in the symphony by the conductor's baton. [Before Mendelssohn, when Matthäi was in control, orchestral pieces were performed without a time-beating conductor.] I agreed with Florestan, who claimed that the orchestra in a symphony should stand like a republic which recognizes no sovereign. And yet it was delightful to watch Meritis as his eye anticipated, in every nuance, the undulations of the composition, from the most delicate to the most powerful, and swam, like a blessed spirit, ahead of the whole, whereas from time to time

[1] Overture by Mendelssohn.
[2] Cantata *Meeresstille und glückliche Fahrt,* opus 112.
[3] "Meritis" was the Davidite name of Mendelssohn.

one encounters conductors who seem to threaten to beat the score, as well as the orchestra and the public, with a scepter! You know how little I care for the quarrels about tempi, and that all that matters to me is the inner pulse of movement. Thus the quicker adagio of a cold man always seems to me more sluggish than the slower one of a sanguine man. In orchestral music one also has to take the instrumental masses into account; coarser, thicker ones are able to give more importance and meaning to details as well as to the whole. But when it comes to smaller, finer ones, like those of our Florentine [Mendelssohn-Meritis], it is necessary to correct the want of sonority with driving tempi . . .

IGNAZ MOSCHELES

(Concert of October 9, 1835)

IT IS RARE that one finds anything new to say about older and well-known virtuosos. But Moscheles in his later works has trodden a path which necessarily had to influence his virtuosity. As once he bubbled, full of youth, in his E-flat major concerto and in his E-flat major sonata; thereafter wrote more carefully and artistically in the G minor concerto and his études; so he now treads more somber, mysterious roads, indifferent whether these be as agreeable to the great masses as were the others. His fifth concerto (C major) showed a leaning toward the romantic; and in the last ones all that hitherto had pendulated between old and new stands forth in complete firmness and form. The romantic vein showing here is not, however, one which like that of Berlioz, Chopin, and others, can be thought far ahead of the general culture of the present. It is a more retrogressive one, a romanticism of the past, of the kind which vigorously confronts us in the Gothic architecture of Bach, Handel, and Gluck. In this respect his works have indeed a similarity to many of Mendelssohn's, even though the latter is still writing with the fresh vigor of youth. Few will believe themselves capable of reaching an infallible verdict concerning that which was heard that evening. The audience was not bacchantic in its applause but seemed thoughtful and anxious to show its sympathy with the master by special attentiveness. It grew enthusiastic, however, after the duo played by Moscheles and Mendelssohn not only like two masters, but like two friends resembling a pair of eagles—rising and falling in turn and alternately encircling one another. We consider this composition, which is dedicated to Handel's memory, as one of the most successful and original of Moscheles' works . . .

No one who has ever heard this master can be in doubt as to his mode of playing, the elasticity of his touch, his healthy power of tone, his poise and certainty in the higher style of expression. And what has been lost of youthful enthusiasm and general sympathy with this newest imaginative way of performance has been replaced by the mature man's sharpness of characterization and intellectual grasp. There were some gleaming moments in the improvisation which concluded the evening.

We remember with great pleasure the treat accorded to us a few days before this concert by the rare union of three masters and a young man who promised to become one. They played Bach's D minor Concerto for Three Pianofortes. The masters were Moscheles, Mendelssohn, and Clara Wieck; the youth Mr. Louis Rakemann from Bremen. Mendelssohn played the orchestral accompaniment. Indeed, it was a joy to hear it!

FRAGMENTS FROM LEIPZIG [1836–1837]

GENTLE READER, it was impossible for us to sit down before today to write to you about the delightful abundance of music and musicians which has been showered upon us during the past two months, precisely because of the delightful abundance which managed to keep us from writing. . . . Chopin's fleeting appearance, . . . Sterndale Bennett, . . . *Israel in Egypt*, . . . Bach motets; indeed, every week, every day brought something new.

To begin with, Mendelssohn, as all know, again conducted the principal events at the head of his faithful orchestra with that power peculiar to him and that love which the general response must inspire in him. If ever an orchestra, without a single exception, believed in, and depended on its director, ours does thoroughly deserve the praise for it. Certainly it has grounds enough for doing so. Here nothing is to be heard of intrigues and the like; and this is as it should be and must profit art and artists.

Seconding him stands David,[1] the pillar of the orchestra, a musician of the finest grain.

It will be impossible here to give an account of more than the most outstanding new compositions and virtuoso performances which were offered us by resident and guest artists . . .

Another novelty, i.e., a piece merely one hundred years old, was J. S. Bach's D minor Pianoforte Concerto, played by Mendelssohn and accompanied by an augmented string quartet. I would like to express some of the thoughts aroused in me by this sublime work as well as those roused by some scenes from one of Gluck's *Iphigenias*, but I am prevented by a mere glance at the long road we have still to travel. One thing, however, the world shall hear, and the sooner the better. Will it be believed that the music shelves of the Berlin *Singakademie*, to which old Zelter bequeathed his library, contains in manuscript, and in good condition, at least seven such concertos as the D minor together with a countless number of other Bach compositions? Few persons are aware of it; nonetheless there they lie. Indeed, is it not about time and would it not be highly desirable that the German nation resolved to make a complete collection of all works by Bach and publish them?[2] One would think so. The words of a certain expert, who speaks of this undertaking on page 76 of this volume of the *Neue Zeitschrift*, might serve as a motto for the collection. They are as follows:

"Your intention to publish Sebastian Bach's works is some-

---

[1] Ferdinand David, famous violinist, the concertmaster.
[2] This idea was realized, to the joy of all artists, in 1852. [Schumann]

thing that warms my heart, which beats wholly for the lofty art of this first father of harmony—I soon hope to see it available to all."

Be sure to look up the quotation! [1]

Among the outstanding artistic pleasures that remain to be mentioned we must not forget Spohr's E minor Concerto, played by David; . . . Beethoven's E-flat major Concerto, and Mendelssohn's in G minor, both played by Mendelssohn, i.e., characteristically cast in bronze by him.

This year's cycle of concerts closed with Beethoven's Ninth. The unprecedented rapid tempo at which the first movement was taken quite deprived me of that rapture which one is accustomed to feel while listening to this exuberant music. My complaint may appear incomprehensible to the conducting master, who knows and honors Beethoven as few will know and honor him again; but, in fact, who other than Beethoven himself could decide here? Provided the execution was faultless, this passionate increase of tempo might perfectly have suited him. Thus I am obliged to count this experience, like so many others, among my most memorable musical ones—and with a certain melancholy that there can be a difference of opinion concerning even the external appearance of the loftiest matters. But when in the adagio all the heavens were opened to receive Beethoven like a soaring saint, it was impossible not to forget the pettiness of this world and not to feel a presentiment of the Beyond thrilling the beholders . . .

Since we point with some pride to three institutions like these [*Gewandhaus*, Euterpe, Quartet Association], developed through enthusiastic devotion to the noblest works of our masters, institutions as scarcely another German city has to show, many of our readers will ask themselves why we have so long postponed an account of their individual performances. The writer of these lines confesses that his double position as editor and musician is responsible for this delay. Only the whole, and,

[1] The "expert" was Beethoven, in a letter dated January 15, 1801!

of the individual performances, only the most significant interest the musician. As an editor he would like to speak about them all; as a musician he ought to remain silent concerning many things, which, for the sake of completeness, as an editor he ought to remark. But where find time to give a thorough account of everything, and to the artist's benefit? Nothing is to be gained with phrases such as "was well received," "met with sympathy," "received much applause"; all color is washed out by them; no one is honored; master and apprentice drawn over the same last. So we will continue—with our eye on the object rather than on the person—to summarize events from ever greater perspectives in which the lesser disappears of itself, and the contours of the whole stand out more sharply—giving the contemporaries and the future a cheering picture of a youthful strength and soaring vitality, unparalleled in the musical history of our city.

A RETROSPECTIVE VIEW

[Leipzig, 1837–1838]

ONE OF THE earlier concerts brought us Beethoven's [cantata] *Glorious Moment*, the history of the origin of which is well known.[1] The performance of this work under Beethoven's personal direction, at a period of historic moment and in the presence of the highest potentates, embassies, etc., must have been an event never to be forgotten by those present; and even without all this ado, as in our performance, there are many passages of the music which will still interest after the lapse of centuries. It would be unjust to compare such works written by great composers for special occasions with their spontaneous inspirations; genius here manifests itself precisely in the transitory and the fortuitous, as for example it does in those little poems which Goethe wrote for special occasions and which were as highly prized by experts as by himself. Such a quality pervades this

[1] It was composed and first performed late in 1814 for the reception of the royal personages attending the Congress of Vienna.

composition, together with an almost ironic breadth and splendor, until at certain moments the master himself suddenly stands before us, smiling and life-sized. Add to this a poem as refractory to composition as is a Pindaric ode, and one will have a faint picture of the embarrassment in which the composer terminated his work—which incidentally must have been distinctly felt by him, decided patriot that he was.

But it was in certain of the last concerts that, finally, something truly *new*, unprecedented, in fact entirely *old*, was offered us; works by masters from Bach to Weber in chronological order. That our ancestors were unable to institute historic concerts of coming times is our fortune! Forsooth, we would have badly stood the test! But one's pleasure in what one was given to hear was equaled by one's displeasure in what one was given, here and there, to hear about it. Many people behaved as though Bach were being honored; as though we today were wiser than they were of old; and thought it all "curious and interesting"! The connoisseurs are the worst in this respect, smiling as though Bach had written just for them—he who can balance us, bag and baggage, on the tip of his little finger—or Handel, steadfast as the heaven above us—or Gluck, no less. And people hear this music, praise it, and think no more about it. I thoroughly prize our own times and understand and respect Meyerbeer. But if anyone should promise me that historical concerts of a hundred years hence, nay of fifty years hence, will contain a single note of Meyerbeer, to him will I say: "Meyerbeer is a god, and I made a mistake."

Respecting the works by Bach that were performed we can say but little; we must have them before our eyes and study them, if possible. Even then does he remain as unfathomable as before. Handel, for his part, appears to me more humanly sublime; in Gluck's case, as we have said, people reject his arias and tolerate his choruses, i.e., they remove from the statue of a god the locks about his forehead and praise nothing but his sinews, his torso. Nevertheless, it would be desirable if such concerts, indeed, several of them, were given every year. The ignorant would learn from them; the wise would smile at them; in short, the retrogression perhaps takes us a step ahead.

To complete the agreeable picture, we will close with an account of the different artists with whose assistance the grander orchestral performances took place.

The most interesting appearance was that of Miss Clara Novello. She came to us from London where she belongs to an artistic circle of the first rank; and Leipzig did not object. For years nothing has refreshed me so much as this voice, conscious and controlled in its entire range, thoroughly lovely in quality, as definite in its tone production as a keyboard; this most noble delivery; this whole simple and modest art which subordinates everything to the work and its creator. She was most in her element with Handel—with whose works she has grown up and become great—to the point that people asked themselves in amazement, "Is that Handel? Can Handel write thus? Is it possible?" The composer himself can learn from such an art of performance; when we hear such a performance we recapture our respect for interpretive artists who so often present us with caricatures because they have run away from school so early. Before such art those stilts on which virtuosity struts about, giving itself airs and looking down upon us, must collapse; in short, Miss Clara Novello is neither a Malibran, nor a Sontag, but very eminently herself, and no one can deny it. . . .

Before taking leave of the *Gewandhaus* Concerts for half a year we must award a laurel wreath to its forty or fifty orchestral members . . . Our musicians form a family; they see one another and practice together daily; the ensemble is always the same, hence they are able to play a Beethoven symphony without notes. Add to these a concertmaster who can conduct such scores from memory, a director who equally knows them inside out, and the wreath is complete . . .

In the concerts of the Euterpe Society we find nearly the same orchestra, or, at least, its younger members, as is well known . . .

As to overtures, we usually had two on the Euterpe evenings;

here we met Weber, Cherubini, and others. Beethoven's in C major, with its truly overwhelming hallmarks of genius, was most successfully performed; it is the one, I think, on the title page of which Beethoven makes use of the words "a poem by" (*gedichtet von*) instead of "composed by." [1]

A treasury of art was also presented this winter by the quartets performed by Messrs. David, Uhlrich, Queisser, and Grenser in the little hall of the *Gewandhaus*. We had four evenings and twenty numbers, among which the gems of the first water were Beethoven's quartets in E-flat major (opus 127), and C-sharp minor, the grandeur of which is inexpressible. They seem to me to stand with some of Bach's choruses and organ compositions on the extreme boundary of all that has hitherto been attained by human art and imagination. But verbal analysis and interpretation would, as we have said, be of no avail here. On the other hand, two quite new quartets by Mendelssohn [2] remained, as was to be expected from him as an artist as well as a human being, in a beautifully human sphere. Here, too, he bears away the palm among his contemporaries; Franz Schubert alone, were he still alive, might have—not contended for it (since everything truly original lives on a par)—but handed it to him as the worthiest of us all. Only the excellence of such a work as Schubert's D minor Quartet—like that of many of his others—can in any way console us for the early and grievous death of this first born of Beethoven; in a few years he achieved and perfected things as no one before him.

And now we draw the curtain over the lively scene. Aspiration everywhere, abundance of talent, the worthiest of aims; may it all repeat itself in higher transformations!

[1] Could Schumann have been mistaken? The *Namensfeier* Overture in C major, opus 115, bears the designation "a poem by," to which Schumann here refers; but the one which has "overwhelming hallmarks of genius," also in C major, is *Consecration of the House*, opus 124, which Beethoven wrote eight years later for the inauguration of the *Josephsstädter Theater* in Vienna.

[2] E minor and E-flat major, opus 44.

MUSICAL LIFE IN LEIPZIG [1839–1840]

As Schumann spent the 1838–1839 season in Vienna, he failed to review the Leipzig concerts during that time.

ONE MUST CONFESS that in this Leipzig which nature treats so shabbily German music blooms to such a degree that, without arrogance, it can compare with the richest and largest orchards and flower gardens of other cities. What an abundance of great works of art were produced for us last winter! How many distinguished artists charmed us with their art! And though the vitality of musical art among us is in a great measure due to our existing concert establishment, yet, as compared with other cities, we also find much that is encouraging in other directions. The opera, like a good fashion shop, at least will provide us with the latest things from Paris, and boasts a few talented performers. Nor is the Church idle, though with the means at its disposal it might accomplish finer things. On the highest level of all, however, stands the concert hall, as I have said before. It is well known to what extent the *Gewandhaus* Concerts, now existing for some fifty years, have provided a worthy focus in particular for German music. At present more than ever is being achieved by this institution. With a famous master at its head, during the last few years the orchestra has brought its virtuosity to still greater perfection. Probably no German orchestra equals it in the performance of symphonies, since accomplished musicians are to be found at many of its desks. This year, too, the direction made such satisfactory engagements with talented singers that we scarcely felt the absence of the famous English singers who visited us last year. Thus variety was always taken into consideration both in regard to the selection of compositions and to the appearances of foreign or native artists. . . . Another novelty was the prayer on the words of Luther, *Grant Us Peace in Thy Mercy,* by Mendelssohn, which was heard here for the first time on the eve of the fête of the Reformation; a composition unique in its beauty; it is scarcely possible to form an idea of its effect by merely reading the score. The composer wrote it among other church compositions during his stay in Rome. . . . The little piece deserves, and will attain, universal fame in the future; Madonnas by Raphael and Murillo cannot long remain hidden.

The same master gave us, on New Year's Day, a lately completed psalm in larger form, to the words of the 114th, *When Israel Went Out of Egypt*. He who successively writes many works in the same style naturally suggests comparisons with himself. And so it was here. Mendelssohn's beautiful older psalm, *As the Hart Pants*, was still fresh in everyone's memory. There was some difference of opinion as to which of the two works was the greater, but the majority of votes went to the older one. We point to this as a proof that our public, in spite of its esteem for the composer, does not admire him blindly. No one entertains any doubt respecting the special beauties of the new psalm, though I cannot deny that in regard to freshness of invention (particularly in the latter half) it falls somewhat short of the other, and also reminds us of music by Mendelssohn we have already heard.

With his ever-fresh mastery Mendelssohn also played Bach's Chromatic Fantasy and Fugue as well as his Five-part Fugue in C-sharp minor. And, accompanied by Mendelssohn, Concertmaster David in his most admirable manner gave us two movements—priceless as compositions—from Bach's sonatas for violin alone. Though it has been said that "an addition of other parts to them is unimaginable," this statement was most emphatically contradicted by Mendelssohn who so adorned the original with further parts that it was a delight to hear.

If we now consider the performances of our different institutions devoted to our art—including the opera, the churches, the different societies—our readers will probably agree with us in what we have said at the beginning of this article: that, in our little Leipzig, music, above all good German music, flourishes to such an extent that it need not fear comparison with what is produced in the most important cities abroad. So may the genius of music long guard and bless this corner of the earth, once consecrated by the name of Bach, now by that of a celebrated young master, who may, we trust, with all those who stand near him, be with us for many years, to the prosperity of true art.

GUTENBERG FESTIVAL IN LEIPZIG

OUR ART, too, helped shed a luster on the festival; for it works miracles, both in joy and sorrow, and can uplift the individual as well as the great mass. And we may consider it a happy chance that at this moment there live in our midst two composers—one of whom, through his successful creations, has already made a reputation for himself throughout Germany, while the other enjoys a European reputation; and that it only needed a suggestion from us to interest them in the festival. Certainly the musical portion of any festival is not the least one, and all arrangements took this into consideration.

For the eve of the festival, Albert Lortzing wrote a new comic opera, *Hans Sachs*, which is said to exceed all his former compositions in point of freshness, lightness, and charm. I was not present at the performance but am told that it was most satisfactory to the audience and gratifying to the composer. Many numbers were encored; and applause through cheers, showers of wreaths, and curtain calls was not wanting. A second performance will take place a few days hence. For the festival itself, which consisted of the unveiling of the working press and the statue of Gutenberg (preceded at 8 A.M. by a church service introduced by a cantata composed by *Herr* Richter, director of the Zittau Choral Society for this occasion), Dr. Felix Mendelssohn composed a cantata for two male choruses with trumpet accompaniment, etc., to words by *Herr* M. Prölz of Freiberg, which was sung early on Wednesday in the open market place. The sky, which at first had threatened, cleared, and the whole scene presented a most impressive aspect. One chorus was directed by Dr. Mendelssohn, the other by Concertmaster David . . .

Yesterday afternoon a great musical performance took place in the Thomas Church, on the spot where Sebastian Bach so often exercised his noble art and where on this occasion it was practiced by his most admiring disciple, who led the great masses with an energetic hand. The performance was very brilliant, and every corner of the church was filled. Chorus and orchestra numbered at least five hundred. The works performed were Weber's *Jubilee* Overture, the *God Save the King* at the close with organ accompaniment; Handel's *Dettingen Te Deum;* and a *Hymn of Praise* by Mendelssohn. It is not necessary to discuss the first two, both world-famous compositions. But as the last was new and completed by its composer with the festival in mind, a few words about it may be welcome to his admirers elsewhere. Mendelssohn, always so correct in the baptism of his works, has named it *Hymn of Praise.* But the hymn itself is preceded by three orchestral symphonic movements so that its form may be compared to that of Beethoven's Ninth Symphony, save for the distinguishing difference that the three orchestral movements proceed without any pause between them—an innovation in the symphonic form. No better form could have been selected for this special purpose. The work was enthusiastically received, and its choral numbers especially must be counted among the master's freshest and most delightful creations; and what this praise means, after his great achievements, will be understood by everyone who has followed the evolution of his compositions. We did not intend to give a detailed description, but we must mention a duet, interrupted by the chorus, "I waited for the Lord," at the conclusion of which a whisper rustled through the entire assemblage—which in a church means more than loud applause does in a concert hall. It was like a glimpse of a heaven filled with Raphaelesque Madonnas . . .

MENDELSSOHN'S ORGAN CONCERT [1840]

WOULD THAT I could record last evening in these pages with gold letters! It was a concert for men, and a good thing, from beginning to end. Again I thought how we have never finished with Bach, how he seems to grow more unfathomable the oftener he is heard. Zelter, and afterwards Marx, wrote excellent and pertinent things about him; and yet, while we listen, we perceive that we can only very remotely approach him through intellectual analysis. The best illustration and explanation of his works will always be found in the music itself. And by whom else can we expect to find this warmly and truthfully performed, if not by the artist who yesterday delighted us; he who has devoted the greatest part of his life to precisely this master; who was the first to refresh, with all the strength of his own enthusiasm, the memory of Bach in Germany! . . .

It is well and widely known how thoroughly Mendelssohn knows how to handle Bach's royal instrument, and yesterday he laid before us the most precious jewels, in magnificent diversity and ever increasing intensity, prefaced by a prelude and closed by an improvisation of his own. After a short introduction he played a fugue in E-flat major, a noble one, containing three thoughts, built upon each other; then a fantasia on the choral *Schmücke dich, o liebe Seele*—as priceless and profound a piece of music as ever sprang from an artist's imagination; then a grandly brilliant prelude and fugue in A minor, both very difficult, even for masters of the organ. After a pause these were followed by the *Passecaille* in C minor, with twenty-one variations, ingeniously interwoven to the point of continuous amazement, and also admirably handled in the registers by Mendelssohn; then a *Pastorella* in F major, a composition thought out as profoundly as any of this type, for its part followed by a Toccata in A minor with a humoristic Bachian prelude. Mendelssohn finished the concert with an improvisation in which he attested the glory of his own mastery; it was based on a choral, if I am not mistaken, with the text, *Head, stained with blood and wounds,* into which he afterwards introduced the name BACH [1] and a fugal movement, rounding everything to such a clear and masterly whole that, if printed, it would have constituted a complete work of art. A lovely summer evening shone through the church windows. Afterwards in the open air many a person must have recalled the wondrous sonorities, and thought that music provides nothing greater than the delight of that twofold mastery: one master expressing the other. Fame and honor to the old as to the young.

MUSICAL LIFE IN LEIPZIG [1840–1841]

[Mendelssohn's Hymn of Praise, December 3, 1840]

THE FEATURED composition of the evening was Mendelssohn's *Hymn of Praise.* Previously performed here on the occasion of the Gutenberg festival, the work had in the meanwhile been successfully revised in some passages for this performance by the composer. All praise for the splendid composition that it was and that it now is! We have called for it before. Everything to ennoble and make men happy may be found here: consciousness of power, its freest, most natural expression; not to speak of the musical skill of the composition and the imagination with which Mendelssohn worked on this piece, especially in the parts where the vocal chorus predominates.

[A Great Singer, March 18, 1841]

IF WE SPEAK last of the climax of the evening, there is a good reason for it. In one word: *Madame Schröder-Devrient* sang. What there is human in a person and an artist of course succumbs to time and its influences: the voice, for instance, and the beauty of appearance.[2] But what there is beyond—the soul,

---

[1] H (German) = B (English).
  B (German) = B♭ (English).

[2] Severe judgment: she was thirty-seven years old at the time.

the poetry—remains fresh throughout all ages in the favorites of Heaven, and thus this artist and poetess will ever enchant us as long as her heart and throat contain one single tone. The audience listened as if under a spell, and when at the close she sang Mendelssohn's *Folk Song* ending with the words "*auf Wiedersehen*," everybody joined gayly in this greeting. It applied as well to the composer who was at the piano, for it was for the last time that his marvelously fluent fingers mastered the keys in this place. So let us not investigate whether the laurels that suddenly appeared in the pit were meant for the master or for the honored guest, and wind up by hopefully calling to all those who have given and received during our evenings of music: "*Auf Wiedersehen!*"

Rossini

Schumann's animosity against Rossini and his followers, reflected in the very introduction to his literary work (p. 25), must be understood as a reaction to the overwhelming fashion of his time. His self-defense as an instrumental composer may almost be compared to the attitude which some contemporary composers assume in regard to popular and operetta music. Added to this chapter are some remarks on the Italian and German school.

IT WOULD BE altogether too one-sided to suppress everything by Rossini in this country; still I could wish that German composers received proportionate encouragement. Rossini is an admirable stage designer; but take away the artificial lighting and the illusion of the theater, and see what remains!

Whenever I hear people speaking about "taking the audience into consideration," about Rossini's school being "consolers and saviors," my fingers just itch. We treat the public with too much laxity; already it is beginning to insist upon having things to its taste; whereas in former times it listened modestly from a distance and was happy enough to receive a morsel from the artist. Is my statement entirely unfounded? Do not people now go to a performance of *Fidelio* to hear Schröder [1] (not entirely without reason), and to oratorios out of pure and simple compassion? And is it not true that Herz, the stenographer, who possesses no heart [*Herz*] save in his fingers, makes four hundred talers by a set of variations, while Marschner scarcely got more for the entire opera of *Hans Heiling?* Again—my fingers itch. *Florestan*

ROSSINI'S VISIT TO BEETHOVEN

The butterfly crossed the path of the eagle, but the latter turned aside in order not to crush it with the beating of his wings. *Eusebius*

ITALIAN AND GERMAN

Behold the lovely fluttering butterfly! But take away its pollen and see how miserably it flaps about, unnoticed, whereas the skeletons of gigantic creatures survive, to the amazement of posterity, for hundreds of years. *Eusebius*

II. BARBIERE DI SEVIGLIA, NOVEMBER 1847

With Viardot-Garcia as Rosina. Witty, enlivening music; the best Rossini ever wrote. Viardot transformed the entire opera into a grand variation; she scarcely left one melody untouched. What a false view of the freedom of the virtuoso! For the rest, this is her best rôle.

[1] Madame Schröder-Devrient, see p. 233.

[ITALIAN AND GERMAN SCHOOL]

I [1]

WHERE ARE they now, the melodies by the celebrated Italian masters prior to Rossini (incidentally, they possessed more genius and knew more than those now living)? Would you care to exchange them for German melodies, for Mozart and Beethoven melodies? These had only lately begun to flower; however they were born in a region lying deeper than the vocal chords: in the musical heart of a German genius, where everything is music. And here you still speak of Italy, of Bellini and the land of song. When will we have done with the naïve superstition that we could learn something about song from them? As though song and music were two different things! As though bad music could be covered over by a good vocal line! As though for the sake of singing one ought first to become a bad musician! I say again that not all that is easy to sing constitutes a melody! There is a difference between melody and melodies. Who possesses melody also possesses melodies, but the reverse is not always true. The child sings his melodies to himself; melody, however, is developed later in life. The first two chords of Beethoven's *Eroica*, for instance, contain more melody than ten melodies by Bellini.

II

Do we Germans possess no melodic style of our own? Has not the most recent past taught us that there are minds and masters in Germany who know how to unite profundity and facility, significance and grace? Do not Spohr, Mendelssohn, and others know how to sing and how to write for singers? We must point this out to the German-Italian hybrid school, which has so many adherents in Vienna. But the union is not natural.

[1] This passage was not included in Schumann's own edition of his literary works.

The highest peaks of Italian art do not reach much beyond the first beginnings of the truly German. How can we stand firmly, with one foot upon an alp, the other on a convenient meadow?

Cherubini

[FIRST AND SECOND QUARTETS IN E-FLAT AND C MAJOR
*As performed during informal quartet matinées
in Schumann's home*]

"WE HAVE HAD the Schuppanzigh, we have the David String Quartet, why should we not also have—" thought I to myself, and assembled four musicians. "It is not so long ago," said I to these, "that Haydn, Mozart, and yet another lived and wrote quartets. Would it be possible for such fathers to have left behind them so few worthy descendants that these have learned nothing from them? Could we not try and feel out whether a new genius were somewhere in bud and required but a touch. With one word, gentlemen, the instruments are ready, and we have many new things, some of which could be played in our first matinée." And without much ado, as befits inveterate musicians, they were already at their desks. I gladly record with which works it was that the morning slipped away; register, if not in a lapidary critical style, at least in a light manner the first impression they made on me; and also indicate the reactions of the quartet, since I often rate the simple curse of a musician higher than entire systems of aesthetics. . . . When I compare the faces of many trembling musicians ascending the *Gewandhaus* staircase, perhaps on their way to a solo performance, with those of my quartet, the latter appear to me by far the more enviable, for they form their own public—and therefore show not the least anxiety—even though no one did anything to drive away a child who was listening outside of the window or a nightingale singing in the trees . . .

We closed with the first of the already long-published quartets by Cherubini. A difference of opinion has arisen even among good musicians in reference to these. The question is not as to whether these works proceed from a master of our art —of this there can be no doubt—but whether they are in the true quartet style, loved and recognized as exemplary by us. We have grown accustomed once and for all time to the art of the three famous German masters and have taken Onslow and, finally, Mendelssohn, into the circle in due recognition of the fact that they are following in the formers' tracks. And now comes Cherubini, an artist grown grey in the highest aristocracy of art and in the conviction of his own views on art; to this day, at his advanced age, superior as a harmonist to all his contemporaries; the refined, scholarly, interesting Italian whose severe reserve and strength of character sometimes leads me to compare him with Dante. I must confess, however, that even I felt a great disquiet on hearing this quartet for the first time; especially after the first two movements. It was what I had expected. Much of it seemed to me operatic, overladen; while other parts of it seemed paltry, empty, and capricious. Of course on my part it might have been the impatience of youth which was unable immediately to grasp the meaning of the often crotchety discourse of the old man; though at other times I certainly felt the complete master to the very soles of his feet. But then came the scherzo with its ebullient Spanish theme; the extraordinary trio; and lastly the finale, which diamondlike throws rays of light to all sides, no matter how one turns it; and now there could be no doubt as to who had written the quartet and whether it was worthy of its master. Many will feel as I: one must first familiarize oneself with the peculiar spirit of this his quartet style. It is not in our mother tongue that we are being addressed; a distinguished foreigner here speaks to us; but the more we learn to understand him, the more highly we must respect him. These remarks, which give but a slight idea of the originality of this work, must suffice to call the attention of German quartet circles to it. Much is required for its performance: artists, above all. . . .

Our third meeting took on a particular radiance through the participation of a pianist and a viola player, found indispensable by us for the performance of a piano trio and a quintet; and I had my reasons for insisting upon this variety. Even the enjoyment of the beautiful has its limits; for instance, I could more easily spend a night listening to dance music by Strauss and Lanner than at a concert at which nothing but Beethoven symphonies were performed, for the tones would end by lacerating us. We must be fresh even to listen attentively to three quartets; nay, even possess special sympathy with this type of composition. Composers are in the habit of leaving after the first one; reviewers, after the second; only the good amateur can stand a third. One of these good amateurs told me that he had once been entirely without music for three months, and that in his great hunger for it, on his first visit to the city, he played quartets for three consecutive days. "To be sure," he added, partly as an excuse, "I play a little myself, and therefore took the second violin." So I insisted that we include compositions related to the quartet; indeed, one can never know whether—reversing the order of things in Haydn's well-known symphony [Farewell]—instrument after instrument will not by and by add itself until at last the little four-leaf clover will have turned into a symphony orchestra. It is scarcely conceivable how the addition of another viola immediately alters the effect of the string instruments as it exhibits itself in a quartet; how greatly the character of the quintet differs from that of the quartet! The middle tints of the spectrum now possess more force and vitality; the single parts give the effect rather of masses; while in the quartet we listen to four individuals, we now seem to have a unified assemblage before us. . . . We turned to the next piece in a somewhat chilled mood; but as it was from Cherubini's hand, it enveloped us so that we quickly forgot what had preceded. This second quartet seems

to me to have been written long before the first in the same
collection, and perhaps even before the symphony which, if I
am not mistaken, pleased so little on its first performance in
Vienna that Cherubini refused to publish it and afterwards
transformed it into a quartet. Thus it has been twice a failure;
for if the music as a symphony sounded too much like a quartet,
as a quartet it sounds too symphonic. (I am opposed to all such
remodeling; it seems to me an offense against the divine first
inspiration.) In its simplicity (which quality distinguishes
Cherubini's older compositions from his later ones), I recognize
its earlier origin. To be sure, were the master himself to enter
and say, "You err, friend; these quartets were written at the
same period, and originally as nothing but quartets," I would
be overruled. Therefore my remarks can stand only as supposi-
tions and should stimulate thought in others.[1] On the whole,
this work is on a level high above that of ephemeral publica-
tions, above that of everything which has been sent us from
Paris; and it would be impossible for anything of the kind to be
produced by any writer who had not earnestly studied, thought,
and written for many years. Some dry passages, parts where the
intellect alone was active, are to be found here, as in most of
Cherubini's works, but even then one always finds something
of interest, be it the texture, a contrapuntal finesse, a canonic
imitation; something that is food for thought. The scherzo and
the last movement certainly contain the greatest amount of
sweep and of masterly vitality. The adagio has a highly original
A minor character, rather like a romance and of a Provençal
flavor; its charms reveal themselves more and more on frequent
hearing. The close is of the kind that makes one listen anew,
although one knows the end to be near. In the first movement
we meet with reminiscences of Beethoven's B-flat major Symphony, an imitation between violin and viola, resembling the
one between bassoon and clarinet in that symphony; and at
the principal return to the theme in the middle we meet the
same figure which we have at the same place in the same move-

[1] Schumann's supposition, however, was correct.

ment of Beethoven's symphony. The movements, however, are so dissimilar in character that the resemblance will strike few people.

Robert Franz

TWELVE LIEDER, OPUS 1

The friendly warning, at the end of the following article, namely not to specialize in LIEDER, remained unheeded. This is one of the instances mentioned by Schumann in his introduction, in which his fears for the future of a young composer came true in later years.

MUCH COULD be said about the *Lieder* by Robert Franz; they are not isolated phenomena, and bear an inner relation to the entire development of our art during the last ten years. It is well known that in the years 1830–1834 there took place a reaction to the popular taste. Essentially, the battle was not hard; it was waged against ornamentalism which showed itself in nearly every branch of art (always excepting the works of Weber, Loewe, and a few others), and especially in pianoforte music. Thus the first attack was launched on piano music; more thoughtful structures began to take the place of mere virtuoso pieces and the influence of two masters—Beethoven and Bach—became perceptible in these. The young musical party grew in numbers, and new life also penetrated into other branches. In the *Lied* the ground had been prepared by Franz Schubert, but more in the Beethovenian manner; while in North German song the influence of Bach was more evident.

What hastened the development was the evolution of a new German school of poetry. Eichendorff and Rückert, though they had begun writing before this time, now became familiar to musicians; Uhland and Heine were very frequently set to music. Thus arose that more artistic and profound style of song of which earlier composers could of course know nothing, for it was due to the new spirit of poetry reflected in music.

The songs of Robert Franz definitely belong to this noble new genre. Hurdygurdy sing-song writing, which recites penny verses with the same satisfaction as a poem by Rückert, for example, is beginning to be estimated at its proper value; and even though this progress has not yet reached the general public, the elite has long been aware of it. Perhaps the *Lied* is the only genre in which a remarkable improvement actually has occurred since Beethoven's time. Should we, for instance, compare the care with which the ideas of the poems have been rendered word for word in the songs before us with the negligence of the former mode of treatment, in which the poem was considered of very secondary importance; the whole harmonic construction here, with the slovenly formulas of accompaniment which earlier times found so difficult to shake off; narrowness of mind alone would be able to perceive the contrary. Robert Franz's characteristics as a *Lied* composer are expressed in the preceding sentence. He desires more than well- or ill-sounding music; he strives to reflect the poem in its true depth. He is most successful in songs of a quiet, dreamy character, but we also find something of the charmingly naïve, as in the first song and in the *Dance-Song in May;* and some ebullience, as in certain songs to texts by Robert Burns. This double volume of songs suggests the most varied pictures and feelings; something of melancholy seeks everywhere to insinuate itself. The performance of these songs requires singers, poets, human creatures; they sound best of all when sung in solitude, and, perhaps, toward evening. A few things vex my ear, for instance, the beginnings of the seventh and twelfth songs, and the often returning E in the last. I wish the seventh had been omitted from the collection; it seems to me too studied in its melody and harmony. The others are interesting, significant, often exquisitely lovely. One could wish for a musically richer close for the *Slumber Song* by Tieck; nonetheless, even without this, it remains one of the most felicitous. The task of individually describing the fine musical features of these songs would be endless: musicians of feeling will discover them for themselves.

These *Lieder*, then, differ remarkably from others. Anyone who thus began ought not be surprised should the future make yet higher demands on him. Success in small forms often leads to one-sidedness, to mannerism. Let the young artist protest against this by trying out new forms of art; let him seek to express his rich inwardness through means other than the voice. He may be confident of our constant interest.

Niels W. Gade

THE FOLLOWING ITEM might lately have been read in a French newspaper:—"A young Danish composer has recently made a sensation in Germany; he is called Gade, and often wanders, with his violin on his back, from Copenhagen to Leipzig and back again; he looks as if he were Mozart himself." The first and last parts of this information are correct; a little romance is mixed up with the middle part of the sentence. The young Dane actually arrived in Leipzig a few months ago (like his violin, however, he came by rail) and his Mozart head, with hair as thick and heavy as if cut in marble, corresponded very well with the good opinions which his *Ossian* Overture and his First Symphony had aroused among our resident artists.

There is little to be told about his external life. Born in Copenhagen in 1817, the son of an instrument-maker of that city, it is possible that he dreamed away his first years among instruments rather than among people. . . . Afterwards he entered the royal orchestra at Copenhagen as violinist, and here had an opportunity to overhear all those secrets of the instruments which he at times allows us to share in his orchestral compositions. This practical school, denied to some, used without understanding by many, was doubtless the principal agent in educating him to that point of mastery in instrumentation which must undeniably be conceded to him. Through his overture, *Reminiscences from Ossian,* which, on the approval of Spohr and Schneider, was crowned with the prize awarded by the Copenhagen Musical Union, he attracted the attention of his art-loving king; like many other talented men in Denmark he then received a really royal grant for a journey abroad; the first place to which he went was Leipzig, where he had first been introduced to a larger musical public. He is still here, but intends shortly to visit Paris, and go thence to Italy. We will therefore take advantage of the moment in which he is still freshly present to us to give a brief sketch of the artistic individuality of this distinguished man who, among the younger generation, has impressed us for a long time as has scarcely another.

Anyone who would straightway conclude from Gade's resemblance to Mozart—which is really rather striking—that these two men resembled each other musically, would be greatly mistaken. We have quite a novel artistic character before us. Things begin to look as if the nations bordering on Germany wished to emancipate themselves from the hegemony of German music. This might annoy a chauvinist German, but it could appear only a natural and cheering phenomenon to the profound thinker and the student of humanity. Thus Chopin represents his country; Bennett, England; in Holland Verhulst gives hope of becoming a worthy representative of his country; likewise in Hungary nationalist endeavors are being felt. But since all these composers seem to regard Germany as their first and favorite teacher of music, no one will be surprised that they try to speak their own musical language to their own nations, without being untrue to their former instructress. For no land

can yet boast of masters that equal our greatest ones, and no
one has sought to deny this.

Manifestations of nationalist tendencies also have cropped up
in the north of Europe. Lindblad in Stockholm has transcribed
its old folk songs, and even Ole Bull, though by no means a
man of the first rank of talent, has tried to make the tones of
his homeland at home with us. Perhaps the appearance of so
many distinguished modern poets of Scandinavia has given
a powerful impulse to musical talent there, even had the artists
of that country not been sufficiently reminded by its lakes,
mountains, runes, and northern lights that the North might
well be allowed to utter its own tones among those of the
world.

Our young composer also has been reared by the poets of his
fatherland. He knows and loves them all; the old fairy tales
and sagas accompanied him on his boyish wanderings, and
Ossian's giant harp gleamed across the sea to him from England's coast. A decidedly Nordic strain for the first time shows
itself in Gade's music, and especially in his *Ossian* Overture;
but Gade would be the first to acknowledge all that he owes to
German masters . . .

Only one wish suggests itself: that this artist may not be submerged in his nationality; that his "northern lights-generating
imagination"—as someone called it—may show itself rich and
varied; that he may direct his glance toward other spheres of
life and nature. Every artist should be advised first to win and
then to reject originality; let him like a snake cast his skin
when the old garment begins to shrink.

But the future is hidden; most things happen differently than
is expected, we can only express that we anticipate the most
perfect and the loveliest things from this distinguished talent.
And as if the accident of his name—like that of Bach's—had
borne an influence in making a musician of him, oddly enough
the four letters of his name are those by which the four open
violin strings are designated. Let no one ignore this little sign

of higher favor; or the other, that his name, by means of four clefs, may be written with a single note,[1] which cabalists will readily discover.

This very month we expect the performance of a second symphony by Gade; it differs from the first, is softer and quieter. It puts me in mind of the lovely Danish beechwoods.

SIXTH SYMPHONY

The following review of a forgotten work has been reprinted here because of its general interest, and at the same time as an example of Schumann's attitude to the less important output of his time.

SUCH MASTERLY ORDER and clarity, lightness and euphony distinguishes this symphony; with one word, so ripe and so sustained is it, that for its sake we are willing to accord to its composer a place in the neighborhood of his beloved model, Franz Schubert. Though he does not approach him in variety of invention, he is at least his equal in talent for orchestration. When this symphony was performed in Leipzig, it was not successful; but the composer need not trouble himself about that since Beethoven, and later Mendelssohn, have somewhat spoiled us; it is no little thing to stand alongside them and receive an honorable mention; besides, the symphony deserves the old reproach of excessive length. Lachner does not always know how to break off at the right moment, in the manner of

[1]

witty men who will send us home with a joke (a method often employed by Beethoven) and who make the audience ask itself—"What did the man mean? But he was probably right." May Lachner often permit himself to be inspired by his good genius to conclusions of this kind. The public must sometimes be imposed upon, for it considers itself the composer's equal as soon as things are made too easy for it. But if a composer from time to time throws a stone in its way and even at its head, all will simultaneously duck, feel terror, and in the end loudly praise him. Beethoven did so in some of his pieces; not all, however, may do so. Only let Lachner read Swift, Lord Byron, Jean Paul; I believe it would be helpful; he would learn how to be brief; he must become less meticulous; not permit himself to repeat his fine ideas so often; not squeeze the last drop out of them but to fit others in with them—new and ever lovelier ones. Everything as in Beethoven! Thus we always return to this divine composer and can think of nothing more to say today save that we hope that Lachner may pursue this path toward the ideal of a modern symphony, which, since Beethoven's death, we are called upon to build along new lines. Long live the German symphony! Fresh prosperity, new flowering to it!

Karl Czerny

INTRODUCTION AND BRILLIANT VARIATIONS ON AN ITALIAN THEME, OPUS 302

NOT EVEN WITH all one's critical speed is it possible to catch up with *Herr* Czerny. Had I enemies, I would, in order to destroy them, force them to listen to nothing but music such as this. The insipidity of these variations is really phenomenal.

Henri Vieuxtemps

In the following two articles, Schumann pays tribute to two great violinists, one of them, Vieuxtemps, merely a boy when Schumann first heard him and hailed him as a genius.

HE WHO PRESENTS himself to the world must neither be too young nor too old, but in full flowering; and not just on one or the other branch but, as it were, over the whole tree. When we listen to Henri, we can safely close our eyes. His playing is like a flower, fragrant and bright at the same time. His execution is perfect, masterly throughout.

When we speak of Vieuxtemps we are apt to think of Paganini. On hearing the latter for the first time, I expected him to begin with a tone such as had never been heard before. But with how small, how thin a tone did he begin! Bit by bit, imperceptibly at first, he threw his magnetic chains into the audience; and the audience swayed with them. Then the links gradually became stronger and more intricate: people pressed closer together. He drew them tighter until the audience was gradually fused into a single entity, meant to be the master's equal, the receiving as' opposed to the giving part. Other wizards of art use other formulas. What fascinated in Vieuxtemps' case were not single beauties which we could grasp; neither was it gradual contraction as in Paganini's, nor the expansion of the scope as in that of other eminent artists. From the first to the last tone we stood as if in a magic circle, the beginning and end of which were hidden from us.

H. W. Ernst

BERLIOZ' prophecy that Ernst would one day make the world talk about him as Paganini had done begins to be fulfilled. I have heard nearly all the great violin players of modern days, from Lipinski down to Prume. Each one had his enthusiastic supporters in the public. Some were constant to Lipinski; his imposing personality impressed at once, and it was only necessary to hear a few of his grand tones to judge him. Others raved about Vieuxtemps, most talented of young masters, who already stands so high that we can scarcely think about his future without experiencing a secret terror. Ole Bull gave us food for thought, like a deep riddle which one can never solve; he in particular found opponents; and De Bériot, Prume, David, Molique, C. Müller, each one has his own public, his own shield bearer among the critics. But Ernst, like Paganini, is able to satisfy, to win all parties whenever he pleases; of a many-sided individuality, he has made himself familiar with all styles and schools. He even approaches Paganini in genius for improvisation—most fascinating of virtuoso gifts!—and this quality may well have been influenced by his early and constant association with Paganini . . . Having traveled through Holland during the past winter, giving sixty to seventy concerts there in a few months, he went straight to Germany after a short stay in Paris. A genuine artist, sure of his art, he disdained to advertise his visit.

At the instigation of Marschner he appeared first in Hannover, and then in many concerts in Hamburg and in neighboring cities. Here we also heard him almost unprepared. The hall was not overly full, but the applause was so rapturous that the public seemed to have doubled its numbers. The climax of the evening was his performance of Mayseder's variations, which he charmingly interwove with some of his own and closed with a cadenza such as we had never heard except from Paganini; in humorous exuberance he let loose all the magic in his bow. The applause which followed exceeded the usual limits of North German enthusiasm; and if wreaths had been prepared beforehand, they would have been showered upon the master by scores. But this yet awaits him, even though, modest man that he is, and rather quiet and plunged in his own thoughts, he would doubtless prefer that it did not. We shall hear him again next Monday. The express train has carried him away for a few days to the neighboring capital [Dresden]. And then, if he plays his own *Carnival of Venice,* we shall have something to report of him; him to whom, it seems, the famous Italian magician, on departing from the world of art, bequeathed the secrets of his power—that masters may make comparisons, youths become emulous, and all the world enjoy.—January 14, [1840]

TANNHÄUSER, AUGUST 7, 1847

A WORK touched with genius, which does not lend itself to a brief discussion. Were he as melodious a composer as he is an intellectual one, he would be the man of our time. There is much to be said about the opera; it deserves that it be said, and I shall wait for the proper occasion.

> *This article was never written, but Schumann's correspondence both clarifies his opinion of the opera and the reason for not continuing its public discussion.*

[*On October 22, 1845, Schumann wrote about* Tannhäuser *to Mendelssohn*]: "Wagner—though certainly a brilliant fellow and full of original, audacious ideas—can hardly set down (and think out) a four-measure phrase beautifully or even correctly.

He is one of those people who have not learned their harmony lessons, or learned how to write four-part chorals, and this their work makes plain. Now that the whole score is under our eyes, nicely printed—including its parallel fifths and octaves—he would probably like to correct and to erase—too late! But enough! The music is not a bit better than *Rienzi;* if anything, more pallid and forced. But should you say this to people, they will suspect you of jealousy, so I say it only to you, aware that you know it all beforehand . . ." [*After seeing the performance, however, Schumann, in a letter dated November 12, somewhat amends this view*]: "I hope soon to be able to talk to you about *Tannhäuser.* I have to take back some of the things I wrote to you after reading the score: from the stage everything strikes one very differently. I was quite moved by many parts of it."

[*A résumé of both these letters is to be found in a letter to C. van Bruyck, written eight years later (May 8, 1853)*]: "I was very interested to read what you wrote about Wagner. He is, if I may say it in one word, a poor musician. He lacks all sense of form and of euphony. But you should not judge him from his piano scores. Many passages of his operas, once heard from the stage, cannot but prove exciting. And if you do not find clear sunlight in them, such as that which radiates from the works of genius, they distil a strange magic which captivates the senses. But, as I said, the music itself (that is, disregarding its stage effect) is poor and frequently amateurish, empty, and distasteful, and praise of his works at the expense of the many great dramatic works previously written by German composers exhibits an unfortunate decline of taste. But enough of this. Posterity will judge these works as posterity ever judges . . ."

[Wagner's arrangement of]
IPHIGENIA IN AULIS, BY GLUCK, MAY 15, 1847

CLYTAEMNESTRA, Schröder-Devrient; Iphigenia, Johanna Wagner; Agamemnon, Mitterwurzer; Achilles, Tichatschek.

251

Richard Wagner was stage director; costumes and decorations were most appropriate. He also edited the music; I believe I have heard indications of it here and there. And he added the close, "To Troy." This is really not permissible. Probably Gluck would have employed the opposite process with Wagner's operas—subtracted, cut out.

What can I say about this opera? As long as the world exists, such music will always come to light again; never grow old. A great, original artist! Mozart plainly stands upon his shoulders; Spontini often copies him, note for note. As in *Armide*, the close of the opera again of the highest effectiveness.

FIDELIO, BY BEETHOVEN, AUGUST 11, 1848

Bad performance; incomprehensible tempi taken by the conductor, Richard Wagner.

Brahms

NEW ROADS [1853]

Schumann's last article, like his first on Chopin's OPUS 2 (see p. 126), was devoted to the introduction of a young genius to the German public.

YEARS HAVE PASSED—almost as many as I once devoted to the editing of these pages—ten indeed, since I have made myself heard in this place so rich in memories. Despite intense productive work I often felt impelled to continue. Many new and significant talents have arisen; a new power in music seems to announce itself; the intimation has been proved true by many aspiring artists of the last years, even though their work may be known only in comparatively limited circles.[1] To me, who followed the progress of these chosen ones with the greatest sympathy, it seemed that under these circumstances there inevitably must appear a musician called to give expression to his times in ideal fashion; a musician who would reveal his mastery not in a gradual evolution, but like Athene would spring fully armed from Zeus's head. And such a one *has* appeared; a young man over whose cradle Graces and Heroes have stood watch. His name is *Johannes Brahms,* and he comes from Hamburg, where he has been working in quiet obscurity, though instructed in the most difficult statutes of his art by an excellent and enthusiastically devoted teacher.[2] A well-known and honored master recently recommended him to me. Even outwardly he bore the marks proclaiming: "This is a chosen one." Sitting at the piano he began to disclose wonderful regions to us. We were drawn into even more enchanting spheres. Besides, he is a player of genius who can make of the piano an orchestra of lamenting and loudly jubilant voices. There were sonatas, veiled symphonies rather; songs the poetry of which would be understood even without words, although a profound vocal melody runs through them all; single piano pieces, some of them turbulent in spirit while graceful in form; again sonatas for violin and piano, string quartets, every work so different from the others that it seemed to stream from its own individual source. And then it was as though, rushing like a torrent, they were all united by him into a single waterfall the cascades of which were overarched by a peaceful rainbow, while butterflies played about its borders and the voices of nightingales obliged.

Should he direct his magic wand where the powers of the masses in chorus and orchestra may lend him their forces, we

[1] I have in mind Joseph Joachim, Ernst Naumann, Ludwig Normann, Woldemar Bargiel, Theodor Kirchner, Julius Schaeffer, Albert Dietrich, not to forget that profound aspirant to great art, C. F. Wilsing, composer of sacred music. As bravely advancing heralds I must also name Niels W. Gade, C. F. Mangold, Robert Franz, and Stephen Heller. [Schumann]

[2] Eduard Marxsen in Hamburg.

can look forward to even more wondrous glimpses of the secret world of spirits. May the highest genius strengthen him to this end. Since he possesses yet another facet of genius—that of modesty—we may surmise that it will come to pass. His fellow musicians hail him on his first step through a world where wounds perhaps await him, but also palms and laurels. We welcome a strong champion in him.

There exists a secret bond between kindred spirits in every period. You who belong together, close your ranks ever more tightly, that the Truth of Art may shine more clearly, diffusing joy and blessings over all things.

Schumann

Schumann reviewed none of his compositions in his journal, with the exception of the Paganini transcriptions, which he discusses as the work of Paganini. This review is followed here by excerpts from letters in which Schumann speaks of his own composing.

SIX ETUDES DE CONCERT AFTÉR CAPRICES BY PAGANINI, OPUS 10

I ADDED an opus number to the above études because the publisher told me that they would "go" better; a reason before which my manifold objections had to yield. In secret, however, I considered the tenth (for I have not yet arrived at the ninth muse) as the symbol of an unknown quantity, and the composition as a genuine work by Paganini except for the basses, the denser German middle parts, the greater fullness of harmony in general, and here and there the smoother finish of the form. And if it may be thought praiseworthy to have lovingly absorbed the thoughts of one higher than oneself, to have re-

Piano Quintet by Schumann, opus 44

worked them, and to have expressed them once again, I may possibly possess a claim to praise.

Paganini is said to have rated his merit as a composer higher than his eminent talent as a virtuoso. If general opinion has not until now agreed with him, it must at least be allowed that in his compositions, particularly in the violin caprices [1] from which the above études were derived, and which, all in all, were conceived and executed with a rare freshness and lightness, there is so much that is diamond-like that the richer setting required by the pianoforte could only fix rather than dissipate it. When once before I had published a book of studies after Paganini,[2] I copied—perhaps only to its detriment—the original almost note for note, and merely enriched the harmony a little. But in the present case I broke loose from the pedantry of the literal transcription and strove to give the impression of an original pianoforte composition which, without sacrificing the underlying poetic idea, permitted one to forget its origin in the violin. It must be understood that to accomplish this I was obliged sometimes to alter, entirely eliminate, or add— especially in regard to harmony and form; but it was all done with the consideration demanded by so powerful and honored a spirit as is Paganini's. It would take too much space were I to point to all these alterations and my reasons for making them. I leave the decision whether my changes have been beneficial to the judgment of sympathetic art lovers, who are at liberty to compare the original with the pianoforte version. Certainly the comparison will not be uninteresting.

With the epithet *"de concert"* I sought to make a distinction between these études and those I had formerly arranged; besides, because of their brilliancy the present ones lend themselves to public performance. But as most of them begin quite brusquely in the middle of things—something to which a mixed

---

[1] The title of the original is as follows: *24 Caprices per il violino solo, dedicati agli artisti. Opus 1. Milano, Ricordi.* [Schumann]

[2] Studies for the Pianoforte, after Violin Caprices by Paganini; with a Preface, Opus 3. Leipzig, Hofmeister. [Schumann]

concert audience is unaccustomed—they had best be introduced with a free, brief, appropriate prelude.

Among other observations, I would like to have noticed:

In No. 2, I selected a different accompaniment, as I thought the tremolo of the original would too greatly fatigue player and hearers. I consider this number especially tender and lovely and sufficient in itself to assure Paganini's position as one of the first among modern Italian composers. Florestan says: "Here he is an Italian river which reaches the sea across Germany."

The effectiveness of No. 3 does not appear to be in proportion to its difficulty; but he who has vanquished this has conquered many things along with it.

In the working out of No. 4 the Funeral March from Beethoven's *Ėroica* Symphony floated before me. Perhaps others will guess as much. This entire number is filled with romanticism.

In No. 5, I intentionally omitted the expression marks, leaving students to seek out for themselves its heights and depths. This will afford a good opportunity for testing the pupil's perceptive faculty.

I doubt whether No. 6 will immediately be recognized by anyone who has played the violin caprices. Played faultlessly as a pianoforte piece, it is charming in the flow of its harmonies. I may mention that the left hand, crossing the right (excepting the twenty-fourth bar), has but one key to strike—that of the highest upward-pointing note. The chords sound fullest when the crossing finger of the left hand sharply meets the fifth of the right hand. The following allegro was difficult to harmonize. The hard and somewhat flat return to E major (pages 20 to 21) could scarcely be softened; one would have to write a new composition.

These études are of the greatest difficulty throughout, every one in a different way. Those who take them up for the first time will do well to read them over before playing, as even the lightning-swift eye and finger will scarcely be able at first sight to carry out the études correctly.

It is not to be expected that the number of those able to perform these études in a masterly manner will ever be very large; but they contain so much of genius that it is impossible for those who have once heard them executed perfectly not to think of them oftentimes with approval.

[FIRST SYMPHONY IN B-FLAT MAJOR]

[Letter to Spohr, November 23, 1842]

"I WROTE this symphony at the end of winter [in 1841] with a spring-like urge—if I may say so—such as is given every year anew to all men, even to the most aged, I think. I did not attempt to depict and to describe anything in it; but I do believe that the season in which this symphony was born influenced its structure and helped make it what it is. You will not find it too easy, but neither will you find it difficult."

[Letter to Taubert, January 10, 1843] [1]

"IF ONLY you could breathe into your orchestra, when it plays, that longing for spring! It was my main source of inspiration when I wrote the work in February 1841. I should like the very first trumpet-call to sound as though proceeding from on high and like a summons to awaken. In the following section of the introduction, let me say, it might be possible to feel the world turning green; perhaps . . . a butterfly fluttering; and in the allegro the gradual assemblage of everything that belongs to spring. However, it was only *after* I had completed the composition that these ideas came to my mind. About the finale I do, however, want to tell you that I would like it to describe a Farewell to Spring and hence do not want it to be taken too frivolously."

[1] This letter (published by Erler, *Robert Schumann's Leben,* Berlin 1886, vol. 1, p. 293) also contains technical suggestions to the conductor which all performers of the work could follow with advantage.

[PIANO WORKS]

[Letter to Klara Wieck, Feb. 12, 1838]

PLEASE WRITE and tell me how you liked the *Phantasiestücke* and *Davidsbündlertänze*—sincerely, please; not as though you were speaking to your fiancé, but as though speaking to your husband, will you? *Traumeswirren*, I believe, could occasionally be played by you in public together with *Des Abends. In der Nacht*, however, is too long, perhaps. . . . In the *Davidstänze* the clock strikes twelve at the very end, as I have discovered:

[Letter to Simonin de Sire, March 15, 1839]

"You INQUIRE so kindly about my new compositions. The following have been published: opus 15, *Kinderszenen;* opus 16, *Kreisleriana;* and opus 17, *Phantasie* in three movements. In four or five weeks Mechietti will publish opus 18, *Arabeske;* opus 19, *Blumenstück;* opus 20, *Humoreske* here. I like *Kreisleriana* the best of all these things. The title can only be understood by Germans. Kreisler is an eccentric, wild and gifted *Capellmeister*, a character created by E. T. A. Hoffmann; you will like him in many respects. The titles of all my compositions never occur to me until I have finished composing. . . . Don't you know Jean Paul, our great writer? I learned more counterpoint from him than from my music master."

[Letter to C. Kossmaly, May 5, 1843]

"IT IS WITH SOME hesitation that I enclose a package containing some older compositions of mine. You will readily discover what there is of immaturity and lack of finish in them. Mostly they are reflections of my agitated former life; the man and the musician at all times attempted to express themselves simultaneously, and I almost believe that this is still the case—except that I have learned to master myself, as well as my art, a little better . . . Unfortunately I was not able to get hold of those piano compositions of mine that I consider the best, that is the *Kreisleriana*, the six [eight] *Phantasiestücke*, four sets of *Noveletten*, and one set of *Romanzen*. These happen to be the latest piano compositions written by me (in 1838). But the earlier ones will also give you an idea of my character and of my aims; nay, in attempts as these there frequently lie the principal germs of future development. . . . These works have received only little publicity—for natural reasons: (1) because of their nature, being difficult in form and content; (2) because I am editor of my music review where it would be impossible for me to mention them; (3) because Fink [antagonist of Schumann's] is editor of the other music review [*Allgemeine Musikalische Zeitung*] and did not care to mention them."

♯

[Letter to Klara Wieck, April 13, 1838]
"ANYTHING that happens in the world affects me; politics, for example, literature, people; and I reflect about all these things in my own way—and these reflections then seek to find an outlet in music. This is also the reason for which so many of my compositions are hard to understand. . . . For this reason, too, so many other recent composers do not satisfy me, because—in addition to all their lack of professional skill—they enlarge on lyrical commonplaces. The highest level reached in this type of music does not come up to the point from which my kind of music starts. The former may be a flower. The latter is a poem; that is, belongs to the world of the spirit. The former comes from an impulse of crude nature; the latter stems from the consciousness of the poetic mind."

SOURCES

ABBREVIATIONS

Robert Schumanns Gesammelte Schriften über Musik und Musiker, 5th edition, Leipzig, 1914. Volume 1 = I, Volume 2 = II.

Robert Schumanns Leben aus seinen Briefen, geschildert von Hermann Erler, Berlin [1886]. Volume 1 = Erler I, Volume 2 = Erler II.

Kerst, *Schumannbrevier,* Berlin and Leipzig, 1905 = Kerst.

B. Litzmann, *Clara Schumann,* Volume 1, 3rd edition, Leipzig, 1906 = Litzmann I.

Schumanns Briefe in Auswahl herausgegeben von Dr. Karl Storck, Stuttgart [1906] = Storck.

263

INDEX

OF NAMES AND COMPOSITIONS

269

273